EVERY
BOOK ITS
READER

ALSO BY NICHOLAS A. BASBANES

A Splendor of Letters

A Gentle Madness

Patience & Fortitude

Among the Gently Mad

HarperCollins*Publishers*

EVERY BOOK ITS READER

The Power
of the Printed Word
to Stir the World

NICHOLAS A. BASBANES

HarperCollins books may be purchased for educational, business, or sales promotional use. For information, please write: Special Markets Department, HarperCollins Publishers, 10 East 53rd Street, New York, NY 10022.

FIRST EDITION

Designed by SH · CV

Except where noted, photographs are courtesy of Nicholas A. Basbanes.

Printed on acid-free paper

Library of Congress Cataloging-in-Publication Data

Basbanes, Nicholas A.
Every book its reader : the power of the printed word to stir the world /
Nicholas A. Basbanes.—1st ed.
p.   cm.
Includes bibliographical references and index.
ISBN 10: 0-06-059323-7
ISBN 13: 978-0-06-059323-0
1. Best books.   2. Books and reading.   I. Title.

Z1035.A1B15   2005
028'.9—dc22   2005046164

05   06   07   08   09   NMSG/RRD   10 9 8 7 6 5 4 3 2 1

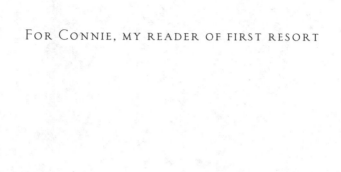

FOR CONNIE, MY READER OF FIRST RESORT

ACKNOWLEDGMENTS

This book benefits greatly from multiple meetings over the years with a number of its principal subjects, most notably David McCullough, whom I have had the pleasure to interview in each of the past four decades, the first time in 1977, on the occasion of his having written *The Path Between the Seas*, a brilliant history of the making of the Panama Canal that for me has been a model of nonfiction writing at its very best.

Additionally, there have been four lengthy interviews with Harold Bloom, and two each with Daniel Aaron, Robert Coles, Robert Fagles, Sherwin B. Nuland, and Helen Vendler. As I was formulating the scope of this book—and thinking about whom I would place on a short list of the best-read people I have ever met—those names came immediately to mind, and it was a joy to meet yet again with each of them. The opportunity to meet for the first time with Matthew J. Bruccoli, William H. Gass, Heather Jackson, Perri Klass, Breon Mitchell, Elaine Pagels, and Christopher Ricks was a great privilege as well, and I express my deep appreciation to one and all for their willingness to share their thoughts, perceptions, and opinions with me, and to do so with such grace and eloquence.

It is with no small measure of satisfaction to note that most of the books used and cited within these pages have come from my own shelves, one small testament to the merits of lifelong accumulation. For the elusive titles that were not within arm's reach, however—and there were dozens of them—I acknowledge with particular gratitude the continuing friendship and support of James E. Hogan, director of library services at the Dinand Library of the College of the Holy Cross in Worcester, Massachusetts, with special thanks to Lynne Riley and Patty Porcaro. My thanks also to the good people at the Robert H. Goddard Library of Clark University in Worcester, and at the Boston Athenæum, one of the nation's great membership libraries.

For their assistance in furnishing images of materials in their collections, my thanks to Joel Silver and Anthony Tedeschi at the Lilly Library of Indiana University, Paul Israel, director of the Thomas A. Edison Papers Project at Rutgers University, and Earle Havens of the Boston Public Library. My appreciation as well to Theresa M. Collins and Lisa Gitelman for permission to quote from their perceptive paper on Edison and his books.

My literary agents, Glen Hartley and Lynn Chu, and their associate Catharine Sprinkel, continue to be champions of my work. At Harper-Collins, I extend deepest appreciation to my editor, Hugh Van Dusen, for the great care he has taken to guide my books so smoothly through the process. I am grateful also to Jane Beirn, Tim Brazier, Marie Estrada, and David Koral, and to copyeditor Bill Harris for such a careful reading of the typescript.

Once again, my eternal gratitude goes out to Terry Belanger, university professor and director of the Rare Book School at the University of Virginia, Charlottesville, whose frank and penetrating comments over the years have enriched my grasp of this fascinating world, and have unfailingly improved the work that has resulted. Jean Fitzgerald of Fort Lauderdale, Florida, and Dimitri Manthos of London, England—each a "common reader" in the rich tradition of Samuel Johnson and Virginia Woolf—read this book in draft and shared their insights, comments, and criticisms, for which I am profoundly grateful.

Acknowledgments

My daughters provided much more than their love and inspiration this time around; Barbara's elegant translations from the French were indispensable, Nicole's careful management of the research materials a godsend. The contributions of my wife, Connie, are evident on every page of every book I write. Everything, she constantly reminds me, is a work-in-progress, words of wisdom that guide my days.

Contents

LIST OF ILLUSTRATIONS

Except where noted, photographs are courtesy of Nicholas A. Basbanes.

1. The historian and biographer David McCullough at the Massachusetts Historical Society in Boston.

2. The marginalia of President John Adams is everywhere apparent in his copy of Mary Wollstonecraft's *Historical and Moral View of the Origin and Progress of the French Revolution*, 1794. *Courtesy of the Boston Public Library.*

3. Thomas Paine's *Common Sense* openly called for separation of the American Colonies from England, and is believed by many historians to have contributed directly to the Declaration of Independence. *Courtesy of the Lilly Library, Indiana University.*

4. Volume 1 of Edward Gibbon's *Decline and Fall of the Roman Empire*, one of several influential books issued in 1776, a "banner year for books," according to David McCullough. *Courtesy of the Lilly Library, Indiana University.*

5. Volume 1 of Adam Smith's *Wealth of Nations*, also published in 1776. *Courtesy of the Lilly Library, Indiana University.*

6. Critic, author, and educator Harold Bloom: "I don't pretend to be a canon maker. I simply say that this is the best that I can make on the basis of what I've read twice."

7. Helen Vendler, "the finest close line reader in the world" of poetry, according to the Nobel laureate Seamus Heaney.

8. Author and critic Christopher Ricks: "The trouble with the word canon is that it sells the past."

9. Robert Fagles, translator of the *Iliad* and *Odyssey:* "A really serious translation becomes a new work of art in its own right." *Courtesy of Mary Cross.*

10. Author and translator of Rainer Maria Rilke's *Duino Elegies,* William H. Gass.

11. Breon Mitchell, scholar, director of the Lilly Library, and translator of Franz Kafka's *The Trial.*

There are perhaps no days of our childhood we lived so fully as those we believe we left without having lived them, those we spent with a favorite book. Everything that filled them for others, so it seemed, and that we dismissed as a vulgar obstacle to a divine pleasure: the game for which a friend would come to fetch us at the most interesting passage; the troublesome bee or sun ray that forced us to lift our eyes from the page or to change position; the provisions for the afternoon snack that we had been made to take along and that we left beside us on the bench, without touching, while above our head the sun was diminishing in force in the blue sky; the dinner we had to return home for, and during which we thought only of going up immediately afterward to finish the interrupted chapter, all those things which reading should have kept us from feeling anything but annoyance at, it has on the contrary engraved in us so sweet a memory of (so much more precious to our present judgment than what we read then with such love), that if we still happen today to leaf through those books of another time, it is for no other reason than that they are the only calendars we have kept of days that have vanished, and we hope to see reflected on their pages the dwellings and the ponds which no longer exist.

—MARCEL PROUST, "ON READING" (1906)

EVERY
BOOK ITS
READER

THE MAGIC DOOR

I care not how humble your bookshelf may be, nor how lonely the room which it adorns. Close the door of that room behind you, shut off with it all the cares of the outer world, plunge back into the soothing company of the great dead, and then you are through the magic portal into that fair land whither worry and vexation can follow you no more. You have left all that is vulgar and all that is sordid behind you. There stand your noble, silent comrades, waiting in their ranks. Pass your eye down their files. Choose your man. And then you have but to hold up your hand to him and away you go together into dreamland.
—ARTHUR CONAN DOYLE, *Through the Magic Door* (1908)

In the early years of the twentieth century a woman named May Lamberton Becker (1873–1958) enjoyed enormous popularity for the "Readers Guide" columns she wrote for the *New York Evening Post*, and later the *Saturday Review of Literature*. "No teacher in any university, no bibliographer or encyclopedist can have helped so many in sudden need of knowledge," the eminent scholar and critic Henry Seidel Canby wrote of Becker's taste and acumen. Her stock in trade, Canby marveled, was an ability to highlight the best books in "well nigh every field of knowledge and imagination in her years of service," matching books with readers "so often with gratifying results that she may well be regarded as an institution." Canby's comments were offered as a foreword to *A Reader's Guide Book*, a 1924 collection culled from hundreds of Becker's columns. Dedicated to "the librarians of America in gratitude for countless kindnesses," she offered her choices in general groupings that included philosophy, music, travel, religion, poetry, economics, and history, along with more discrete categories, such as "a bride's bookshelf," "teaching English to foreigners," "studying social work," "the baby's first books," and "getting over the grippe."

In its day, getting the May Lamberton Becker stamp of approval carried the same cachet for a book that a nod from the television personality Oprah Winfrey does today. Most of the titles Mrs. Becker recommended speak for their times. Each section of her guide—and there are one hundred and eleven—is prefaced by an inquiring letter from a reader. My copy, purchased for $2 at a secondhand bookstore in Oberlin, Ohio, in 1996, bears the bookplate and the signature of a woman, Grace Kelser Willett, along with the date, 1925, written in ink on the front pastedown. Mrs. Willett had lightly marked in pencil a number of choices that piqued her interest: *The Happy Traveller* by the Reverend Frank Tatchell; *Geography and World Power* by James Fairgrieve; *Our Poets of To-day* by Harold Cook; *West Broadway* by Nina Wilcox Putnam, along with several novels of faraway places and a few anthologies of short stories. To a young man who asked for a list that would give him "something of a background equivalent to a college education," Becker replied that she could, if she wanted, "dispose of this question by saying truthfully that there are no such books. But it would not be fair." Then, ever so gently, she suggested a menu of reading material that would give her correspondent confidence, broaden his reach, and encourage him to go serendipitously in search of other titles. "To read like that is one of the high delights of being a human being, and like all high delights, there must be a certain noble recklessness about it, something quite different from 'calculating profits, so much help from so much reading.' "

My favorite piece in the collection is an essay Becker wrote about a correspondence she had with a woman she never met face-to-face, but considered a kindred spirit all the same. Rarely has the therapeutic power of reading been expressed more poignantly than by this lovely exchange. The friendship began, Becker wrote, when she returned from a month's vacation in the autumn of 1921, and "found on the top of a mountain of mail" a letter written on a single card, "packed in with the skill that comes in only one way—literary tastes early in life combined with a paper shortage." The return address indicated a rural delivery route—an R.F.D.—that elicited yet another bond of sympathy from Becker. "I remember when there were none of these, and I have lived to see a secondhand Ford come climbing the hill to the door of a farmhouse that I knew when it was isolated, bringing all the world to the door with yesterday's newspaper. I watched it wheezing up the valley one calm August morning with not a notion that it was carrying the World War. So I can't even take the letters R.F.D. just as letters; they have too much meaning."

The writer, a farm woman in Pennsylvania whose frugal budget allowed her very little in the way of personal luxuries, had a simple enough request for Becker: "May I ask you to tell me of a few books that you have *loved*, that have made you sit up and just shout with delight? I am going to buy four new books this winter and I want four friends to stay by me, to read over and over." The woman explained that her family's horses were always needed elsewhere when she wanted to go into town, making trips to the library difficult, if not impossible; what she sought was some can't-miss recommendations for books she could acquire through a mail-order purchase. "It was when she began to give me samples to order from that I realized what books must mean to her on the farm," Becker continued, and thereupon provided a brief summary of the woman's reading, along with her sage comments on the literary fashions of the day. "Now I would not have been a human being had I not packed up four books and sent them off with a note saying that I had too many and she too few and that before we could talk business we'd have to make some effort to restore the balance of nature. They were, as I explained, a somewhat haphazard choice because all book lovers should have a little margin and she was running too close to the edge, but it so chanced that every one fitted in to some particular place."

Among the books she sent along was *Dodo Wonders*, a newly issued novel by the prolific English author E. F. Benson, which Becker later learned went right on the woman's shelf next to Sarah Grand's controversial novel of 1893, *The Heavenly Twins*. As for the copy of Louis Untermeyer's *Modern American Poetry*, the woman in Pennsylvania immediately began reading choice selections to her grandchildren, but set aside for later examination Padraic Colum's *Wild Earth* and Réné Juta's *Cape Currey*. Touched deeply by the correspondence, Mrs. Becker decided to let her readers in on what was happening, and devoted a column to the exchange. "I printed part of her letter and turned the choice of the four books over to the readers of the *Guide*, saying that perhaps now some people would see that I did not have to work up interest in a mail that might, at any minute, and generally did, hold a letter as alive as this. The only suggestion I offered was that under the conditions I thought my old rule in the Sunday-school library would apply, which was, as between a thin one and a fat one always take the fat one." Before long, letters were coming in from all over the United States, each one offering thoughts and opinions on which four books the woman might enjoy. "Everyone took the choice of those four books to heart in the proper way. 'I should be miserable,' said one, 'if through me that woman bought a book and then hated it.'"

Mrs. Becker did not tell her readers about another letter she had received from the daughter of the woman she called R.F.D., informing her that the very day the first shipment of books arrived on the farm, her mother had just come home from major surgery. "I learned what they both knew and what I never told the readers of the *Guide*—that the malady was only checked, and that, in a few months at most, agony and death were waiting. All she said about that was how much it meant 'to have four books *all at once* to pass the hours when I must lie still.' " As the weeks passed, many carefully selected books were sent the woman's way, many literary letters were exchanged, and for the only time in the history of her column, Becker gave out the name and address of a correspondent to readers who wanted to write R.F.D. directly.

"If you only know how shameless I am where books are concerned you would not need to be so tactful—making me feel I merit all this because I cannot control my desire for the exquisite pleasure of reading," R.F.D. wrote after several weeks had passed. "I suspect you of a good deal in this. *Why* should you care so much? Have you known book-hunger and loneliness? I never cared for the theatre, dancing or society as most women do. With books I slip out of my life and am with the choicest company. I am grateful to the ones who have reached out their hands to me, but I do not know how to say it so it will sound right. I must wonder if I am awake and really hearing from people who care for books as I do. And now that I am in pain it seems as if they had come in my greatest need."

Realizing that time was running out, the woman confided how desperately she wanted to "hang on until Arnold Bennett's *Mr. Prohack*" was released, "and perhaps that will give me another lease on life, eh? You love him too. I can always re-read *Clayhanger*." Becker knew from her sources that *Mr. Prohack*, though in the press, was nowhere near publication, "but within five minutes" she had Bennett's publishers on the phone, "and within two hours the first copy anyone saw in America, even the reviewers, was on its way to R.F.D. She began to read it by herself and then the daughter whose tenderness enfolded her took up the reading." In the intervals of consciousness that remained, the book was finished, "and with the last words a blessed haze of opiates rose around her bright spirit," and then the woman died. "In life I never met Mrs. Katherine Hilliard Young," Becker concluded. "But if ever I go to Heaven I know where to find her. I shall go straight over to the corner by the bookcases."

I was reminded of May Lamberton Becker and R.F.D. in June 2004 when word spread through the book world that A. David Schwartz, the greatly admired second-generation owner of the Harry W. Schwartz Bookshops in Milwaukee, Wisconsin—one of the truly great independent bookstores remaining in the United States—had died at the age of sixty-five after a long and painful battle with lung cancer, an especially shocking development since Schwartz had never been a smoker. Established in 1927 by an idealistic man whose founding principle was that "books are the physical representation of ideas," the Schwartz stores, now in their third generation of family ownership, have maintained a firm dedication to the centrality of literature in modern society. Indeed, a mission statement posted on the company's Web site expresses that sentiment precisely. "We continue to believe that books embody the ideas that turn us from isolated souls into a powerful community," it declares. "At Harry W. Schwartz Bookshops, books are more than merchandise. We are a staff of serious readers, passionate about our favorite authors and subjects. Some of us are writers and many of us have spent our adult lives in book-selling. Living as we do in a time when alienation from one's job is the norm, we feel privileged to spend our days in an occupation we love. Providing readers with the books they seek is a commitment we do not make lightly."

As moving as that statement is—and I consider it a profoundly touching expression of intellectual purpose in these early years of the twenty-first century—it was a profile of David Schwartz published in the *Milwaukee Journal Sentinel* three months *before* his death that I found particularly revealing, coming as it did at a time when I was still considering the scope and direction *Every Book Its Reader* would take. Schwartz had told his interviewer that one of the first things he did when he learned the previous year that he was gravely ill was to pick up a small octavo edition in four compact volumes of Leo Tolstoy's great novel of the nineteenth century, *War and Peace*, a set of manageable size that he could handle easily while hospitalized. Though he had read the novel as a young man decades earlier, something about the work attracted him in his hour of mortal crisis. "It was something I had always wanted to go back to. I saw the physical size of the book and I thought, I can actually hold this book. I saw the actual amount of words and pages and I thought, well, this would be a good book to die with."

Schwartz said that he was not turning to Tolstoy for inspiration, that he had answered for himself many of life's toughest questions years earlier, issues dealing with spirituality, the finality of death, and the great beyond. Though by no means in agreement with Tolstoy's thoughts on existence, Schwartz found the opportunity he had to engage with the author's fertile mind totally stimulating. "He is so smart, he's in enough places that you can find whole avenues that you can walk down together with him before he branches off. And that's why it's an endlessly fascinating book even though I come from a different perspective." What made the exercise of reading the novel anew after the passage of more than four decades especially meaningful was an offer that came from a good friend, John Gilligan, to share it with him. Together, they took turns reading aloud to each other from the same version, and when they had finished that, they moved on to Seamus Heaney's 1999 translation of *Beowulf.* An obsessive worker for most of his life, Schwartz by then had reduced his time at the bookstores to twenty or so hours a week, preferring instead to stay at home and read. "I was somebody who never thought I would retire, surely not at sixty-five. I'm now quite satisfied to spend time at home reading, and talking to my friends, and being with my wife. I'm simply not an unhappy man." And the example he set apparently had an impact on those around him. "I have been able to convince close to a dozen people and, finally, my wife, to read *War and Peace*. I'm not sure they all have the equal enthusiasm that I had, and some of them are bewailing their commitment to it, but they have read it. So I have remained a bookseller through and through." David Schwartz died on June 7, 2004, and was buried on June 11, the same day Ronald Reagan was laid to rest in California, but with far less ceremony.

The idea of a book coming forward in an hour of pressing need is appealing to consider, but it would be misleading to suggest that such a moment is driven entirely by the imminent prospect of death. I think in this regard of Terry Waite, the Anglican churchman held hostage in Beirut for 1,763 days during the 1980s, who retained his sanity partly by composing in his mind a memoir that he committed to paper upon his release, and by reading books that his captors begrudgingly doled out to him in his final year of captivity. "I was forced to depend upon memory and traveled back across the years to recall books I had read during my life," he wrote later of his first months chained in a room. On the day he was finally given something to read—*Beyond Euphrates*, by Freya Stark, a travel book—he was filled with joy:

> First, I hold it to my face to capture the lingering smell of new volumes in the bookshop in Wilmslow. Next I see how many pages there are and count the words on each page so that I will know exactly how long it will take me to read the book. I tell myself that I must read slowly, but I know I am not capable of such discipline. Once beyond the first page, I will want to continue until the whole joyous experience is complete. Along with the book, the guard has given me a small plastic magnifying glass as I have no reading glasses. It's hardly sufficient, but it does the job, and that's all I need.

When Waite was given another book, he was ecstatic, since it was Alexander Solzhenitsyn's *The First Circle*, a work he had always wanted to read. Again, he counted the number of words. "I want to savour the book, to enter into the mind of the writer." When the lights in his room were turned off, Waite lit the stub of a candle with one of three remaining matches he had been rationed by his captors, and stumbled across a quotation from Thomas à Kempis: "I have sought for rest everywhere, but I have found it nowhere except in a corner with a book."

What has to be regarded as one of the most influential books of the twentieth century, *The Diary of Anne Frank*, met its readership by pure happenstance. When German soldiers arrested the fourteen-year-old girl and seven others in the Amsterdam apartment annex they had occupied for two years, the notebook and loose sheets containing the journal were overlooked, and left on the floor. The papers were locked away for safekeeping until the war was over by Miep Gies, a friend who had helped the group while they were in hiding. If any one piece of writing can be said to have given a habitation and a name to the human loss of the Holocaust, it is this journal, well known today by millions of readers in many languages, and by many more who have seen the 1959 Academy Award–winning film that was based on it. Determined to be a professional writer when she grew up, young Anne Frank (1929–1945) worked at developing her skills at shaping narrative. On May 11, 1944, less than three months before her arrest on August 4, 1944, she wrote directly to her diary, which she called "Kitty," confiding her most fervent aspiration:

Now about something else; you've known for a long time that my greatest wish is to become a journalist someday and later on a famous writer. Whether these leanings toward greatness (or insanity?) will ever materialize remains to be seen, but I certainly have the subjects in my mind. In any case, I want to publish a book entitled *The Secret Annex* [*het Achterhuis*] after the war. Whether I shall succeed or not, I cannot say, but my diary will be a great help.

When Anne was not making such entries in her notebooks, she was absorbed in whatever books were available. On October 29, 1942, she wrote how her father had made a key decision: "I'm allowed to read more grown-up books lately. I'm now reading *Eva's Youth* by Nico van Suchtelen. I can't see much difference between this and the schoolgirl love stories." Further on, she reported that "Daddy has brought the plays of Goethe and Schiller from the big cupboard," and that he planned to read them aloud to her every evening. Anne discussed several dozen books, including novels, works of history and biography from which she copied out sections that interested her. On July 3, 1943, she reported how Miep was bringing five library books every Saturday for the group to read, a great event that was eagerly anticipated by all. "We always long for Saturdays when our books come. Just like little children receiving a present. Ordinary people simply don't know what books mean to us, shut up here." And on April 6, 1944, while telling "Kitty" what she regarded as her hobbies, she shared this: "I can hardly wait for the day that I shall be able to comb through the books in the public library."

At the other extreme, there is the uplifting story of the Pack Horse Library Project, which was established in 1935 by the Works Progress Administration (WPA) to provide books to isolated regions of eastern Kentucky that had no access to public libraries. Designed primarily to give needy women work during the years of the Great Depression— qualified men got the more desirable jobs in construction, building roads, schools, health clinics, and community centers—the project served 100,000 residents of the rural Appalachian area, with librarians riding horses and mules up and down dirt trails, through mountain basins and along rocky creek beds, delivering reading material to some of the most destitute people in the United States. Because the government only funded salaries, all books and magazines were discards that had been donated by schools, churches, or libraries, and when demand far exceeded supply, scrapbooks containing magazine and newspaper clippings were compiled by the staff for distribution, such was the hunger. "The book woman's coming, she's coming down the creek," was a shout often heard echoing up the hollows. The program was terminated in 1943, when money ran out; ten years would pass before another innovation—the bookmobile—was introduced to the region.

One of the great surprise best-selling works of recent years was a memoir by Azar Nafisi, an Iranian national who is now a professor of literature at Johns Hopkins University in Baltimore, titled *Reading Lolita in Tehran*; released in 2003, the book went through numerous printings and was translated into more than a dozen languages. The idea of a group of people—in this instance eight Iranian women—gathering once a week in someone's living room to discuss books is not, at first glance, a particularly momentous event. It happens all the time, of course, as the great success of reading groups makes abundantly clear. But Nafisi hosted her book group during the postrevolutionary days of the Islamic Republic in Tehran, when people who were discovered reading the works of Henry James, Jane Austen, F. Scott Fitzgerald, or Vladimir Nabokov faced serious reprisals, possibly hard time in horrific jail cells. "That room, for all of us, became a place of transgression," Nafisi wrote. "What a wonderland it was! Sitting around the large coffee table covered with bouquets of flowers, we moved in and out of the novels we read." Looking back on that clandestine group's meetings, which began in 1995, she was amazed at how much they all learned together. "We were, to borrow from Nabokov, to experience how the ordinary pebble of ordinary life could be transformed into a jewel through the magic eye of fiction."

The epiphany for the great American man of letters of the Harlem Renaissance, Langston Hughes (1902–1967)—a person described in his time as the "Poet Laureate of the Negro Race"—came when he was a lonely second-grader living with his maternal grandmother in Lawrence, Kansas, and seeking the kind of direction that he could find nowhere else. "Then it was that books began to happen to me, and I began to believe in nothing but books and the wonderful world in books—where if people suffered, they suffered in beautiful language, not in monosyllables, as we did in Kansas," he wrote years later. Hughes read voraciously, from the Bible, from the essays on African-American life of W. E. B. DuBois, and was influenced greatly by the poetry of Henry Wadsworth Longfellow and Walt Whitman. When he dropped out of Columbia University in 1923, he took a job as an able seaman on a merchant freighter bound for West Africa from New York, and in a gesture of youthful rebellion, Hughes dumped a box of textbooks over the side of the SS *Malone* off Sandy Hook, a symbolic severing of ties to a difficult past that he recalled in the opening scene of his autobiography of 1940, *The Big Sea*. "Melodramatic maybe, it seems to me now. But then it was like throwing a million bricks out of my heart when I threw the books into the water." Noticing that one volume failed to make it over the side—a work by H. L. Mencken, he recalled—Hughes tossed the straggler far into the night sky. "You see, books had been happening to me," he repeated. "Now the books were cast off back there somewhere in the churn of spray and night behind the propeller. I was glad they were gone." Hughes was twenty-one at the time, and he would come to realize that it was through books—not apart from them—that he would make sense of his life.

That literature is fundamental to our cultural heritage and our shared patrimony is a given. The Greeks have their *Iliad* and *Odyssey*, the Chinese their *Tao te Ching*, the Indians their *Mahabharata*, the Italians their *Divine Comedy*, the Spanish their *Don Quixote*, and each of these works is a literary masterpiece that is transcendent, every one an *epic* in the most fundamental sense of the word. Even among cultures that have not survived to our time, great works that helped define who these people were live on—the Mesopotamians with their *Gilgamesh*, the Persians with their *Shahnameh*, the Anglo-Saxons with their *Beowulf*, the Romans with their *Aeneid*, the Maya with their *Popol Vuh*, to cite just a few examples. But books not only define lives, civilizations, and collective identities, they also have the power to shape events and nudge the course of history, and they do it in countless ways. Some of them are profoundly obvious, as in the case of Harriet Beecher Stowe's *Uncle Tom's Cabin*, the 1852 novel that, some believe, moved Abraham Lincoln to remark, "caused this great war," or Rachel Carson's *Silent Spring*, an eloquent condemnation of the pesticide DDT issued in 1962 that questioned the sureness of technological progress and ushered in the environmental protection movement.

Those books were read by millions of people, and their impact was immediate. Other books, though read by only a few in their time—Nicolaus Copernicus's *De Revolutionibus Orbium Coelestium* (On the Revolutions of the Celestial Spheres) of 1543 being a prime example—were read all the same by an *important* few, and thus altered the way humanity views the world, in this case the entire solar system and the vast universe that contains it. *Civil Disobedience* was published in 1866, four years after its author, Henry David Thoreau, had died at the age of forty-four. The essay had little influence on nineteenth-century thinkers at first, prompting the Russian novelist Leo Tolstoy to wonder why Americans paid very little attention to its thesis, which advocated the principles of passive resistance. Adherents of this approach in the twentieth century, though, included Mahatma Gandhi and Martin Luther King Jr.

One of my favorite examples along these lines involves an obscure monograph written in 1919 by the pioneering physicist Dr. Robert H. Goddard (1882–1945) titled *A Method of Reaching Extreme Altitudes*, and issued in a sixty-nine-page pamphlet by the Smithsonian Institution as a "miscellaneous publication." Regarded today as the generative document in the development of modern rocketry, the essay was mocked in the United States as naïve and fanciful when it appeared, with the *New York Times* going so far as to declare that Goddard's ideas lacked such basic knowledge as "ladled out daily in high schools." Some readers in Germany, most notably Dr. Wernher von Braun and the scientific team he assembled to develop the V-1 and V-2 guided missiles, were not so dismissive of Goddard's experiments, and pored over all of his writings, including the dozens of patents he had filed that in turn became matters of public record. When questioned at the end of World War II about their work with liquid propellants and sophisticated guidance systems, one German engineer told his captors: "Why don't you ask your own Dr. Goddard? He knows better than any of us." As a youngster growing up in Worcester, Massachusetts, Goddard's favorite book was Jules Verne's *From the Earth to the Moon* (1869), and he claimed that it was those fanciful musings of extraterrestrial flight that inspired him to develop achievable ways of probing the heavens, in the process becoming the modern world's first bona fide rocket scientist. As an undergraduate student at Worcester Polytechnic Institute in 1907, he submitted his first piece of writing on the subject to *Scientific American*, an essay titled "Possibility of Investigating Interplanetary Space." On the day in 1969 that Apollo 11 left earth's atmosphere and headed for a rendezvous with the moon, the *New York Times* humorously reconsidered its contemptuous rejection of the ideas the brilliant Clark University professor had put forth fifty years earlier: "Further investigation and experimentation have confirmed the findings of Isaac Newton in the seventeenth century, and it is now definitely established that a rocket can function in a vacuum as well as in an atmosphere. The *Times* regrets the error."

In my 2003 book, *A Splendor of Letters*, I wrote about a small monograph with a long title that had been enormously influential in its time, but through a variety of factors—mainly the embarrassing circumstance of its hateful message of legalized euthanasia—was nowhere to be found in any North American institutional library, though copies had once been held in profusion throughout the land. The book—*Die Freigabe der Vernichtung lebensunwerten Lebens* (Permitting the Destruction of an Unworthy Life) by Dr. Alfred Hoche and Dr. Karl Binding—was published in 1920, and has been described by Robert Jay Lifton in *The Nazi Doctors* as "the crucial theoretic work" that paved the way for the "medical killing" of 200,000 chronically sick, physically disabled, and mentally ill adults, and helped shape a "psychology of genocide" that led ultimately to the mass murders of the Holocaust. In this instructive instance, a book had a decided influence on the course of history, but in ways that were anything but positive, a cautionary tale for the ages.

In 1923, a man named S. R. Ranganathan (1892–1972) applied for a position as chief librarian at the University of Madras in India. Of the nine hundred people who sought the job, none, including Ranganathan, had been trained for the work. What gave this quiet academic the edge was a background in research—he had two degrees in mathematics—and a smattering of information about librarianship gleaned from an essay in the *Encyclopædia Britannica* he had read a few days before being interviewed for the job. Appointed in 1924, Ranganathan was bored at first by the apparent tedium of the routine, but was persuaded to soldier on when offered an opportunity to pursue advanced study in London. When Ranganathan returned to India, he was determined to make books a more powerful force in Indian life, with ideas for the establishment of public and national libraries at the forefront of his agenda. In time he wrote fifty monographs in his field, most notably *Five Laws of Library Science* (1931), which outlined a set of principles that has become a guiding code among professionals. Three of the laws—Books Are for Use, A Reader's

Time Is Precious, and Libraries Are Growing Organisms—were directed primarily at his colleagues. The other two—Every Reader His Book and Every Book Its Reader—have meaning for anyone with an abiding respect for the written word. They also form the guiding premise, and suggested the title, for this book.

ONE OUT OF MANY

In anything fit to be called by the name of reading, the process itself should be absorbing and voluptuous; we should gloat over a book, be rapt clean out of ourselves, and rise from the perusal, our mind filled with the busiest, kaleidoscopic dance of images, incapable of sleep or of continuous thought.
 —ROBERT LOUIS STEVENSON, "A Gossip on Romance" (1882)

What has sometimes been called the greatest exhibition of rare books ever assembled was mounted jointly in the summer of 1963 by the British Museum and a confederation of printing press manufacturers, an odd alliance of bibliophiles and entrepreneurs gathered in common purpose to celebrate the milestones of Western thought. The occasion for the event was the Eleventh International Printing Machinery and Allied Trades Exhibition, a gleaming assortment of industrial and technical equipment crammed into two sprawling convention halls over a ten-day period, with the books added on as a kind of afterthought to trumpet clear and convincing proof of just how much civilization "owes to print," imparting a little class, as it were, to what might otherwise have been perceived as a dull trade show. More than a few eyebrows were raised by the unlikely union, and even the event organizers themselves were bemused by what in some circles seemed to have been a distraction to the no-nonsense task at hand, as two of the guiding spirits readily acknowledged several years later in a lavish retrospective of the extravaganza, aptly titled Printing and the Mind of Man. "*Why*, it might be asked (and was asked), should an association of shrewd and powerful industrialists, engaged on a very expensive, toughly competitive international trade exhibition, waste time and space, let alone money, on a 'cultural' sideshow dreamed up by a couple of visionary antiquarians?" wrote the London booksellers John Carter and Percy H. Muir, two of the "visionary antiquarians" who had coordinated the landmark event.

There were other important people besides Carter and Muir whose enthusiastic support for such an undertaking was necessary before such an idea could get off the ground, most notably Stanley Morison, a leading authority on the history of printing and typography, and the author Ian Fleming, creator of the wildly successful James Bond 007 spy novels, which were at the peak of their popularity in the early 1960s. Morison was described by his colleagues as "the conscience and the mentor" of the London project, though some credit certainly belonged to Fleming, who had formed a fabulous private library centered around the loose premise of identifying books that were notable for having "started something" significant in the world, books that had "made things happen." Though known primarily for his spy novels—he had worked in naval intelligence during World War II—Fleming was a confirmed bibliophile who in 1952 had founded a quarterly journal, *The Book Collector*, that is still regarded as the most important journal in the field. For the collection he built, Fleming's principal adviser had been Percy H. Muir, who called his involvement in the project "one of the proudest achievements of my life."

Muir had begun buying for Fleming in the 1930s, and by the time the Printing and the Mind of Man spectacular was being discussed several decades later, the collection was respected for its originality and comprehensiveness, and it was these books that shaped the concept of the exhibition that ultimately emerged. Pretty much given a free hand to decide what was worthy of inclusion and what was not, Muir had assembled a modest number of high spots, works of unquestioned social and cultural impact that included Charles Darwin's *Origin of Species* (1859), Friedrich Nietzsche's *Also sprach Zarathustra* (Thus Spake Zarathustra, 1891), Albert Einstein's general theory of relativity, *Grundlage der allgemeinen Relativitätstheorie* (1916), and Karl Marx's *Manifest der Kommunistischen Partei* (Communist Manifesto, 1848). But the greater thrust of their activity had been directed more to the lesser-known works than the certifiably famous, the thinking being that everyone knew that Nicolaus Copernicus and Isaac Newton had altered worldviews on astronomy and calculus, and that first-edition copies of their signature works were sure to be expensive, since Fleming's scheme was to build the collection on a modest budget. Thus it was that among the thousand books assembled in his collection were such diverse titles as Alessandro Volta's treatise of 1800, *On the Electricity Excited by the Mere Contact of Conducting Substances of Different Kinds*, Wilhelm Conrad Röntgen's reports documenting his experiments with the penetrative powers of a certain kind of radiation, *Eine neue Art von Strahlen* (A New Kind of Ray, 1895–96), and Robert Baden-Powell's *Scouting for Boys* (1908), the founding document of the Boy Scout movement.

Sixty-three libraries and individuals from more than a dozen countries lent 424 works for display in the King's Library of the British Museum and at Earls Court. Forty-four titles were borrowed from Ian Fleming, a number exceeded only by King's College, Cambridge, with fifty-one. The Lilly Library of Indiana University—which ultimately would purchase the Fleming collection in its entirety from the spy novelist's estate—sent thirty-one. Since *print* was the guiding concept, the exhibition aptly began with the only known surviving proof sheet of the Gutenberg Bible; it concluded with a printed copy of Churchill's famed

Battle of Britain speech, delivered just twenty-three years earlier in the House of Commons, on June 4, 1940.

Thinkers through history who gave their names to words, processes, axioms, laws, movements, or concepts by virtue of their writings—Karl Baedeker, Alexander Graham Bell, Jeremy Bentham, Robert Boyle, Louis Braille, Louis Daguerre, Daniel G. Fahrenheit, Sigmund Freud, Thomas Gresham, John Maynard Keynes, Niccolo Machiavelli, Thomas Robert Malthus, Louis Pasteur, Georg Simon Ohm, Ivan Petrovich Pavlov—were richly represented. A lesser known writing selected on the basis of having "made things happen" was John Napier's 1614 tract *Mirifici Logarithmorum Canonis Descriptio* (Description of the Wonderful Table of Logarithms), a pioneering book of mathematical technique that the exhibition's curators proclaimed to be "unique in the history of science in that a great discovery was the result of the unaided original speculation of one individual without precursors and almost without contemporaries in his field," the key thought there being "without precursors," as so much technical advancement is predicated on what has gone before. Included as well: Francis Galton's breakthrough study that revolutionized police investigations, *Finger Prints* (1892); and Florence Nightingale's *Notes on Matters Affecting the Health, Efficiency, and Hospital Administration of the British Army* (1858), a painstakingly detailed evaluation of ghastly medical conditions in military facilities during the Crimean War that occasioned drastic improvements in hospital care throughout the world.

The selection process was overwhelmingly centered on works of nonfiction, though products of the imagination were not left out entirely. "Creative literature has elevated and inspired the *spirit* of man," the curators wrote of their methodology, which was why they restricted fictional works to writings that had brought about "the propagation of ideas," such as *The Pilgrim's Progress*, *Utopia*, *Candide*, and *Alice's Adventures in Wonderland*, or of characters such as Hamlet, Don Quixote, or Faust, "which have sensibly affected" humanity's *"thinking* and actions—though in fact the accident of typographic distinction has earned a number of pieces of pure literature a place in the aesthetic section."

Of the artifacts displayed, just fourteen, or barely 3 percent of the total, were American in origin. They were: The Eliot Indian Bible (1661); Benjamin Franklin's *Experiments and Observations on Electricity* (1751); the Declaration of Independence (1776); *The Federalist Papers* of Alexander Hamilton, James Madison, and John Jay (1788); Meriwether Lewis and William Clark's journal of their expedition to the Pacific Ocean (1814); Noah Webster's *American Dictionary of the English Language* (1828); Francis Parkman's remarkable history of a continent about to change forever with western expansion, *The California and Oregon Trail* (1849); Harriet Beecher Stowe's abolitionist novel, *Uncle Tom's Cabin* (1852); the first edition of Walt Whitman's pathbreaking collection of poems, *Leaves of Grass* (1855); Abraham Lincoln's Gettysburg Address (1863); Mary Baker Eddy's *Science and Health* (1875), which established a religious movement; Frederick Winslow Taylor's studies of "time and motion" in the workforce, *Principles of Scientific Management* (1911), credited with forming the modern concept of industrial production; the text of Frederick Jackson Turner's *Significance of the Frontier in American History* (1894), a brief address delivered at the Chicago World's Fair in 1893 that "initiated a novel interpretation of the course of American history"; and Woodrow Wilson's "Fourteen Points" (1918), a document of "high idealism" meant to make the world safe for democracy, which "caught the public ear, not only in the United States but everywhere."

Thomas Paine (1737–1809), whose writings were read on both sides of the Atlantic and were arguably as influential in England and France as they were in America, was represented in the exhibition, but not for *Common Sense*, the spirited pamphlet issued in thousands of copies in 1776 that openly called for separation of the American colonies from

England and the formation of an independent republic. Instead, Paine was chosen for his 1791 tract, *Rights of Man*, written and published in England two years after the fall of the Bastille in Paris as a direct response to the conservative Parliamentarian Edmund Burke, whose *Reflections on the Revolution in France* (1790) stressed the dangers implicit in mob rule. Paine's argument—dedicated to "George Washington, President of the United States of America," an entity "which your exemplary Virtue hath so eminently contributed to establish"—offered a lucid discussion of revolutionary politics. Despite determined government attempts to discredit and suppress it, the book was a huge bestseller in England, and thus more consequential in the eyes of those who decided which printed works should be featured in a London exhibition.

A prevailing European attitude on the relevance of American writing in the early nineteenth century was expressed rather succinctly in 1820 by a British critic writing in the *Edinburgh Review*: "In the four quarters of the globe, who reads an American book?" Even the great New England thinker who would become the leading exponent of an American cultural identity, Ralph Waldo Emerson (1803–1882), had very little to do with books written on his native soil in the early years of his development. "Young Emerson was highly susceptible to American oratory, but generally contemptuous of American print culture," the Harvard professor Lawrence Buell wrote in an incisive examination of the person he called the "first public intellectual" in the United States. "Before 1835 not a single American book touched him deeply apart from James Marsh's edition of Coleridge's *Aids to Reflection* (1829) (because of its interpretation of Coleridge) and Sampson Reed's visionary pamphlet *Observations on the Growth of the Mind* (1826) (which led him to the Swedish mystic Emanuel Swedenborg)."

So while fourteen titles may well indeed have been perceived as short shrift for the New World, the imbalance was not entirely out of line. Indeed, the organizers of an exhibition held at the Grolier Club in New

York in 1946, seventeen years *earlier* than Printing and the Mind of Man, tacitly embraced that logic themselves when they were planning an effort that totally *excluded* European writings. Called One Hundred Influential American Books, selections for the New York show had been restricted to works published in North America before the twentieth century, and immediately apparent was the utilitarian aspect of so many of the selections, a circumstance that one of the organizers felt essential to explain in an address to the membership on opening night. In his remarks, Frederick B. Adams Jr., director of the Pierpont Morgan Library from 1948 to 1969, compared the American books embraced by his group with those chosen by the Grolier Club in 1902 to honor One Hundred Books Famous in English Literature, a listing that took books published on both sides of the Atlantic into account, the one criterion applied then being the common tongue. "They were concerned with *famous* books, with *literary* books," Adams said, "we are concerned with books that influenced the life and culture of the American people." For those in the predominantly American audience who needed a further explanation as to why the earlier selection was so top-heavy with British books, Adams offered this:

The small number of American books admitted to the 1902 list on their literary merits has often been remarked, but the naked truth is that prior to 1800 our forebears were too concerned with mastering their strange and often hostile environment and with building a new country to find much leisure time for literature. A glance at the books for this exhibition will make it immediately obvious that theology, science, education, law, Indians, and political propaganda were our standard subjects before 1800, a far more practical fare than was set before contemporaries in the mother country. While we were struggling with the bare and awkward translation of the *Psalm Book*, England produced Browne's *Religio Medici* and Donne's *Sermons* and *Poems*; while Wigglesworth was terrifying us with his foretaste of hell's torments in his *Day of Doom*, our English contemporaries were elevated and inspired by *Paradise Lost* and *Pilgrim's Progress*; while Mather glorified God and New Englanders with his *Magnalia*, Congreve amused ungodly London audiences month after month with his sophisticated *Way of the World*; and while our children struggled over the *New England Primer*, their English cousins of all generations rejoiced in *Robinson Crusoe* and *Gulliver's Travels*. The contrast was most marked between the two most-famous mid-eighteenth-century books written by churchmen: in America Edwards's earnest philosophical treatise on the *Freedom of Will*; in England [Laurence Sterne's] light-hearted, worldly-wise *Life and Opinions of Tristram Shandy*. When we finally produced Irving and Bryant, we began in earnest to compete with England on her own literary terms.

The Grolier 100 list of 1946 by no means ignored America's evolving literary canon prior to 1900, paying respectful tribute to works by a number of writers, each of which deserves mention here. They included: William Cullen Bryant (*Poems*, 1821); Nathaniel Hawthorne (*Twice Told Tales*, 1837, and *The Scarlet Letter*, 1850); Edgar Allan Poe (*Tales*, 1845, and *The Raven, and Other Poems*, 1845); Herman Melville (*Moby-Dick*, 1851); Mark Twain (*The Adventures of Tom Sawyer*, 1876); Louisa May Alcott (*Little Women*, 1868, and *Little Women, Part the Second*, 1869); Henry James (*The Portrait of a Lady*, 1881); William Dean Howells (*The Rise of Silas Lapham*, 1885); Emily Dickinson (*Poems*, three series, 1890, 1891, 1896); Ambrose Bierce (*Tales of Soldiers and Civilians*, 1891); and Stephen Crane (*The Red Badge of Courage*, 1895). Other poets and writers of fiction represented were: James Fenimore Cooper (*The Last of the Mohicans*, 1826); Washington Irving (*The Sketch Book*, published in seven parts, 1819–20); Henry Wadsworth Longfellow (*Ballads and Other*

Poems, 1842, and *The Song of Hiawatha*, 1855); John Greenleaf Whittier (*Snow-Bound*, 1866); and Bret Harte (*The Luck of Roaring Camp*, 1870, a greatly esteemed collection of short stories). Works selected for this exhibition that were later represented in the Printing and the Mind of Man show of 1963 were *Uncle Tom's Cabin* and *Leaves of Grass*.

Though few critics could assail the literary merit of those choices, gray areas developed with the selection of Ann Sophia Stephens and her book *Maleska, The Indian Wife of the White Hunter* (1860). This, the first of the Beadle Dime Novels, was chosen, the Grolier committee wryly pointed out in its notes, "not for what it is, but for what it started," a backhanded way of recognizing the impact on the mass market of what today might be regarded as "trash fiction." The same rationale, presumably, was used to justify inclusion of Susanna Haswell Rowson's *Charlotte, a Tale of Truth* (1794), "the first American fiction best-seller," with 59 editions published through 1830, and another 102 by 1932, by which time the book was known more familiarly as "Charlotte Temple," after the heroine, but which is virtually unknown today except to specialists. A number of other works that survived the cut did so for what has to be assumed was their influence, not their enduring literary merit. Clement C. Moore, for instance, was selected on the strength of "A Visit from St. Nicholas," a workmanlike ballad published anonymously in 1823 that introduced a rotund man in a red suit whose once-a-year exploits with a team of flying reindeer bring joy to millions of children worldwide. But by far the most utilitarian item of all—to call it a "book" is a decided stretch—was the first mail-order broadside, issued in 1872 by Montgomery Ward & Co. of Chicago; two years later, the first pamphlet mail-order catalog in the United States was issued by Montgomery Ward, featuring 573 items. Seventeen years after that, the first Sears, Roebuck catalog appeared, and continued appearing through most of the twentieth century, earning recognition as "The Farmer's Bible" and "The Nation's Wish Book."

The mail order catalogue has been perhaps the single greatest influence in increasing the standard of American middle-class living. It brought the benefit of wholesale prices to city and hamlet, to the cross-roads and prairie; it inculcated cash payment as against crippling credit; it urged millions of housewives to bring into their homes and place upon their backs and in their shelves and on their floors creature comforts which otherwise they could never have hoped for; and, above all, it submitted sound quality for shoddy. As a final bow, the mail order catalogue was, in too many homes, the only illustrated book.

Edward Bellamy's utopian romance, *Looking Backward: 2000–1887* (1888), was chosen because its vision of a socialist state stirred tremendous controversy in its time, but it is largely forgotten today. Timothy Shay Arthur's *Ten Nights in a Bar-Room* (1854) was described as the "literary spear-head of the temperance movement in America," with sales during the 1850s and 1860s that were surpassed only by *Uncle Tom's Cabin*. It would not be polite to call Horatio Alger Jr. a "hack," though even his most devoted fans—and I have given keynote addresses at two annual meetings of the Horatio Alger Society—acknowledge that his 119 books of rags-to-riches success were formulaic at best, yet *Ragged Dick* (1868), the first of these confections preaching that virtue is always rewarded with happiness and honor, was selected for inclusion among the Grolier 100. Though few people read these tales today, the phrase a "Horatio Alger character" still pops up in daily discourse, most recently—and most appropriately, perhaps—in obituaries written of Ronald Reagan in 2004.

The key word in the Grolier exhibition was the adjective "influential." It was on the basis of this premise that *The Farmer's Almanac*, begun by Robert Bailey Thomas in 1792, and which is still printed annually more than two hundred years later, became one of the chosen. Its first appearance came during the eighteenth century, when almanacs were "second only in importance to the Bible," and "entered largely into the life of the people, especially of those living in the country." They contained pithy prescriptions for everything from pickling carrots and cucumbers to predicting the weather and tracking the movements of the tides. A similar thinking justified the selection of William Holmes McGuffey's *Eclectic First Reader* (1836), a school text with forty-five lessons that "by its nature, was read to destruction." It is said that, on average, one million copies were sold every year from 1852 to 1894, and that the total sale of spellers, printers, and readers produced through 1920 was 120 million copies. *Mrs. Lincoln's Cook Book*, published in Boston in 1884, and its immediate successor, *Fannie Farmer's Cook Book*, became standard kitchen companions throughout the United States, inaugurating an industry of food-preparation books that has thrived ever since.

One of the three Grolier selectors, John T. Winterich, the author of several books on book collecting, had the nettlesome assignment of playing devil's advocate, a task he handled with wit and aplomb. "The announcement of this meeting declares that I am to 'present the case for the opposition,'" he said in his remarks. "Opposition to what? To the Declaration of Independence? To the Constitution of the United States? To *Walden* and the Gettysburg Address and *Little Women*?" He mused that while selecting the one hundred most influential American books certainly was an admirable undertaking, "I venture the opinion that if the whole membership of the Grolier Club were divided into committees of equal size with this one, no two committees would come up with the same list of books by ten or twenty or perhaps even more titles." After sharing a few of his personal "quibbles"—was the selection of William Gilmore Simms's antebellum novel of life in South Carolina, *The Yemassee* (1835), for instance, a "concession to the Southern faction of the committee"—

he mildly questioned the whole concept of "influence," and wondered how such a quality can possibly be assessed on the impact of print alone, at least for some of the selections:

> The physical fact of print did not of itself initiate the influence exerted by the Declaration of Independence, the Constitution of the United States, or Monroe's message of December 2, 1823. I will grant that it expedited and extended that influence, but it did not induce it. I know what the Dred Scott decision was and what it did, but I have never read the text of it. I can look at the exhibition copy unmoved. I cannot look unmoved at the copy of [Frances Hodgson Burnett's] *Little Lord Fauntleroy*, because it once determined the kind of clothes I wore. There indeed is a printed book that influenced "the life and culture of the people."

In 1989, an ambitious exhibition at the Bibliothèque nationale in Paris presented a French compilation of four hundred books, with a thousand-year range that did not restrict itself to the printed word, but also included manuscripts in the mix. Just one condition was imposed, as the name of the show, *En Français dans le texte: dix siècles de lumières par le livre* (The Text in French: Ten Centuries of Illumination by Books), suggested: every writing had to have had an indelible impact on the world, but most particularly on France, and all had to have been originally in French. A writer did not have to be French to qualify, though the vast majority of those selected were, with Simone de Beauvoir, Denis Diderot, Louise Labé, Molière, Montaigne, Rousseau, George Sand, Jean-Paul Sartre, and Voltaire among the many names to be featured. A few foreign authors who wrote in French were included as well, most notably the thirteenth-century adventurer Marco Polo, the tell-all Venetian diarist Giacomo Casanova, the Irish expatriate Samuel Beckett, the Romanian-born playwright Eugene Ionesco, and the German mathematician, philosopher, scientist, and librarian Gottfried Wilhelm Leibniz, who composed his discourses on metaphysics in the language.

The introduction to the exhibition catalog was written by Yves Bonnefoy, a widely admired man of letters whose poems and translations had brought him many honors over the previous fifty years, including a seat on the illustrious Collège de France. His preface is filled with imagery of the vastness of the heavens and light, and asks more questions than it can possibly hope to answer, though one message is clear, that "books have given our country its civilization." He compared books to stars in a summer sky. "They have illuminated, guided, and announced a certain moment in time," he declared. "They show our civilization the way of the future. These four hundred brighten the countless other works that are out there, other stars, each one different, each waiting patiently to be discovered." He then asked a series of questions: "What awaits the intrepid explorer who negotiates the empty space and attempts to understand the darkness? What does a book strive to be against the night that constantly threatens to envelop it? Is it something more than thoughts hiding between two pieces of leather, waiting for someone to allow the light to shine? Will books one day transcend language itself? Where does it all lead? We remain in the dark of night, limited by our range of vision, waiting. Why do we always want these books in our hands? Because they are our guides into the unknown."

Among the guiding "stars" to illuminate the Paris gallery was the 1658 collaboration of Nicolas Sanson and Melchior Tavernier on *Cartes générales de toutes les parties du monde* (General Maps of Every Place in the World), an atlas that French travelers relied on for close to a century, and *l'Histoire des deux Indes* (The History of the two Indias) by Abbot Guillaume Thomas Raynal and Denis Diderot, which first appeared anonymously in 1770 and dealt with exploration and commerce in the Indies and in America. Diderot's strident denunciations of slavery and exploitation in the colonies prompted the French parliament to ban the work and send Raynal into exile. Republished in 1780, it contributed to the fall of the ancien régime, but by the end of the eighteenth century Raynal was forgotten. Only in recent years have his writings been reexamined.

Déclaration des droits de l'homme et du citoyen—the French counterpart of the American Declaration of Independence—was ratified by the national assembly on August 26, 1789. Although limited in scope—it guaranteed rights only to men, for example—the charter continued to nourish social upheaval in France throughout the nineteenth and twentieth centuries. It found new life in 1946 as *Déclaration Universelle des droits de l'homme*, when it was used as a model document for the chartering of the United Nations. Napoleon Bonaparte, a voracious reader, carried books with him into battle, but he was not overly solicitous of contrary views. When Germaine de Staël, the wife of the Swedish ambassador to France, wrote *De l'Allemagne* in 1810, a work strongly critical of his Code Civil, Napoleon had the work suppressed and ordered her sent into exile. Published and disseminated in 1804, the code spelled out in 2,281 articles the rights of citizens, and remained in force through 1880.

Of the making of books, Ecclesiastes reminds us, there is no end; second only to the production of books in the world of letters, perhaps, is the making of lists, most of them focusing on "best" efforts, some decrying the "worst." One of my favorites is *The Best Books of Our Time: 1901–1925*, written and compiled by Asa Don Dickinson (1876–1960), a career librarian who studied under Melvil Dewey at the New York State Library School in Albany and served variously at the Brooklyn Public Library, Brooklyn College, Union College, Washington State College, the Leavenworth, Kansas Public Library, and from 1919 until his retirement in 1944, at the University of Pennsylvania. During World War I he was responsible for gathering more than a million books for the American Library Association to distribute among the troops in Europe, a program that he personally supervised from a warehouse in Paris. A prolific writer and editor, he enjoyed some success in 1924 with *One Thousand Best Books*, which encouraged him to undertake *The Best Books of Our Time*. His lengthy subtitle pretty much summarized the ambitious task at hand: *Another Clue to the Literary Labyrinth Consisting of a List of One Thousand Best Books Published in the First Quarter of the Twentieth Century Selected by the Best Authorities Accompanied by Critical Descriptions.*

Until the moment I found this book gathering dust in a secondhand bookstore I knew nothing whatsoever about it. Truth be known, I did not know very much about Asa Don Dickinson or his oeuvre either, but I instantly admired the verve and deep sense of purpose of the project, and I even liked his dedication "to the readers of 1975," who might one day pick up his compilation in search of guidance and inspiration. As it happened, I came to it in 2000, and the price I paid, $2, was probably about what the sturdy hardcover had cost when issued. Even the methodology Dickinson used had some charm to it. "The titles included have been chosen by no single person, but according to a consensus of expert opinion," he made clear, emphasizing that "no book has been included unless at least four sponsors for it have been found." The list of "sponsors" he consulted fills nine pages, and includes such authorities as A. St. John Adcock, author of *Gods of Modern Grub Street: Impressions of Contemporary Authors* (1923); positive reviews that had appeared in the *Book Review Digest*, an important periodical of the time; books discussed in the twelfth edition of the *Encyclopædia Britannica*; the observations of John Macy, author of *Story of the World's Literature* (1925); Carl Van Doren and Mark Van Doren, authors of *British and American Literature Since 1890* (1925); and books chosen by former president Theodore Roosevelt for the "Pigskin Library" he took with him on a hunting expedition to Africa. The epigraph used for the book, from Proverbs 11:14, is pertinent to Dickinson's scheme: "Where no counsel is, the people fall: but in the multitude of counselors there is safety," a delightfully cautious way of saying that strength comes in numbers. But then does it always?

Dickinson singled out the work of 378 authors, 309 of them British and American, the remaining 69 coming from thirteen countries, and each of them notable for "surmounting the barrier of language which lies between them and the English-speaking peoples for whose use this guide has been prepared." What is really great fun here is the structure Dickinson employed. He opened with a traditional alphabetical listing of authors, beginning with Henry Adams, Jane Addams, George Ade, and Mildred Aldrich, and continued on through Anzia Yezierska, Israel Zangwill, Alfred Eckhard Zimmern, and Charles Zueblin. The number of endorsements each author received from the various "sponsors" was listed and the books they wrote were succinctly summarized, with snippets of favorable reviews included as a kind of additional validation of high esteem. Following that is a list of the "ten favorite authors of our day"—they are, in order of their popularity, John Galsworthy, H. G. Wells, Arnold Bennett, G. Bernard Shaw, Edith Wharton, Joseph Conrad, Booth Tarkington, Rudyard Kipling, W. H. Hudson, and Joseph Hergesheimer—followed by the "twenty-five favorites," with fifteen names—Hugh Walpole, Eugene O'Neill, G. K. Chesterton, Stewart Edward White, Willa Sibert Cather, Sir James M. Barrie, Jack London, Winston Churchill, Henry James, Gamaliel Bradford, William J. Locke, James Branch Cabell, J. M. Synge, May Sinclair, and Theodore Dreiser—added to the top ten.

I cite each of these authors individually to make the point that while some of the names have fallen out of favor over time—Hudson, Hergesheimer, White, Bradford, Locke, and May Sinclair are almost totally off today's reading lists—Dickinson and his "sponsors" have still acquitted themselves rather decently with their first twenty-five selections. In the following section, each author is listed in order of endorsements received: Galsworthy earned number one by garnering 197 votes; H. G. Wells came in second with 172; Arnold Bennett was third with 127.

But it is at this point where the numbers begin to wander in curious directions, and we begin to see the fickle nature of contemporary fame. A writer named Percy MacKay, for instance, got more support for his writing than Sherwood Anderson, O. Henry, and Owen Wister. The names Zona Gale, Robert Herrick, Margaret Deland, H. A. Franck, Hamlin Garland, and Agnes Repplier, bibliographical blips at best today, handily outpolled the likes of Sinclair Lewis, William James, Anton Chekhov, Thomas Hardy, Robert Frost, Henry Adams, Amy Lowell, William Dean Howells, and William Butler Yeats, whose eighteen votes seem particularly egregious. And the further down the list we go, the "best" authors become more and more remote to a reader in the first decade of the twenty-first century. Eugène Brieux, Ellen Key, Henri Barbusse, Antonio Fogazzaro, W. F. Moneypenny, Ludwig Lewison, and Prince von Buelow verily jump off the pages, each and every one of them new to my eyes, yet all acclaimed in their day as having given life to some of the "best books" of their time, which may well have been the feeling eighty years ago, but is almost laughably embarrassing today when measured against authors whose names appear in the same compilation *beneath* these now-marginal luminaries of the past. Near the bottom of the list are to be found Albert Einstein, Thomas Mann, Sigmund Freud, Havelock Ellis, Helen Keller, Luigi Pirandello, A. A. Milne, and Marcel Proust, a ringing commentary on the lasting nature of genuine influence.

Dickinson's miscalculation, it seems to me, was that he allowed himself no wiggle room. He picked a thousand books, which was certainly ambitious, but instead of declaring them to be the "most noteworthy," or the "most beloved," or even the "most resonant" or the "most readable," he chose without equivocation to declare them "the best." For readers of today who are conversant with John Collis Snaith's *Araminta* (1909),

Feodor Sologub's *Little Demon* (1907), Carl Van Vechten's *Peter Whiffle* (1922), or Mrs. Humphrey Ward's *Testing of Diana Mallory* (1908), I tip my hat, but I have not seen them assigned as required reading on any college syllabus I have perused, nor have I seen them discussed in any scholarly journal or literary periodical of recent vintage, nor can I find any evidence of any of their still being in print. This does not detract in any way from any impact they may have had on their time, or their intrinsic literary merit, for that matter—the title of this book, after all, is *Every Book Its Reader*, which takes prevailing fashion into account—but merely suggests how dangerous it is to make pronouncements intended to be eternal on the basis of ephemeral data.

A far safer approach was taken in 1986 by three recent Harvard graduates who had asked 113 professors at their alma mater to discuss "the books that have shaped their thinking" with an idea toward compiling a "guide to reading for the future." What C. Maury Devine, Claudia M. Dissel, and Kim D. Parrish came up with was *The Harvard Guide to Influential Books*, with the *Harvard* imprimatur—and a dedication to the memory of John F. Kennedy, A.B. '40, "a passionate reader, a student of life"—giving it exactly the kind of texture it needed to make readers in search of authoritative advice take notice.

Their choices are eclectic, and in some cases revealing. Anyone who ever met the late paleontologist Stephen Jay Gould, for example, would not be surprised by the choices this vibrantly curious man offered. Sure, Gould was suitably impressed as a youngster with the writings of Charles Darwin, but as a kid who grew up playing stickball in New York—and he gleefully showed me some of the autographed baseballs he kept on the bookshelves of his SoHo town house when I met him there for an interview in 1996—he was equally smitten with Joe DiMaggio's 1946 memoir, *Lucky to Be a Yankee*. Bernard Bailyn, whose extensive writings on American history earned him numerous honors, including a Pulitzer Prize in 1968 for *The Ideological Origin of the American Revolution*, singled out three works of fiction—Thomas Mann's *Doctor Faustus* (1947), William Faulkner's *Absalom! Absalom!* (1936), and *The Stories of William Trevor* (1983)—among his six choices. Of the Mann selection, he declared it a "brilliant commentary, in fictional form, on German culture—its great achievement and deadly disease," while Faulkner's "multigenerational saga of Southern life, woven in an elaborate narrative structure, swept me along by its wildly imaginative storytelling." The poetry critic Helen Vendler—the first woman ever to be named a University Professor at Harvard, and the subject of a profile elsewhere in this book—chose not to make any specific recommendations. "The stuff of poetry, the life of the affections, the speculations of the mind and the contradictions of existence, are as alive in Homer as in us, for readers and writers alike," she responded. "The patterning of language—present in every culture—seems likely to be with us 'til the end of time." So what advice did Professor Vendler have to offer? "I think others should find for themselves," she suggested. "For one reader, it will be Whitman, for another, Marvell, for another, Dickinson. As Dickinson said, 'The Soul selects her own society—Then—shuts the Door.' "

In 1939, Malcolm Cowley, poet, critic, editor, and chronicler of the Lost Generation, joined Bernard Smith, an editor at the publishing firm of Alfred A. Knopf who in time would make a name for himself as a Hollywood producer, in convening what they described as a symposium of ideas to determine which nonfiction works of the twentieth century had "profoundly affected the intellectual climate of our era." The results of their queries were published in *Books That Changed Our Minds*, an erudite effort that is notable for the fine focus of its premise, and for the discursive nature of the contributions they gathered. Given that the century had barely run a third of its course, this was quite a challenge they had set for themselves, one that Cowley, a towering intellect in his own right who would serve as chancellor of the American Academy of Arts and Letters from 1966 to 1976, put in some perspective. "By confining itself to the twentieth century," he allowed, the project left "no place for the nineteenth-century books that continue to mold our thinking, not even for the two with the deepest influence on our own time," those being Karl Marx's *Communist Manifesto* of 1848 and Charles Darwin's *Origin of Species* of 1859. That significant qualification aside, Cowley, Smith, and the editors of the *New Republic* who conceived the project, saw merit in singling out a dozen books that had been powerful enough in the relatively few years since their first release to impact contemporary thought in meaningful ways. Calling on some of the most eminent critics of the day—Lewis Mumford, Max Lerner, George Soule, Clarence E. Ayres, Charles A. Beard, Louis Kronenberger, Rexford G. Tugwell, and Paul Radin—Cowley and Smith took the pulse of America, as it were, highlighting books that had helped formulate "ideas that are changing the modern American mind." Cowley explained the motivation for the exercise:

> Sooner or later the life of our time is summarized in its books. Our new ideas are expressed there, whatever may be their original sources or the first mediums through which they reached us. It is books that form the permanent record, and books that furnish the most convenient basis for describing the mind of the world in which we live. In many ways it is a different mind from that of the world in which our fathers lived, and books at the very least have contributed to the change.

On everyone's short list was Sigmund Freud's *Interpretation of Dreams*, published in 1900 and thus just qualifying for twentieth-century consideration. "The important question is whether Freud is correct, not whether one deplores the truth he found," George Soule observed of the tremors the Vienna psychoanalyst's explorations into the mysteries of the subconscious had evoked three decades after they were first postulated, and still reverberate now. It was for similar reasons that Thorstein

Veblen, the Wisconsin economist who coined the phrase "conspicuous consumption," did not make the cut for his best-known work, *Theory of the Leisure Class*, since that major monograph was issued in 1899, but was singled out instead for his *Theory of Business Enterprise*, which appeared in print in 1904. The time gap was explained away through a convenient loophole, though it took a bit of hedging by the critic Rexford G. Tugwell to explain. "It would be difficult to say which of his books influenced us the most," he wrote, noting that *Theory of Business Enterprise* was the third volume in what he suggested was a seamless trilogy, with a series of articles including an important essay, "The Preconceptions of Business Enterprise," appearing second, thus making it possible to perceive a clear pattern that extended into the twentieth century. "All these, as can be understood from unmistakable likenesses melting into and illuminating one another, emerged from the same mind during one period of an uninterrupted stream. So that if one book can not be centered on, one creative design is quite easy to distinguish." That is what is known as splitting hairs, but obviously they wanted Veblen in, and they got him in.

Few observers today could question the logic of including Henry Adams, Frederick Jackson Turner, and Vladimir Lenin in a group of influential twentieth-century writers, though it is interesting to note that the Adams book chosen was *The Education of Henry Adams*, a work never intended by its author for public distribution. Henry Adams issued his introspective memoir in 1907 in an edition of one hundred copies, and circulated it exclusively among his close friends. It did not appear in a trade edition until six months after his death, in 1918; the following year it won a Pulitzer Prize. How a book never intended by its author for public consumption could in twenty years be regarded by intellectuals of formidable stature to be one of the seminal autobiographical writings of its time is pertinent, especially when the premise being argued is that influence is not always measured by the number of people a work may reach, but *who* it reaches.

The grandson and great-grandson of two American presidents, John Quincy Adams and John Adams, and the eldest son of Charles Francis Adams, a Massachusetts congressman who served as Abraham Lincoln's ambassador to Great Britain, Henry Adams (1838–1918) broke with family tradition by eschewing public service and dedicating his life to scholarship. Speaking of himself throughout the autobiography in the third person, Adams wryly acknowledged that being born with such a distinguished pedigree had allowed him to be "ticketed through life" with the "safeguards of an old, established traffic," though such safeguards, he quickly pointed out, "are often irksome, but sometimes convenient, and if one needs that at all, one is apt to need them badly." His dilemma—and it became the mantra of his memoir—was that he was *not* driven to follow the expected path, and that he felt lost at the crossroads. "What could become of such a child of the seventeenth and eighteenth centuries," he asked plaintively, "when he should wake up to find himself required to play the game of the twentieth?"

For the critic Louis Kronenberger, Adams's book "found its most responsive readers in those years following the World War when they too had reason to believe that American life had failed them; and to every American intellectual who still retained inside him vestiges of the American moralist, Adams's grim citation of a century's crimes and blunders helped explain the plight of the modern world." And what gave the book special relevance, Kronenberger argued—and what continues to give it such resonance today—is that "not a dozen Americans of any period were intellectually and morally of a stature to produce it." Adams, Kronenberger reminded his readers, was a person "who came to know everything within the reach of the cultivated man of the world, everything to be had of drawing-rooms and libraries, colleges and clubs, churches and ruins, senates and courts." And though forced by circumstance to regard the twentieth century with a discerning eye, he was clearly of the nineteenth. Not liking what he saw, he issued a warning to those who in due course would give full shape to the decades that remained. It was a book, quite obviously, that changed people's minds.

Not nearly as obvious from today's perspective are the five works that rounded out the 1939 selection, titles that are likely to send many readers scurrying to their encyclopedias or launching Google searches on their computers for further clarification. *Folkways* (1907), by the Yale sociologist William Graham Sumner, was cited for having charted the evolution of human customs and introducing such terms as "mores" and "ethnocentrism" to the language. The German-born ethnologist Franz Boas pioneered a scientific approach to anthropology in *The Mind of Primitive Man* in 1911, though the critic Paul Radin acknowledged in his commentary that it had "little immediate effect on his contemporaries, outside the circle of his students and professional colleagues." But one of Boas's most salient arguments—that no race is innately superior to any other—would in time generate considerable comment, especially when balanced against what Radin called "the presence of the fascist threats to civilization" then evident throughout the world. In the realm of literary discourse, the judges were mightily impressed by Vernon Louis Parrington's *Main Currents in American Thought*, published just a decade earlier, in 1928, and *Principles of Literary Criticism*, by the Cambridge University scholar I. A. Richards, released in 1924.

If popularity was a criterion for selection, then Charles A. Beard's *An Economic Interpretation of the Constitution* (1913) would never have made the list, Max Lerner wrote, since its influence was "not to be measured by its sales, which, after the initial flurry on publication, dribbled along year after year until new interest was awakened by the New Deal constitutional crisis." Instead, Lerner felt, "Beard's book on the Constitution is one of those books that become a legend—that are more discussed than read, and are known more for their title than their analysis. But in a quarter-century its thesis has increasingly seeped into our history-writing—although a recent study shows that most of the primary and secondary school textbooks either ignore it or mention it only for refutation. It is not hard to guess that this is because school supervisors are still fundamentalists."

The twelfth author selected, the philosopher John Dewey, was perhaps the most problematic of them all, with the editors citing him generally for a body of work that had spanned most of the century to that point, but specifically for *Studies in Logical Theory*, a volume of essays published in 1903 that was by then out of print and largely being ignored when Cowley and his colleagues were putting together their list. "It will be interesting to see what the world does with such a book," C. E. Ayres wrote about it, noting paradoxically that a good deal of the philosopher's growing obscurity derived from the success of his earlier views, and that the "dwindling of Dewey's fame," it reasonably followed, had resulted from "the growing familiarity of his ideas."

Especially interesting about this symposium in print was Cowley's tacit acknowledgment that a good number of the selections were *not* known by a high percentage of the reading public, and that some of the authors, like Dewey, had already drifted off center stage into obscurity. Indeed, Cowley felt it necessary to explain in an afterword why *Books That Changed Our Minds* had ignored entirely the most popular and widest read books of the day. "By confining itself to scholarly and speculative works, it leaves no place for works of the imagination. And people might say that even if poems and plays were omitted, novels should certainly be included on our list, on the ground that about five-sixths of American reading is fiction. To that criticism, there is a fairly simple answer. We are not concerned here with American reading habits, or with literature as such, but chiefly with the source of our ideas." With the book appearing as it did in 1939, and with global conflict looming on the horizon, Cowley was mindful of the power certain books have to define their times, yet the focus of his effort was on *American* thought, not what was shaping ideas in Europe.

By now the Italian and German fascists, who started with almost no philosophy at all, have adopted a long line of intellectual step-parents—for example, Count Arthur de Gobineau, with his "Essay on the Inequality of Races," and Houston Stewart Chamberlain, who was Gobineau's apostle, and Richard Wagner, with his blond-beast heroes out of the Nibelungenlied, and Friedrich Nietzche, with his pitiless supermen, and Georges Sorel, the French syndicalist who converted Mussolini to his belief in social myths and the beauties of violence, and Gaëtano Mosca, the Italian sociologist who outlined the theory of the elite that Pareto would develop in systematic detail. The house of fascist thought, as Max Lerner said, has become a death-house of all nations. Yet among the scores of fascist and pre-fascist thinkers, only Spengler is discussed in this series. A place might have been found for at least one other, and preferably for Hitler himself. By forcing us to defend the ideas that we once took for granted, he has affected us more deeply than many authors whose opinions agree with ours.

As coincidence would have it, within a matter of months a place was found for the American people to have an unfiltered look at the thinking of Adolf Hitler, with the publication that same year of the first English translation of *Mein Kampf.* "The most important book in the world," the publisher proclaimed darkly on the dust jacket, urging the American people to "read and judge for themselves" a work "which has sold in Germany by the millions, and which is probably the best written evidence of the character, the mind, and the spirit of Adolf Hitler and his government." The publisher inserted a commentary at the front of the book by the writer Dorothy Thompson—who eight years earlier had written *I Saw Hitler*—that explained why such a "deeply barbarous book" was being released at that time to an international audience:

Americans can now read the text of the book that has shaken Western civilization. The reader will find the English writing rhetorical, turbid, and digressive, and the text disorganized. Do not, however, criticize the translators. Hitler's first battle was with the German language, and this fight at least he has never won. Let it be said that if the world is overthrown by this document and the man behind it, it is overthrown without benefit of grammar or literary style.

In the late 1990s, as the second millennium drew to a close, people everywhere were offering up itemizations of innumerable things that had helped define the era about to end, with books being no exception. In the United States, among the more interesting were results published by the Modern Library, a division of Random House, listing the top one hundred works of fiction and nonfiction published since 1900, as determined by separate boards of eminent scholars, with James Joyce's *Ulysses* coming in as the number-one novel, and *The Education of Henry Adams* heading up the nonfiction side. "The goal was to get people talking about books," the sponsors said in response to criticism that inevitably came in regarding some of their choices—incredulity over some books that were on the list, dismay over others that were not—prompting an invitation to the reading public to submit their own choices in an online poll. Some 400,000 responses were received by e-mail, resulting in selections that bear little resemblance to the compilations prepared by the experts, illustrated best, perhaps, by the two first choices. The favorite novel of the respondents: Ayn Rand's *Atlas Shrugged*. Their favorite work of nonfiction: *The Virtue of Selfishness*—also by Ayn Rand. (The complete lists are posted on the Random House Web site; see endnote for link.) A rival list to the Modern Library selections, meanwhile, was prepared by the Radcliffe Publishing Course of Radcliffe College, with F. Scott Fitzgerald's *Great Gatsby* and J. D. Salinger's *Catcher in the Rye* taking the top two spots, pushing *Ulysses* all the way down to fifth, behind John Steinbeck's *Grapes of Wrath* and Harper Lee's *To Kill a Mockingbird*.

In Britain, fifty thousand members of the Folio Society, a book club, overwhelmingly chose J. R. R. Tolkien's cycle of Middle Earth novels, *The Lord of the Rings*, over all comers, agreeing with a *London Times* survey conducted in 1997 that ranked it as "Britain's Favourite Book" of the twentieth century. The following year, the English author Martin Seymour-Smith weighed in with *The 100 Most Influential Books Ever Written: The History of Thought from Ancient Times to Today*, a decidedly high-brow compilation listed chronologically (from *The I Ching*, 1500 BC, to B. F. Skinner's *Beyond Freedom and Dignity*, 1971) that one reviewer in the *New Statesman* called much "too serious," with little lee-way having been allowed for "the effect of imaginative writing on people's lives." In England, the journal *LOGOS* compiled a list of lists, a number of them quite compelling, including one from a Moscow publisher suggesting "the most influential books of the century *from the Russian point of view*," which led the editors of the publication to seek out other regional lists, and to produce its own multinational compilation, published in 1999 as *1900–2000: Books That Shaped the Century*.

For myself, it happens that my wife, Connie, and I, as a literary project we share together, have been reviewing children's books since the early 1990s for a number of newspapers, and have developed what we immodestly regard as a sense of connoisseurship for the genre. Thus it happens that a favorite list of ours is *100 Best Books for Children*, a thoughtful, erudite, fully annotated list gathered by Anita Silvey, a long-time editor and reviewer for the *Horn Book Magazine*—the acknowledged "bible of children's literature"—and a publisher of children's books for Houghton Mifflin Company. "For over fifty-five years I have read, and reread, about 125,000 children's books," she pointed out in her foreword, giving new meaning to the concept of "critical mass," and putting in some context her qualifications for the task. To her credit,

Silvey's choices are not numbered one to one hundred, but are presented thematically and by reading level. "Because children are young for such a short time, we need to give them their literary heritage during these brief years," she explained of her effort. "Just as every literate adult knows certain books, every child should know specific children's books. If we fail to present these books to children, they reach adulthood without a basic literary heritage."

The word "heritage," of course, suggests the past, and if there is anything every book on each and every one of these lists has in common it is that they all, to one degree or other, reflect on what has happened, not necessarily on whatever may lie ahead in the future. Breon Mitchell, director of the Lilly Library of rare books and manuscripts at Indiana University in Bloomington, Indiana, and custodian of the Ian Fleming books that were used in the Printing and the Mind of Man exhibition among multiple other remarkable collections, told me that the concept of looking backward needs to be redefined, at least on an institutional level, to incorporate works whose impact remains unproven, especially when the mission of these institutions is charged with gathering materials that will be of historical and cultural significance generations from now. This is especially pertinent at the Lilly, a research library that is renowned for collecting the manuscripts, archives, correspondence, and books of living writers, not just those of recognized merit. "Once you have this canon established, its impact, in a sense, is finished—well, not finished, of course, its impact continues—but somehow that whole exercise about establishing a canon is looking back at it. Here we try to collect books that we think people will care about three hundred years from now."

One way to do this, he said, is to buy new books on standing order in a broad range of British and American authors, "and to have all of the first editions of those authors in very nice condition, and not to have missed out on them in some way simply because we didn't have the foresight to get them three hundred years earlier. So collecting broadly is one way of doing this." Another aspect that concerns Mitchell is the need to take a global approach to collecting. "We bought the first Chinese edition of Mao Tse-tung's Little Red Book," he said, an exceedingly scarce item, it happens, given that many millions of the book have been distributed since its first appearance in May 1964 in an initial printing of 200,000 copies; by 1967, some 720 million copies of the book formally titled *Quotations of Chairman Mao* (*Mao Zhu Xi Yu Lu*) were in print. Several billion more have appeared since then, the precise figure pretty much guesswork, but in numbers that certainly would put it in company with the Bible as the most circulated book of all time.

"There probably aren't a lot of libraries looking for that first issue, or collecting it right now," Mitchell said of his copy. "But I think there's no doubt that if someone were planning, let's say, a Printing and the Mind of Man extension—an updated exhibition—that's got to be one of the books that would be interesting to have represented. Most of our Printing and the Mind of Man material is really Eurocentric, and centered in the past; the future is going to be much more global, and therefore a work like Mao, coming out of China, is going to be very important. And there are undoubtedly many other important things appearing around the world that we will be interested in having here at the Lilly."

As to whether future writings will come to research libraries as printed books or in some kind of electronic form, Mitchell said he expects to receive material of mixed media. "We have many authors now who say to me, 'You want my papers, does that mean you want the disks also?' Or, 'You want my electronic files? You want my e-mail?' Right now I'm saying yes, send us your disks, copy out your e-mails, send them by attachment, whatever. That's the correspondence we have, and we have to figure out how to preserve it, but I'm one of the people who believes that the book will last forever. The book is such a wonderful thing, and it has so much to it beyond the text itself, the physical artifact, the book is absolutely going to last for hundreds of years."

3.

EYE OF THE BEHOLDER

The meaning of any beautiful created thing is at least as much in the soul of him who looks at it, as it was in his soul who wrought it. Nay, it is rather the beholder who lends to the beautiful thing its myriad meanings and makes it marvellous for us, and sets it in some new relation to the age, so that it becomes a vital portion of our lives, and a symbol of what we pray for, or perhaps, of what, having prayed for, we fear that we may receive.

—OSCAR WILDE, *Intentions* (1891)

As a former book editor whose job it was to cultivate a diverse corps of reviewers for a Sunday newspaper, I learned early on that when people share their reading habits with you, what they are really granting is privileged access to their deepest interests and predilections, even their dreams, needs, and anxieties. Causing me the most anxiety by far, I must say, was the responsibility to pair the right book with the right reader, since just as important as playing matchmaker with reviewers was the obligation I felt to be fair with the authors, who deserve to be evaluated intelligently on the merits of the work at hand, and nothing else. But that, as they say, is another story entirely. One of my old job's most satisfying perks, on the other hand, was the opportunity I had to meet with hundreds of writers, an exercise I enjoyed so much that I still write literary profiles periodically for a number of publications. At last count, I had conducted more than a thousand of these interviews, some of them in various cities around the United States, a few abroad, but most of them in Boston.

For years the hotel of choice to lodge "front-list" authors out on tour was the Ritz-Carlton. Most of my interviews took place in the authors' rooms, though occasionally arrangements were made to talk in the café, the lounge, or the dining room. Only on three occasions—when I had breakfast with the actor Leonard Nimoy, lunch with the television newsman Walter Cronkite, and dinner with everyone's favorite gourmet cook, Julia Child—was there an obvious celebrity buzz among staff and patrons. If any of them recognized Margaret Atwood, Pat Conroy, Michael Crichton, Robertson Davies, E. L. Doctorow, Mary Gordon, Joseph Heller, George V. Higgins, P. D. James, or William Kennedy, they did not show it. Sometimes, if the weather was especially nice, we might go across Arlington Street and talk in the Public Garden, where the character is decidedly Back Bay, and the setting most conducive to candid conversation.

To prepare, I always relied primarily on my reading of the new book being released, supplemented by whatever background material seemed pertinent at the time, along with an immersion in other works the authors had written. My goal was to have a focused dialogue. Usually, I formulated about a half dozen questions in advance, more often than not during the hour's drive from my home in central Massachusetts into Boston. In the course of making hundreds of these trips, I confess to having daydreamed every now and then about how I would go about conducting the ultimate literary interview of them all. Fueled by a lifelong love for the works of William Shakespeare, I admit a whimsical desire to discover something new and meaningful about the man, a daunting challenge in a field heavily populated by professional scholars who have devoted their careers to the task. From time to time—it became something of a project over the years—I would ask people who were authorities on various aspects of the great playwright and his oeuvre what question above all others *they* would ask Shakespeare if given the chance.

The challenge clearly interested the critic Harold Bloom in the first of four interviews I have had with him since 1994—the year his book *The Western Canon* became a best-selling work of literary criticism—prompting him to set forth an entire menu of questions he would want to ask. "I would like to talk to him not so much about the sonnets, which I am content to have remain basically a mystery, but I would very much like to talk to him about some of the characters in some of his plays. I would like to talk to him about the relationship between Macbeth and Lady Macbeth as he understood it. I would very much like to talk to him about whether or not, as I deeply suspect, there's a kind of absolute nihilism that underlies the four major tragedies. I guess I'd like to ask him how he really felt about Christopher Marlowe, since I feel increasingly that is the clue to Shakespeare. I think Marlowe for him was both a blessing and a curse."

Of primary interest to Bloom, though—the question he would ask if limited to just one—would be to elicit a comment on his belief that Shakespeare wrote two versions of *Hamlet*, the one known to many millions of admirers over the centuries, and an "Ur-*Hamlet*" that he suspects was written by Shakespeare at the very beginning of his career, not by a contemporary, Thomas Kyd, as has been suggested by others. "I am at variance with most Shakespeare scholars on this point, and I would delight in being proven right from the horse's mouth, as it were," Bloom said. "I believe it was a play that he turned against in its initial form, that he then revised completely and made into a very different *Hamlet*." Indeed, two years after Bloom and I had this discussion, the issue was discussed at length in the book he claimed at the time was the magnum opus upon which he expected his reputation to rest, *Shakespeare: The Invention of the Human.*

The British author Anthony Burgess told me that he would not want to limit himself to one question either, in fact nobody I engaged on the matter did, but he expressed particular interest in nailing down the biographical details of Shakespeare's life. "I'd rather have a laundry list than a lost play, to tell you the truth," he said when we spoke in 1979, noting that he needed "no convincing at all about the magnitude of his genius." My astonishment at this response was palpable, prompting Burgess—whose dozens of writings on a stunning variety of subjects and in multiple genres over a long career, including numerous examples of literary criticism at the highest levels of accomplishment, had made him a genuine hero of mine—to laugh out loud. He then suggested that I read Michel de Montaigne's essay "On Books" for my "general stimulation," and to find in particular a section where the old master reflected on a book he wished *he* had read, if only it had survived the ravages of time. I took his advice, of course, and located the passage. Here it is:

> I have regretted hundreds of times that we have lost the book which Brutus wrote about virtue: it is a beautiful thing to learn the theory from those who thoroughly know the practice; yet seeing that the preacher and the preaching are two different things, I am just as happy to see Brutus in Plutarch as in a book of his own. I would rather have a true account of his chat with his private friends in his tent on the eve of a battle than the oration which he delivered next morning to his army, and what he did in his workroom and bedroom than what he did in the Forum or Senate.

Warming to the subject, Burgess then said he would also want to know if Shakespeare had done any work on the King James Bible, something he had speculated about several years earlier in his own book about the man from Stratford. Burgess had theorized that Shakespeare was recruited in 1610—at a time when he would have been forty-six years old—to work with a team of eminent scholars on preparing what would become known as the King James Bible; Burgess had speculated further that Shakespeare retooled the 46th Psalm to insert the word "shake" forty-six words from the beginning and the word "spear" forty-six words from the end ("if we leave out the cadential *Selah*"), a clever way to secure a modicum of immortality for himself. "This was the Bible, after all, and it was forever," Burgess said over his eggs Benedict. "So you can be sure I would ask him about that."

What may be regarded as a related line of interest, since it also probes, in a way, Shakespeare's sense of self-esteem, would have come from the noted New York publisher Robert Giroux, the author of a 1982 book on the sonnets. "What totally baffles me is why he had no apparent interest in publishing his plays during his lifetime," Giroux said unhesitatingly when we spoke at the Players Club in New York, a beautiful building opposite Gramercy Park that was once the home of the famed Shakespearean actor Edwin Booth, where quotations from Shakespeare are on the walls of every room, and a perfectly appropriate setting for this conversation.

In 1979 I asked the question of the Renaissance scholar Samuel Schoenbaum, the author of several studies of Shakespeare's life and work; his proposal for a single query came the closest to what I believe would be my opening strategy. "I am not at all interested in the identity of the Dark Lady or anything like that," he said. "What I would like to identify in a few succinct sentences are the wellsprings of his creativity, if something like that is at all possible. Where in the world did all this genius come from? That is the direction I would probe."

The British critic Christopher Ricks, who like Harold Bloom is famed for having committed most of Shakespeare to memory, told me in the summer of 2004 that he would ask the dramatist to explain an apparent contradiction in the structure of the play *Measure for Measure* that has bothered him for years. "Entertaining beliefs that you do not hold is an imperative of individual and social training," he began, putting in context the direction he would pursue. "It is very difficult to *train* people to entertain beliefs. It is much easier to get them to *believe* things than to get them to *entertain* beliefs. So if I had the chance to put questions to Shakespeare, I think they'd go something like this: 'Am I incorrect to think there is something wrong with this work of yours, *Measure for Measure*? I would like to have it explained to me that I've got it wrong, because I think this is a very great play. Why is it all right for Angelo to have been, and to be known to the duke to be, a duplicitous or treacherous person? What does it mean to say, "Hence we shall see / If power change purpose, what our seemers be," if all along the person who says that—Duke Vincentio—knows that Angelo had previously, dishonorably, justified the breaking of his engagement with his fiancée, Mariana, by "pretending in her discoveries of dishonor," while really it was because she no longer had a dowry? Now I don't believe that about Angelo's past. I think it is the opening of the play that tells the truth.' So, anyway, I would engage Shakespeare in this manner."

In my wistful agenda, Shakespeare makes a day-trip to Boston, I am there to greet him, and clever literary journalist that I am, I have assembled a short list of probing questions from a cadre of eminent scholars, just in case things bog down and I need to lean a bit on outside authority. It is a lovely summer day and I suggest we talk in the Public Garden, where children's voices trill in the background and ducks scramble for scraps of bread. For shade, we sit beneath one of the ancient mulberry trees that line the artificial pond designed by Frederick Law Olmsted in the 1870s, a nice little touch, I think, given that Shakespeare is said to have planted a mulberry at New Place in Stratford that stood well into the eighteenth century, and a perfect location from which to admire the rickety swan boats as they paddle by in slow procession, something else that might make the man Ben Jonson called the Sweet Swan of Avon break into an appreciative smile.

There is no note taking for this exchange—I want to see the fire in the great man's eyes—although, if I am lucky, he allows me to tape the con-versation on the pocket-sized microcassette recorder I always have with me. Undoubtedly, there will be some small talk to start—I expect he might notice the statue of George Washington mounted on a horse that faces Arlington Street and comment on how British the American general looks—but time is precious, and I need a strong opening question, some-thing with a little bite to get things headed in the right direction, so this is how I begin: "There are some people, Mr. Shakespeare, who refuse to believe you wrote your plays, and one of the reasons they always give is that you never attended college; perhaps we can start with you telling me a little bit about your reading, and how it was that you secured access to these books." And we continue on from there, one unexpected answer after another giving way to one unscripted question after another, all of it a revelation. But Shakespeare's reading is where I would start.

One interesting book collection of fifty-five hundred titles, assembled by the Elizabethan scholar Thomas W. Baldwin and now housed at the University of Illinois in Urbana-Champaign, includes a rich variety of books that were available in Shakespeare's lifetime, and which could have influenced his work. But since nothing survives to document precisely what books Shakespeare may have owned or read, there will always be speculation, and questions will continually be asked how someone with his simple and unsophisticated background could be sufficiently inspired to read and absorb such challenging material on his own. It is largely for this reason that whenever some new theory regarding the "true author-ship" of the Stratford playwright's works comes along, one of the chief arguments inevitably put forth by hard-core skeptics is the absence of a secondary education, and the implication that nobody could possibly have written so beautifully, so incisively, and so knowledgeably of the human condition without university instruction.

Denigrations to that effect are by no means a recent phenomenon; they began to appear, in fact, during Shakespeare's lifetime—indeed, in the very first essay in which his name appears in print—with the publication in 1592 of *Groatsworth of Witte*, a pamphlet in which the impoverished writer Robert Greene complained bitterly of an "upstart crow" who stole his feathers from university men such as himself. This was a jab so petty and malicious that the phrase "green with envy" made its way into the language as a consequence, by way of Shakespeare himself, no less, when Iago reminds a seething Othello that jealousy is the "green-ey'd monster which doth mock the meat it feeds on." Shakespeare's authorship has been questioned often since then, yet again in 1984 with *The Mysterious William Shakespeare*, a tedious argument served up ponderously in 892 pages by Charlton Ogburn, Harvard Class of 1932, who favored anointing Edward de Vere, the 17th Earl of Oxford (1550–1604), the holder of degrees from both Oxford and Cambridge, as the true author of the timeless plays. This theory was first put forth in an aggressive way in 1920 in *"Shakespeare" Identified in Edward de Vere, the Seventeenth Earl of Oxford*, by J. Thomas Looney, yet again in 1997 in *Alias Shakespeare*, by Joseph Sobran, a columnist for the *National Review*, and in the summer of 2005, *"Shakespeare" by Another Name*, by Mark Anderson, a freelance writer.

A determined band of de Vere champions calling themselves the Oxford Shakespeare Society and operating under the slogan *Vero Nihil Verius* (nothing is truer than truth), now has a Web site to argue its case. Each of these arguments follows various threads of the same position, many of them using the same basic premise, none of them terribly different from that of Charlton Ogburn, whose line of attacking Shakespeare began predictably: "No mention is found of the subject's ever having had a day's schooling." To support the argument, he quoted other disbelievers, a doubting cast that over the years has included Walt Whitman, Mark Twain, Henry James, John Galsworthy, Sigmund Freud, Charles Chaplin, Benjamin Disraeli, and Charles de Gaulle.

Ogburn cited a succession of scholars who argue that the person who wrote the plays evinced intimate knowledge not only of the literature of his native England but of ancient Greek and Latin as well, and also what were, in his time, "modern languages and literature." The "myriad-minded man" of the English Renaissance who wrote the plays was familiar with medicine, nature, warfare, the law, the sea, and the European continent, and his alert eye missed nothing of importance. So how, Ogburn wondered, "do orthodox scholars assimilate this vast reading to the life of the Stratfordian 'Shakespeare,' who arrived in London from the literary desert of a provincial town, presumably, without means, speaking the crude Warwickshire dialect?" To frame an answer to his own question, Ogburn quoted the late Elizabethan historian A. L. Rowse's belief that Shakespeare was an "avid," "rapid" reader, blessed with the enviable ability "to grasp at lightning speed what could be attained only after dull years of work by ordinary minds," one way of saying, pure and simple, that the man was a genius. Ogburn's response to such a straightforward position: "That, we may suppose, would have left him time to master French and Italian just to fill up the empty hours."

Ogburn's case for Edward de Vere relied heavily on his refusal to accept that the son of an illiterate glover from Stratford had the intellectual capacity to read insatiably on his own, and to use that knowledge as the foundation for a transcendent body of work. De Vere's early life and education, in contrast to Shakespeare's, are well documented. A bright young man with an impressive lineage, he demonstrated an early facility with language. Ogburn gushed that by the time he was nineteen, "Edward was buying not only the Geneva Bible, Chaucer, Plutarch's works in French, and other books, coming in all to two pounds, seven and ten, but subsequently, 'two Italian books' and later 'Tully's and Plato's works in folio, with other books, paper and nibs' in the amount of four pounds, six and four—then a great deal of money," proof positive that the young man was acquiring the kind of material that would prepare him for bringing into existence the great dramatic works to come.

As for the lad from Stratford, all scholars have to go on is conjecture, such as Rowse's suggestion that most of the time from 1585 to 1592, the famous "lost years" in which nothing is known of Shakespeare's activities, were spent laying in "a considerable stock of reading" and becoming "soused in the classics." There was little in Shakespeare's upbringing, so far as anyone knows, that would have nurtured the curiosity of an inquisitive mind. His mother, Mary Arden, heiress to some land in Warwickshire, may not have been the illiterate most scholars assert she was, though his father, John, a glove maker who became actively involved in Stratford village politics, signed all legal documents bearing his name with the "mark" of a person who could neither read nor write. With next to nothing known of William's formative years, there remains no way of pinpointing what books he may have read as a young man, yet any number of energetic speculations have been advanced, including inventories of primers and texts known to have been used in elementary schools of the period. Samuel Schoenbaum suggested in a 1985 essay, "Shakespeare and the Book," that a grammar school education during Elizabethan times was surprisingly rigorous, and formed the foundation for what was to come, but even he readily acknowledged that this by no means offered a full explanation. "What Shakespeare did acquire in his youth," Schoenbaum surmised, "was a taste for reading, an interest in ideas, and a quick and retentive memory. His own genius and the bookstalls of St. Paul's Churchyard—center for the London book trade—furnished the rest."

William Shakespeare died in 1616, indifferent, apparently, to any thought of ever seeing his dramatic works published during his lifetime, leaving that task to his faithful colleagues from the London theater, John Heminges and Henry Condell, to whom he left small sums to buy rings they could wear in his memory. Their dedication resulted triumphantly with release in 1623 of the book known as the First Folio. Using an almost identical text, the Second Folio of 1632 included a brief poem by John Milton, who was just seven years old when Shakespeare died. Milton himself was soon to embark on a fruitful literary career of his own, one that continued to flourish after the loss of his eyesight, the kind of personal tragedy that has stopped many creative spirits in their tracks, none more poignantly than Eratosthenes of Cyrene (276–194 BC), director of the great library at Alexandria and the first person to determine the correct diameter of the earth. When failing eyesight left the aging scholar unable to make sense of his beloved books—eyeglasses would not be invented for another thousand years—Eratosthenes refused to eat and starved himself to death; when Milton lost his vision in late middle age, the staid Puritan began dictating his prose and poetry to his youngest daughter, Deborah, creating in this manner the poems *Paradise Lost*, *Paradise Regained*, and *Samson Agonistes*.

In a memoir of his life dictated to Deborah, Milton reflected that he read tirelessly among his father's books as a child, and that "from my twelfth year I scarcely ever went to bed before midnight, which was the first cause of injury to my eyes." As a brilliant young student at Christ's College, Cambridge, he is said to have spent his days in the university library immersed in Greek and Hebrew texts, and the evenings in his dormitory quarters poring over books he had brought with him from home. What titles, specifically, he may have had with him are unknown, although undergraduates at nearby Trinity College were required at this time to have copies of Plato, Aristotle, Demosthenes, Cicero, and the Greek Testament, or face expulsion; the likelihood is high that similar requirements applied for Milton at Christ's College.

Considered arrogant, lofty, and snobbish by his classmates, Milton found college anything but fulfilling, and he was suspended at one point for disagreeing with his tutor over the curriculum. He finally received his BA in 1629 at the age of twenty-one, and an MA cum laude three years later. Eschewing the life of a minister, a profession that his mother had championed, Milton nurtured a profound yearning to write poetry. By the time he left Cambridge, he already had composed elegies to several prelates who had died, a number of sonnets in Italian, and "On the Morning of Christ's Nativity." But instead of embarking immediately on a career in letters, he went to live with his parents at their country house in Horton, seventeen miles outside London. Years later, Milton explained how he spent his time there from 1632 to 1637: "I enjoyed an interval of uninterrupted leisure, which I devoted entirely to the study of Greek and Latin authors; though I occasionally visited the metropolis either for the sake of purchasing books, or of learning something new in mathematics or in music, in which I, at that time, found a source of pleasure and amusement. In this manner I spent five years till my mother's death," leading Samuel Johnson to quip how it "might be supposed that he who read so much should have done nothing else." But Milton's biographers and admirers—including Johnson—agree that he was using this reading to prepare himself for the creative works of his own he knew would come. "Milton had read the whole of English poetry, most of Latin, Greek, French, and Italian poetry," A. N. Wilson wrote in his life of the poet. An examination of Milton's journal from that period makes clear how deeply he felt that the "great poem which he will one day write must be prepared for, by learning, by scholarship, by solitude, by withdrawal, by prayer."

A cynic might argue that while Milton's most consequential reading probably did come through independent inquiry, he was mentored from an early age by an acutely alert father, and guided at university in the rigors of disciplined inquiry by seasoned instructors, his recalcitrant nature notwithstanding. In addition to taking her father's dictation, Deborah and her older sister, Mary, were required to read aloud to Milton, not just from works in English that they understood but in languages they could only pronounce, but not comprehend. In his *Lives of the Poets*, Samuel Johnson quoted the poet John Philips (1676–1709), on the demands

Milton placed on his daughters, which the young women did not always find to their liking:

> [They] were condemned to the performance of reading, and exactly pronouncing of all the languages of whatever book he should, at one time or other, think fit to peruse, viz., the Hebrew (and I think the Syriac), the Greek, the Latin, the Italian, Spanish, and French. All which sorts of books to be confined to read, without understanding one word, must needs be a trial of patience almost beyond endurance. Yet it was endured by both for a long time, though the irksomeness of this employment could not be always concealed, but broke out more and more into expressions of uneasiness; so that at length they were all (even the eldest also) sent out to learn some curious and ingenious sorts of manufacture, that are proper for women to learn, particularly embroideries in gold or silver.

Books have been analyzed from every imaginable perspective over the years—how they are written, the ways they are made, distributed, collected, preserved, condemned, banned, or destroyed, a profusion of fascinating approaches. Fear of books is as old as the book itself, and is a subject that has been written about by novelists that range from Miguel de Cervantes in the seventeenth century to Elias Canetti and Ray Bradbury in the twentieth. On a shelf by the desk where I write is a piece of publishing ephemera I received in the mail in 1981, a cardboard placard sent out to book-review editors to commemorate what was then the thirtieth anniversary of the publication of *Fahrenheit 451*. Now yellowed with age, the message printed on the front panel remains clear enough: "Books are dangerous—they make you think!" In 1932, the British author Holbrook Jackson devoted an engaging study to this concept, and used a word, "bibliophobia," to describe the many ways that people have expressed their fear of books over the centuries, in some instances condemning them to incineration, but most spectacularly, perhaps, in 213 BC, when the Chinese prime minister and senior historiographer, Li Ssu, "set out to abolish the past and start history afresh" by ordering every book in the empire "except works of agriculture, medicine and divination" to be destroyed. "Those who refused to give up their books for destruction were branded and condemned to slavery on the Great Wall for four years."

Long before the British physician Thomas W. Bowdler (1754–1825) and his sister, Henrietta Bowdler (1754–1830), took it upon themselves to make the plays of William Shakespeare "safe" for innocent eyes, the wholesale editing of another author's writing so that it might be more palatable to prudish tastes was known as "castration" to some, "winnowing" by others. But with the publication of the first edition of the *Family Shakespeare* in 1807, the world of letters got a new verb—*bowdlerize*—to identify the process of literary expurgation. Inheriting a fortune at the age of thirty-one, Bowdler retired from medicine and undertook a campaign to bring about the "erasure of indecent" passages from Shakespeare's works while taking steps, in his words, "to retain the spirit and fire" of the original. Immensely popular in their time, these sanitized versions of the plays were the principal text by which England's national poet reached thousands of impressionable readers for close to a century, the dialogue discreetly pruned of any references to God or Jesus, with every hint of sexual pleasure or misconduct snipped out. The goal of the Bowdlers was stated rather emphatically on the title page of the *Family Shakespeare*: "In which nothing is added to the original text; but those words and expressions are omitted which cannot with propriety be read aloud in a family."

Some discriminating readers were outraged, to be sure. A writer for the *British Critic* railed that the Bowdlers had "purged and castrated" Shakespeare, "tattooed and beplaistered him, and cauterized and phlebotomized him." But bowdlerism was far from being abandoned, and was adopted by numerous successors, Noah Webster and his heavily expurgated American dictionaries and William Michael Rossetti's watered-down British edition of Walt Whitman's *Leaves of Grass* among the more egregious examples. "Three or four generations in England and America grew up with a moderately inaccurate idea of their own literature as a result," Noel Perrin wrote in *Dr. Bowdler's Legacy*, a discursive history of expurgated books in the two countries. And as belittled as the practice has been since, it has by no means disappeared, Perrin wrote in a 1991 foreword to an updated edition of his book, which was first published in 1969. "Traditional bowdlerism aimed to get sexual terminology out of books, and, as a secondary goal, profanity. Modern bowdlerism exists to get references to race and ethnicity out of books. There were early traces of racial expurgation back in 1971, but there was nothing like the present major force in children's literature."

In the decade and a half that has passed since that assessment, increasing attention has been focused on textbooks that are sanctioned for use in the public schools, with districts in some sections of the United States, to cite just one continuing example, steadfastly refusing to allow the ideas developed in Charles Darwin's *Origin of Species* to be read by high school students as anything other than a "theory." In *Lies My Teacher Told Me* (1995), James W. Loewen, a professor of sociology at the University of Vermont, scrutinized a dozen American history textbooks that were currently in use, and found instances ranging from outright omission to subtle shadings of the facts, books that routinely avoid mentioning such embarrassing issues as Thomas Jefferson and George Washington having owned slaves, or Helen Keller having been a radical socialist.

In *The Language Police* (2003), Diane Ravitch, a historian of education at New York University and a senior fellow at the Brookings

Institution in Washington, D.C., documented numerous instances of how "pressure groups" go about the practice of restricting what high school students are allowed to read in classrooms, not just in history, which was Loewen's principal concern, but in every area of letters, including such fictional works as Mark Twain's *The Adventures of Huckleberry Finn*, Aldous Huxley's *Brave New World*, even Watty Piper's *The Little Engine That Could*, rejected for use in some districts because the locomotive of the story was portrayed as a male, and thus, allegedly, a flagrant example of gender bias. A similar judgment was levied against the venerable Aesop tale from antiquity "The Fox and the Crow," since the crow—a female—"is vain and foolish, while the fox—a male—is intelligent and clever." Some of this censorship, Ravitch demonstrated in numerous examples, is "trivial, some is ludicrous, and some is breathtaking in its power to dumb down what children learn in school." Even more sobering was evidence she marshaled showing that the pressure to limit what children can read comes from many directions. "Both right-wingers and left-wingers demand that publishers shield children from words and ideas that contain what they deem 'wrong' models for living. Both assume that by limiting what children read, they can change society to reflect their worldview."

Deciding what books people are allowed to read is one highly contentious issue; surreptitiously monitoring what they actually do read is something else yet again, and the practice did not begin in the United States with the Patriot Act of 2001, which in certain instances allows federal investigative agencies to require librarians and bookstore owners to turn over records of any books patrons may have borrowed or bought, and forbids them to disclose any details of having done so, making objective oversight of the practice impossible. One of the lesser-known consequences of the relentless hunt for Communists undertaken by Senator Joseph McCarthy in the 1950s was the selective destruction of thirty thousand books acquired by the State Department for use in its Overseas

Libraries Program operated by the United States Information Agency, books condemned in the aftermath of a whirlwind "fact-finding" trip to Europe by Roy Cohn and G. David Schine that has been roundly derided ever since for its pathetically laughable ineptitude.

"McCarthy's lists would arrive, he would want to know how many books we had by a given author or a given list of authors located in all the libraries overseas," Catherine Heniford Lewis, a librarian with the State Department in the 1950s assigned the task of removing books maintained in about two hundred USIA libraries abroad, said in an oral history. "The lists he sent to us were of the most respectable names in almost any field you want to mention. There would be clergymen on the list, there would be journalists, whose names were in the news all the time, on a given list. There would be lists of actors, or people associated with the theater. These people were not Communists." One name on the list was the San Francisco novelist Dashiell Hammett, creator of the private detective Sam Spade, who refused to answer any questions about his political activities during the 1930s before McCarthy's House Un-American Activities Committee, or to "name names." Declared to be in contempt of Congress, Hammett was imprisoned for six months and blacklisted from writing scripts in Hollywood, and suffered the further disgrace of having all of his books, including *The Maltese Falcon* and *The Thin Man*, removed from USIA libraries and unceremoniously sent up in flames.

This travesty of justice from the last half century aside, the question remains: Can the books people buy or read, especially in these post-9/11 days of heightened security awareness, help prevent unspeakable crimes, or provide evidence to solve them after they have been committed? There are a few instances from the recent past that bear on the question, most notably the case of Theodore Kaczynski, known as the Unabomber, who sent sophisticated "letter bombs" through the mail to all reaches of the country over an eighteen-year period, in the end killing three people and injuring twenty-three others. Kaczynski taunted authorities with mocking letters, making the unprecedented offer to end his campaign if the *New York Times* and the *Washington Post* would agree to print his 35,000-word manifesto, the only time in history where it can be demonstrated that an author secured publication of a manuscript by promising to stop murdering people. Referring to himself as "we," Kaczynski admitted as much in what came to be known as the Unabomber Manifesto:

> If we had never done anything violent and had submitted the present writings to a publisher, they probably would not have been accepted. If they had been accepted and published, they probably would not have attracted many readers, because it's more fun to watch the entertainment put out by the media than to read a sober essay. Even if these writings had had many readers, most of these readers would soon have forgotten what they had read as their minds were flooded by the mass of material to which the media expose them. In order to get our message before the public with some chance of making a lasting impression, we've had to kill people.

This long, angry, sometimes rambling, but all the same more-than-capably-written screed was published on September 19, 1995. An anarchistic polemic, it railed against every manner of social convention and called for worldwide revolution against the effects of modern society's "industrial-technological system." From an investigative standpoint, what was truly significant was how much detail the Unabomber had exposed of himself in the context of what he had written.

A full text of Kaczynski's manifesto is available on the Internet—indeed, a reading of the text on a computer by his younger brother, David Kaczynski, is what led ultimately to his arrest—so a detailed summary is not needed here, and the substance of what he had to say is irrelevant in this context anyway. What is germane is that four books were discussed in the manifesto. Kaczynski twice cited *Violence in America: Historical and Comparative Perspectives* (1969), edited by Hugh Davis Graham and Ted Robert Gurr, in one instance quoting a substantial passage from the work verbatim. Other books he discussed were: *The Ancient Engineers* (1963), by L. Sprague De Camp; *Chinese Political Thought in the Twentieth Century* (1971), by Chester C. Tan; and *The True Believer: Thoughts on the Nature of Mass Movements* (1951), by Eric Hoffer. Elsewhere, Kaczynski mentioned an article that appeared in the magazine *Omni*, and discussed an article that appeared in *Scientific American*, furnishing the name of the author of the essay, and giving the date of its appearance.

Seven months elapsed from the time the manifesto was published to when Kaczynski was arrested in a one-room wooden cabin in rural Montana. A grand jury investigating the crimes had authorized a sub-poena of literary records in various areas of the country with the hope of learning whether anyone had checked out the specialized books he had cited, but none of the libraries contacted, it turned out, were at all close to where he was living. Investigators, meanwhile, asked various academics who had been allowed to read the document before it was published by the two newspapers to evaluate his writing. A few of their comments are revealing. "It's clear that the writer has thought about a lot of things and read a lot of things, but I don't see much specifically related to the scholarly discipline of the history of science," John E. Lesch, a professor at the University of California, Berkeley, who has written extensively on the history of science, told a reporter for the *Sacramento Bee*. "His vision of things is not scholarly in any sense," Lesch surmised. "It's kind of apocalyptic. He's seeing things rushing toward disaster for the human race. Certainly you can find academics who view certain aspects of society as damaging, but his kind of radically pessimistic vision of the future is usually not built into an academic discipline."

David C. Lindberg, chairman of the Department of the History of

Science at the University of Wisconsin and president of the History of Science Society, called the discourse "extraordinarily well-written," with "good prose," and sentences that "flow well into one another," and paragraphs "that are coherent." The Unabomber "even knows how to punctuate," he said, "and that's a very rare gift." Based on what Lindberg had been shown, however—and he saw only excerpts—the bomber was not, in his view, an academic or someone with an extensive formal education in the history of science or in technology. "I'm pretty sure the Unabomber didn't come through our program," he told *Bee* reporter Cynthia Hubert. "But that is not at all to suggest that the FBI is barking up the wrong tree. This is really a long shot, but it might pay off. If enough professors read this, someone might say 'I remember a guy in our program who felt that way.' I applaud the attempt, but it's like looking for a needle in all the haystacks in Nebraska."

The headline the *Sacramento Bee* ran over the article made what would prove to be an embarrassing declaration: "Scientists: Unabomber Lacks Formal Schooling." When the case was broken, it was disclosed that Kaczynski had received a bachelor's degree in mathematics from Harvard in 1962, and two graduate degrees from the University of Michigan at Ann Arbor in mathematical science, a master's degree in 1964 and a doctorate in 1967. "Boundary Functions," his dissertation for his doctorate, dealt with a pure mathematics problem of quantities whose value depends on other quantities, and was declared "brilliant." Several articles Kaczynski wrote while living in Ann Arbor had been published in professional publications, including the *Journal of Mathematics and Mechanics* and the *Michigan Mathematics Journal*. On May 26, 1996, in an exhaustive profile that filled three pages of the newspaper and drew on reporting submitted by several dozen journalists, the *New York Times* described Kaczynski as being an "obsessive reader" from the time he was a child growing up in Chicago. "When he was 10, the Kaczynskis went on a camping trip—the father often took them out in the summer and taught them to appreciate the woods, plants and animals—and for vacation reading Teddy took along a volume of *Romping Through Mathematics from Addition to Calculus.*"

The ultimate irony, of course, is that the arrest of the Unabomber did not result from professionals evaluating his reading or investigators getting the break they needed from library records, but the eerie similarities David Kaczynski saw between what he read on the screen of a computer terminal and what he knew to be the troubling views of his brother. "I was prepared to read the manifesto and be able to dismiss any possibility that it would be Ted, but it continued to sound enough like him that I was really upset that it could be him," David Kaczynski said. In one instance, he recognized the curious phrase "cool-headed logicians" as one his brother had used in a letter sent to him some months earlier, and applied in a similar context here. Elsewhere, there was the observation that "you can't eat your cake and have it, too," a variation of the popular expression, "you can't have your cake and eat it, too," that Ted had written in a letter to their mother, Wanda, who saved all of her son's correspondence. David Kaczynski told the *Times* that when he finished reading the manifesto—the actual title was "Industrial Society and Its Future"—his "jaw dropped." It was at that point that he realized he had one option; two and a half weeks later, his brother was arrested by a team of FBI agents, ending the nightmare.

4.

SILENT WITNESSES

❦ ❦

To help my defective and treacherous memory a little—and it is so extremely bad that I have more than once happened to pick up again, thinking it new and unknown to me, a book which I had carefully read several years earlier and scribbled all over with my notes—I have for some time now adopted the practice of adding at the end of each book (I mean of each book which I intend to read only once) the date when I finished reading it and the general judgment I drew from it, in order to show me again at least the general idea and impression I had conceived of its author when reading it.

—MICHEL DE MONTAIGNE, "On Books" (1580)

❦ ❦

The idea that people are products of the things they read, that they are, to a great extent, shaped by their books, is an endlessly fascinating notion to consider. For historians and biographers concerned with motivation, it is an especially fruitful concept to pursue, offering insights not always available from traditional sources. Sometimes, if we are lucky, observations scribbled in books survive as telltale inklings of thought, yet the practice is abhorred as desecration by some bibliophiles obsessed with acquiring pristine copies, and reviled by librarians the world over, most famously articulated, perhaps, in the solemn oath every reader at the Bodleian Library has been required to swear over the past four centuries before privileges are issued. For others, marginal writings squirreled away in books and comments left in journals can be pointers that guide the way to a deeper understanding of purpose.

As a young seaman plying the South Pacific on board the New Bedford whaler *Acushnet* in 1841, Herman Melville borrowed another sailor's copy of *Narrative of the Most Extraordinary and Distressing Shipwreck of the Whale-Ship Essex, of Nantucket* (1821), a firsthand report of the only documented instance of a whale ever turning the tables on its hunters by deliberately ramming their vessel, in this instance sending it to the bottom of the ocean. The harrowing tale of the *Essex* was written by Owen Chase, first mate of the three-master during its ill-fated cruise, and his recollection of the attack on November 20, 1820, had lost none of its immediacy for Melville. "The ship brought up as suddenly and violently as if she had struck a rock and trembled for a few minutes like a leaf," Chase had written. "We looked at each other with perfect amazement, deprived almost of the power of speech."

Though severely damaged, it was a second ramming by the giant sperm whale that sealed the vessel's fate, and the one detail above all others that gave Melville the raw material for the climactic scene in the magnificent novel he would write a decade later. "This was the first printed account of it I had ever seen," Melville wrote of the *Essex* incident in the back of his own copy of Chase's narrative, which he acquired while writing *Moby-Dick*. "The reading of this wondrous story upon the landless sea, and close to the very latitude of the shipwreck, had a surprising effect on me." Little else that befell the survivors of the *Essex* over the ninety-three days of their subsequent ordeal at sea in lifeboats—how they had turned to cannibalism to stay alive, how they drew straws to decide who among them would be sacrificed—made its way into *Moby-Dick*, providing a valuable glimpse into the exquisitely selective workings of the novelist's art.

Certainly one of the most influential literary themes in the Western tradition is the legend of King Arthur, an icon of popular culture over the course of fifteen centuries, whose apocryphal exploits in Celtic Britain were legitimized by the Oxford scholar Geoffrey of Monmouth (c. 1100–c. 1155) in *Historia Regum Britanniae* (History of the Kings of Britain), a work completed in 1148 that became a medieval best seller. Loosely combining some fact with lots of fancy, Geoffrey formally placed Arthur in the forefront of British royalty, and introduced the character of Merlin to the narrative. Arthur became an extremely popular figure throughout Europe, inspiring the writing of romances in no fewer than eleven languages, most notably four tales written in the twelfth century by the French court poet Chrétien de Troyes, and *Tristram and Isolde* early in the thirteenth century by the medieval German poet Gottfried von Strassburg. An anonymously written poem from the fourteenth century in English, *Sir Gawain and the Green Knight*, survives by way of a single manuscript copy now in the British Library.

About 1470, near the end of his life, Thomas Malory (1420–1471), a colorful character whose real-life activities were alleged to have included extortion, robbery, rape, and attempted murder, was incarcerated in Newgate Prison in London on charges of conspiracy, not an infrequent offense during the Wars of the Roses. It was during this confinement that he drew liberally on some Old French tales of Lancelot, the Quest for the Holy Grail, and the death of Arthur compiled in the thirteenth century and known as the Vulgate Cycle, to produce *The Book of King Arthur and His Noble Knights of the Round Table*. These thrilling tales of knight-errantry and derring-do achieved immediate popularity, persuading England's first printer, William Caxton (c. 1422–1491), to make it one of the major productions of his Westminster press, adapting Malory's chivalric tales freely for his 1485 edition and changing the title to *Le Morte d'Arthur* (The Death of Arthur).

Though the source material and the title were French, *Morte d'Arthur* was written in English prose, prompting the curators of the Printing and the Mind of Man exhibition to declare it the "only true" English epic. "The matchless style, the humor, the magnificence, the magic that takes away the breath, combine in a masterpiece of legendary narrative. Each century has produced its own version of the Arthurian legend, but Malory's will never be forgotten." *Idylls of the King*, the outstanding nineteenth-century version, was written in 1859 by Alfred, Lord Tennyson (1809–1892), England's poet laureate for forty-two years. A younger contemporary of Tennyson, Samuel Langhorne Clemens/Mark Twain (1835–1910), was moved to try his own take on the classic in the most serendipitous of ways. During the winter of 1884 and 1885, Twain and George Washington Cable, a prominent writer of the period, barnstormed more than seventy American cities in a series of programs dubbed the "Twins of Genius" tour that were attended by thousands of admirers. After a public reading one night in Rochester, New York, the pair visited a bookstore, where Cable noticed a copy of *Le Morte d'Arthur* lying on a table, prompting him to urge the creator of Tom Sawyer and Huckleberry Finn to buy it, boldly predicting that he would consume the enthralling work in a single sitting. When *A Connecticut Yankee in King Arthur's Court* was published in 1889, Twain called his traveling companion of four years earlier the "godfather" of the novel.

A book casually encountered by an imaginative mind, lighting a spark that ignites a flame of creativity—undoubtedly it has happened on countless occasions. I run across interesting examples often, most recently in an essay the novelist Philip Roth wrote for the *New York Times Book Review* about the premise for his 2004 novel, *The Plot Against America*, in which the hero aviator Charles A. Lindbergh defeats Franklin D. Roosevelt in the 1940 presidential election and institutes a pro-Nazi agenda. Known to be a true reader of the old school—Roth has been quoted, in fact, as saying that one of the reasons literary fiction is in decline in postmodern America is that "serious readers" are dying off faster than they can be replaced—the notion for the novel came in December 2000 while he was reading *A Life in the Twentieth Century*, the autobiography of the historian Arthur M. Schlesinger Jr., which had just been released.

> I came upon a sentence in which Schlesinger notes that there were some Republican isolationists who wanted to run Lindbergh for president in 1940. That's all there was, that one sentence with its reference to Lindbergh and to a fact about him I'd not known. It made me think, "What if they had?" and I wrote the question in the margin. Between writing down that question and the fully evolved book there were three years of work, but that's how the idea came to me.

On May 1, 1913, the London auction company of Sotheby, Wilkinson and Hodge began a six-day sale of pictures, drawings, engravings, autograph letters, manuscripts, works of art, and books accumulated by Robert Browning (1812–1889) and his wife, Elizabeth Barrett Browning (1806–1861), a massive sell-off of more than five thousand items that would realize £28,000. "The resulting dispersal," Philip Kelley and Betty A. Coley wrote in an ambitious attempt seventy years later to reconstruct a detailed inventory list of the holdings, has ever since been regarded as a disaster, having "condemned" scholars in search of material that might illumine the lives of the poetic couple "to wander eternally from library to library like moaning restless shades."

When the biographer Leon Edel (1907–1997) set out to research what would become a benchmark life in five volumes of the novelist Henry

James (1843–1916), he took pains to immerse himself in the books once owned by his subject. In 1937, Edel traveled to Lamb House in Rye, where James had done much of his work while living as an American expatriate in England. "I climbed the hill and for the first time crossed the threshold into an important part of Henry James's past," he recalled in an introductory essay to *The Library of Henry James*, an inventory of books known to have been gathered, treasured, consulted, and consumed by a writer whose formidable oeuvre bears the unmistakable stamp of a widely read thinker. Described by his father as a "devourer of libraries," James was not a connoisseur of rarities in any antiquarian sense, but rather a "highly informed reader, a 'professional' who somehow sniffed out certain interests in volumes as soon as he glanced at them." In his examination of the books, Edel discovered "hundreds of informal little messages" James had written to himself, jottings that "now become messages to us."

> Important for posterity is the way in which James used his books. They were auxiliary to his writing; and this gave them importance above the autograph content which delights collectors. A line drawn down a page, a single word and page number, set down in the front of a book, a tiny cross at the beginning of a paragraph to enable him to find the place when he wanted it—an entire signal system exists in his library. In one volume there can be found the schema for a novel he wrote shortly after making this primitive outline. In my life of James I speak of these volumes—especially when they have a place, a date, a name—as "silent witnesses."

On the title page of a novel by Nathaniel Hawthorne (1804–1864), Edel found the signature of the author, beneath which James had inscribed his own name, a gesture of profound respect the biographer found particularly moving. "Two great American novelists of their time, the older and the younger, here keep eternal company. Perhaps the special message to posterity had been willed by at least one of the parties." Though Edel wrote the essay for this slim monograph fifty years after seeing James's library, which had since been broken up and dispersed, he vividly recalled its contents in their original setting. He remembered the selection as being "strangely miscellaneous, as if gathered from other shelves, consulted and left mixed up with those tenanted here," books on many subjects that were in no way predictable, books that were "heterogeneous and comparatively modern." Standing in no discernible order were Alfred, Lord Tennyson, Robert Browning, James Fenimore Cooper, Hugh Walpole, a volume of Edward Fitzgerald's letters, several George Sand novels, Dante in a Florentine edition, a copy of *Les Fleurs du mal* "in an edition of 1872, that is about the time of James's essay on Baudelaire." Edel noted volumes on every floor of the large house and in every room, yet for all the apparent disorder, "I suspect he knew where each volume was."

As exciting as it was for Edel to examine the notes Henry James had jotted in his books—the "silent witnesses," as he called them—even greater satisfaction came from finding echoes of what his subject had read in his own published works. They are so numerous that Edel conceived of an imaginary collector, an admirer of Henry James, who sets out on a mission to gather every book mentioned or hinted at in the twenty novels and 112 tales that his hero saw through the press. "Our mythical collector," Edel surmised, would "have to acquire the entire *Comédie humaine* of Balzac in its original 23-volume edition, for it was probably here that James first read *Louis Lambert*, unless he had had some earlier edition. It would be safe to acquire that many-volumed edition, because the collector would soon discover that James is constantly using Balzac; in fact there are probably more allusions to Balzac novels than to most other works, allusions direct and indirect."

Edel mused that if completism were the ultimate goal, the quest for material would prove inexhaustible, taking in many ephemeral writings and minor works of popular fiction now forgotten. "Henry James demonstrates in this use of literature and of the past—with a finesse perhaps unequalled in fiction—how literature comes out of literature, and how much it is nonsense to think of literature as coming exclusively out of life. If we could gather in one immense library all the works of the human imagination written since the beginning of writing, what we would have would be a vast record of human imaginings and overwhelming proof of our myth-creating powers."

Adeline R. Tintner, a scholar who worked with Leon Edel on compiling the *Library of Henry James*, carried this line of inquiry a step further in *The Book World of Henry James*, a meticulous example of literary detection that has as its subtitle the phrase *Appropriating the Classics*, an unambiguous reference to the use of reading as vital to the creative process. "Throughout his life Henry James made it quite clear to his intimates and his readers that his devouring interest in fiction lay in measuring his mind against the works of others and that his pleasure arose from rewriting them in his own way," she wrote, and provided a series of statements James made over half a century expressing that very point. "I have doubtless simply, with violence and mutilation, *stolen* it," he admitted boldly in an 1899 letter discussing the genesis of one book. "I take liberties with the greatest," he declared three years later in yet another. Because James destroyed his personal correspondence and papers "so that no one would penetrate the secrets of his personal life," locating the sources of his work involved a good deal of speculation, an "archaeological expedition into James's fiction" that Tintner undertook with admirable gusto, the product of which very definitely would occupy a lifetime of sleuthing for any mythical book collector bent on acquiring a copy of every text he had drawn on. But the key point on which both Tintner and Edel agree is that what James read—and he was, by his own admission, a "ferociously literary" person—he transformed entirely into new works of the imagination, leading both to perceive the outlines of a pattern.

"The greatest artists have understood that the best thing they can do is renovate old forms by creating new ones, *using* the past rather than relinquishing it," Edel wrote. "Ezra Pound was doing this when he turned to Provençal poetry or rewrote Propertius. T. S. Eliot did it by grafting lines out of classic poetry into his own, representing a continuity of thought and allusion, a feeling of profound kinship, a peculiar personal intimacy with a dead author—as when Eliot made poems out of Lancelot Andrewes's old sermons."

And the exercise was not one of trickery, as Tintner sought to demonstrate; it was a collaboration involving writer and reader. She quoted James on the matter, citing an essay he wrote in 1866, when he was twenty-three years old, on the necessity of shaping his own audience:

In every novel the work is divided between the writer and the reader; but the writer makes the reader very much as he makes his characters. When he makes him ill, that is, makes him indifferent, he does no work: the writer does all. When he makes him well, that is, makes him interested, then the reader does quite half the labour. In making such a deduction as I have just indicated, the reader would be doing but his share of the task; the grand point is to get him to make it. I hold that there is a way. It is perhaps a secret; but until it is found out, I think that the art of story-telling cannot be said to have approached perfection.

During the early years of the nineteenth century, no less an intellect than John Quincy Adams—a man the historian and biographer David McCullough believes to have been the most intellectually astute president of them all—decried the paucity of books in the young republic by attempting to gather every source cited by the British historian Edward Gibbon (1737–1794) in *The History of the Decline and Fall of the Roman Empire*, "not half of which," according to an 1855 survey of American libraries, were at the time "to be found on this side of the water." Even more remarkable is the fact that most of the books Gibbon used to produce his monumental history came from a storehouse of material that he personally formed over the course of his eventful life. "I have always endeavoured to draw from the fountainhead; my curiosity, as well as a sense of duty, has always urged me to study the originals; and if they have sometimes eluded my search, I have carefully marked the secondary evidence on whose faith a passage or a fact were reduced to depend," he wrote in the preface to the fourth volume of his history. Because most of Gibbon's books were dispersed after his death, a full inventory of his library is impossible to compile, though a number of records were kept during his lifetime, including entries written on the backs of 1,676 playing cards, a number of them in the former owner's hand, all now preserved in the British Library.

Seeing wisdom in attempting a reconstruction, the surgeon and scholar Sir Geoffrey Keynes (1887–1982) set about the task in the 1930s with the zeal of an obsessed detective, determined to offer documentation for what he asserted were the underpinnings of Gibbon's remarkable work, which was published in six volumes between 1776 and 1788. Though Gibbon wrote other books, it is upon this effort that his fame and reputation rest. Notable for its extensive crediting of primary sources—the Princeton University scholar and writer of book history Anthony Grafton credited Gibbon with elevating the footnote to a "high form of literary art"—the *Decline and Fall* is one of the first books to indicate precisely where its factual material came from, making an inventory of the books he owned a fruitful exercise. "The mind of Man is recorded in his books, and the catalogues of the great libraries enable the individual to consult the universal mind on any limited subject that happens to interest him," Keynes explained of his reconstruction. "The library collected by one man, on the other hand, expresses only his own mind and special interests, and a catalogue of the books it contains can have no value unless the mind that it reflects is one of very unusual distinction."

In *Memoirs of My Life*, Gibbon detailed a lifelong need for books that began in a childhood that was marked by frequent periods of sickness. He called Mrs. Catherine Porten, an aunt with whom he stayed in his grand-father's house in London after the untimely death of his mother, "the true mother of my mind as well as my health." He treasured the woman's memory, not only for having granted him full access to whatever books his fertile inquisitiveness had desired, but for the "indulgent tenderness" that allowed the two to communicate on equal terms. It was Mrs. Porten's "delight and reward to observe the first shoots of my young ideas," he wrote. "Pain and languor were often soothed by the voice of instruction and amusement: and to her kind lessons I ascribe my early and invincible love of reading, which I would not exchange for the treasures of India."

Gibbon was eleven years old when he arrived in her care, and already he was reading Alexander Pope's translation of Homer and John Dryden's rendering of Virgil. "I derived more pleasure from Ovid's *Metamorphoses*, especially in the fall of Phaeton, and the speeches of Ajax and Ulysses," he confessed, and with an abundance of books in his grandfather's library to browse, "I turned over many English pages of poetry and romance, of history and travels. Where a title attracted my eye, without fear or awe I snatched the volume from the shelf, and Mrs. Porten, who indulged herself in moral and religious speculation, was more prone to encourage than to check a curiosity above the strength of a boy." He regarded 1748, the first year with Mrs. Porten, to have been "the most propitious to the growth of my intellectual stature," decidedly more stimulating than the fourteen months of "idle and unprofitable" study that he undertook at Magdalen College, Oxford, several years later, because it offered assurance that he would never become, as he had once feared, "an illiterate cripple." By his sixteenth year, Gibbon's health had improved dramatically, and along with renewed vigor came an acceler-ated appetite for reading in multiple areas, which he indulged with undis-guised relish. "Our family collection was decently furnished: the circulating libraries of London and Bath afford rich treasures: I borrowed many books, and some I contrived to purchase from my scanty allowance. My father's friends who visited the boy were astonished at finding him surrounded with a heap of folios, of whose titles *they* were ignorant and whose contents *he* could pertinently discourse."

It was not long before Gibbon's youthful program of "vague and mul-tifarious" reading had "exhausted all that could be learned in English, of the Arabs and Persians, the Tartars and Turks, and the same ardour urged me to guess at the French of d'Herbelot, and to construe the barbarous Latin of Pocock's *Abulpharagius*." After his brief, unpleasant stay at Oxford, he studied for five years under a tutor at Lausanne in Switzerland, returning there several decades later while working on the final volumes of his monumental history. It was in Lausanne where he began to read the Latin authors in such earnest that thirty years later he could still read flu-ently "a dissertation of eight folio pages on eight lines of the fourth Georgic of Virgil." When he returned to London, Gibbon was indifferent to the glitter of the city, and he continued to immerse himself in reading. "While coaches were rattling through Bond Street, I have passed many a solitary evening in my lodging with my books. My studies were some-times interrupted by a sigh, which I breathed toward Lausanne," where many of his books had been left behind. Fortified with a comfortable inheritance upon the death of his father in 1770, Gibbon was free to buy what he wanted, and it was from "this slender beginning," he reported proudly, that he "gradually formed a numerous and select library, the foundation of my works, and the best comfort of my life both at home and abroad." The "manufacture of my History," he emphasized—the writing of the *Decline*, some million and a half words, fully a quarter of them devoted to 7,920 scrupulously documented footnotes—"required a various and growing stock of materials." The books contained in the residences Gibbon occupied during his lifetime numbered, by his own accounting, between six and seven thousand volumes, not one of which, he emphasized in his memoir, had been acquired frivolously. "I am not conscious of having ever bought a book from a motive of ostentation, that every volume before it was deposited on the shelf was either read or sufficiently examined, and that I soon adopted the tolerating maxim of the elder Pliny, *nullum esse librum tam malum ut non ex aliquâ parte prodesset* [No book so bad but some part may be of use]." One book we know was in Gibbon's library—a 1755 Paris edition according to the Keynes compilation—was Charles de Secondat Montesquieu's *Considérations sur les causes de la grandeur des Romains, et de leur decadence* (Considerations on the Greatness of the Romans and Their Decline). Gibbon wrote in his memoir of having discovered the work early in life, asserting that its "energy of style, and boldness of hypothesis were powerful to awaken and stimulate the Genius of the Age." One recent scholar was unambiguous in the impact the treatise had on the historian's work. "Montesquieu was clearly the most important Enlightenment influence on Gibbon," Patricia B. Craddock wrote in a 1989 monograph. The *Decline and Fall*, she asserted, "would not exist if Gibbon had been entirely satisfied with Montesquieu's sketch."

Gibbon devoted considerable space in his autobiography to tracing the arc of his reading, explaining how he developed a facility to condense what he consumed and to prepare extracts for future reference, even attempting at various times to develop a grasp of mathematics, anatomy, and chemistry, though those pursuits were elementary at best. He journeyed extensively, and on those trips he carried with him a "traveling library" of twenty-four volumes of the classical authors—compact editions of Horace, Virgil, Sallust, Lucretius, Lucan, Tacitus, Ovid, Terence, and others—contained in a mahogany box fitted with brass handles. A routine Gibbon developed early remained with him through-out his life, and bears quoting here: "After glancing my eye over the design and order of a new book, I suspended the perusal until I had fin-ished the task of self-examination, till I had revolved, in a solitary walk, all that I knew or believed, or had thought on the subject of the whole work, or of some particular chapter: I was then gratified to discern how much the author added to my original stock; and if I was sometimes satis-fied by the agreement, I was sometimes armed by the opposition of our ideas."

Gibbon acknowledged that an early model for his approach to read-ing, particularly in the keeping of what were known as commonplace books, was the seventeenth-century philosopher and founding spirit of the English Enlightenment, John Locke (1632–1704), whose own library of thirty-five hundred books has been the subject of a modern recon-struction. Locke's first scholarly publication, in fact, was a work pub-lished in England in 1706, but written twenty years earlier for a French enterprise, *Bibliothèque Universelle*, and titled *Méthode nouvelle de dresser des recueils*. Translated into English, it became *A New Method of a Common Place Book*, in which techniques for entering proverbs, quota-tions, ideas, speeches, and other forms of written or spoken words in an album were formulated, setting in motion a trend toward the systematic management of information that now, four hundred years later, is han-dled most efficiently by the database, a word—and a concept—that did not exist in the seventeenth century.

In the primer, Locke gave specific advice on how to arrange material by subject and category, using such key topics as love, politics, or reli-gion. Commonplace books, it must be stressed, are not journals, which are chronological and introspective, though Locke also maintained detailed notebooks with great enthusiasm, filling dozens of them with his thoughts and perceptions. To document what he had read, Locke's inno-vation was to file the writings that interested him under conventional

headings called *loci communes*, or "common places," in which a significant excerpt was copied down verbatim. Original expression was not the
goal of this exercise, as it was in the journal; what mattered here was easy
access to material that had been deemed worth saving for future reference. Some of history's greatest readers kept commonplace books,
Desiderius Erasmus, John Milton, and Virginia Woolf among them, the
latter quite famously eschewing the practice of annotating books as a
form of defacement. A prime collection of the genre is in the British
Library, with examples representing every major academic field and profession, politics, law, medicine, history, geography, and rhetoric among
them. One of the highlights is a notebook kept by Sir Walter Raleigh
(1552–1618) during a long incarceration in the Tower of London containing library lists, poetry, and an illustrated guide to the Middle East.
Another, attributed to the mathematician and astronomer Thomas
Harriot (1560–1621)—founder of the English school of algebra, whose
friends included Sir Walter Raleigh, and the playwright Christopher
Marlowe—contains the earliest known quotation from Shakespeare's
Henry IV Part 1. One of the more curious examples is a twelve-hundred-
page commonplace book maintained by Sir Julius Caesar (1558–1636), a
seventeenth-century judge and politician who recorded in meticulous
detail a determined program of reading he sustained over a forty-year
period. Locke was painstaking in describing how he prepared commonplace books for his use:

> I take a [blank] paper book of what size I please. I divide the two
> first pages that face one another by parallel lines into five and
> twenty equal parts, every fifth line black, the other red. I then cut
> them perpendicularly by other lines that I draw from the top to the
> bottom of the page, as you may see in the table prefixed. I put
> about the middle of each five spaces one of the twenty letters I
> design to make use of, and, a little forward in each space, the five

vowels, one below another, in their natural order. This is the index
to the whole volume, how big soever it may be.

Having thus prepared his index—which itself was something of an
innovation—he then proceeded with the arrangement of his material:

If I would put any thing in my Common-Place-Book, I find out a
head to which I may refer it. Each head ought to be some important and essential word to the matter in hand, and in that word
regard is to be had to the first letter, and the vowel that follows it;
for upon these two letters depends all the use of the index.

Further on, Locke explained how he documented his reading:

To take notice of a place in an author, from whom I quote something, I make use of this method: before I write any thing, I put the
name of the author in my Common-Place-book, and under that
name the title of the treatise, the size of the volume, the time and
place of its edition, and (what ought never to be omitted) the number of pages that the whole book contains. For example, I put into
the class M. a. "Marshami Canon Chronicus Ægyptiacus, Græcus,
& disquisitiones fol." London 1672, p. 626. This number of pages
serves me for the future to mark the particular treatise of this
author, and the edition I make use of. I have no need to mark the
place, otherwise than in setting down the number of the page from
whence I have drawn what I have wrote, just above the number of
pages contained in the whole volume.

In this manner, Locke set down "tens of thousands of quotations"
from more than a thousand works, according to one study. To the great
chagrin of scholars, the books he owned and handled, of which about a

third survive and are now housed in the Bodleian Library at Oxford University—a gift of the late American philanthropist and collector of many things important and beautiful, Paul Mellon—are surprisingly void of extensive annotation. In cases where Locke did insert some telltale mark in a volume, it was put there as a reminder that a record should be made in his notebook. Occasionally, Locke would make references to notes he had already made on the inside back cover of a book. In his autobiography, Gibbon acknowledged adopting Locke's precepts when he was young, and confirmed that he kept "a large Commonplace book" during his most formative years, but he judged the exercise to be a practice "which I do not strictly recommend," for reasons that he frankly explained: "The action of the pen will doubtless imprint an idea on the mind as well as on the paper: but I much question whether the benefits of this laborious method are adequate to the waste of time; and I must agree with Dr. Johnson (*Idler* Number 74), 'that what is twice read is commonly better remembered that what is transcribed.' "

A great contemporary of John Locke, Sir Isaac Newton (1642–1727)—indeed, an acquaintance with whom he exchanged correspondence—also kept commonplace books, but not with nearly as much dedication. Interestingly, the author most extensively represented in the libraries of both Newton and Locke was Robert Boyle (1627–1691), the pioneering Oxford scientist often called the "father of chemistry," who, with his younger colleague, Robert Hooke (1635–1703), built the first pump to create vacuums, and carried out trials to determine the nature and importance of air. Of the thirty-nine works published by Boyle between 1655 and 1691, Locke had thirty-four on his shelves. Of the twenty-four titles known to have been owned by Newton, those that survive—the locations of sixteen are known—"show clear signs of having been minutely studied," with many containing notes in his hand, according to John Harrison, who compiled a reconstructive catalog of Newton's library. Because Newton achieved great fame in his lifetime, he received many presentation volumes from authors as gifts, a number of which have survived. He occasionally annotated those books, usually to indicate mistakes he had found, by writing "error" in the margins, though he rarely rendered an opinion of any writing by underlining or sidelining of the text.

Trinity College, Cambridge, has 862 volumes formerly owned by Newton, of which 52 bear his annotations; another 24 are in other collections; 8 were classified by Harrison as "whereabouts unknown." Thirty-two of these annotated volumes deal with chemistry and alchemy, 24 with mathematics, 8 with physics, 7 with theology, 6 with astronomy, and 1 each on a variety of other disciplines. Newton's most heavily annotated theological volume is a 1660 edition of the English Bible printed in London and bound together with a 1639 *Book of Common Prayer*. This material is regarded as key to understanding Newton's spiritual thinking, and includes a personal note attached to the volume stating that it was "given by Sir Isaac Newton in his last illness to the woman who nursed him." The first edition of his personal copy of *Principia Mathematica* is heavily annotated with revisions in his hand for inclusion in later editions. Of particular interest to scholars is the system of "dog-earing" notation Newton used to mark passages he deemed to be of special significance. If something interested him, he would fold the upper or lower corner of a page down or up so that the tip of the paper would precisely locate a sentence or phrase in the printed text he wanted highlighted. Of the Trinity College volumes known to have been Newton's, 122 have dog-eared pages, while another 152 indicate they were once creased, and then folded back. "Though book lovers may deplore this ugly habit," Harrison noted, "it clearly reflects Newton's attitude that books are working tools to be used as convenient." The value of these books, he concluded, is evident: "Its potential importance to Newton scholars as an index to the direction of his mind as he read the books in his library has certainly not yet been fully realized."

Newton's father, also named Isaac Newton, signed his name with a mark, suggesting quite persuasively, as was the case also with Shakespeare's father, that he could not write, and quite possibly could not read, either. A yeoman about whom very little is known, the senior Newton took ill and died before his son was born. Always a bright lad, the youngster was sent to Trinity College, Cambridge, as a student known as subsizar, who earned his keep by performing household tasks for more affluent classmates. Newton was exposed to many philosophical texts and ideas at Cambridge, especially those of the French philosopher René Descartes. Though Newton wrote more than a million words, only a few of his writings were published during his lifetime, most spectacularly the *Philosophiae naturalis principia mathematica* (The Mathematical Principles of Natural Philosophy) in 1687, a benchmark work in the history of science in which the presentation of the laws of gravitation and Newton's rules for reasoning from physical events were demonstrated.

At his death, Newton was accorded a state funeral, the first time England had extended such an honor to a person whose accomplishments came neither from rank nor privilege, but from intellectual accomplishment. In 1676, Newton wrote a letter to Robert Hooke, a bitter rival who by then had already invented the microscope—his *Micrographia* (1665) was one of the books featured in the Printing and the Mind of Man exhibition—to comment on the influences in his own work, famously expressing the debt he felt he owed to those who had come before him with a sentence that has been quoted on countless occasions ever since. In this instance, Newton was referring specifically to work that had laid the groundwork for his findings on optics—he was angered by Hooke's demands that Newton furnish proof for his theories—but in a much broader sense he could easily have been referring to Nicolaus Copernicus, Galileo Galilei, Johannes Kepler, Robert Boyle, or René Descartes, each of whom contributed in demonstrable ways to his studies in the mysteries of planetary motion, infinitesimal calculus, mechanics, mathematics, and gravity. "If I have seen further," Newton wrote—and he was anything but a humble man, according to his numerous biographers—"it is by standing on the shoulders of giants." Less frequently quoted, but equally revealing and decidedly more poignant, is an observation the lifelong bachelor made of himself toward the end of his life, seemingly satisfied with his accomplishments, and at peace with the choices he had made:

> I do not know how I may appear to the world, but to myself I seem to have been only like a boy, playing on the sea-shore, and diverting myself, in now and then finding a smoother pebble or prettier shell than ordinary, whilst the great ocean of truth lay all undiscovered before me.

IN THE MARGINS

In the same way you will write some brief but pithy sayings such as aphorisms, proverbs, and maxims at the beginning and at the end of your books; others you will inscribe on rings or drinking cups; others you will paint on doors and walls or even in the glass of a window so that what may aid learning is constantly before you.
—DESIDERIUS ERASMUS, *On the Method of Study* (1511)

T hroughout his life, Samuel Taylor Coleridge (1772–1834) kept notes on everything he read, and what he learned from his books, the Harvard University scholar John Livingston Lowes (1867–1945) wrote in a classic examination of the poet's primary sources, "stuck like limpets in his memory." The central topic of inquiry for Lowes in *The Road to Xanadu* (1927) was the making of "The Rime of the Ancient Mariner" and "Kubla Khan," but the regimen he perceived was consistent in everything Coleridge did, his penetrating essays and celebrated lectures included. "I have read almost everything," the poet once said, leading Lowes to conclude that any scholar "who sets out to track him through his reading leaves unread at his peril anything readable whatsoever that was extant in Coleridge's day." Because Coleridge detailed his reading so fully, Lowes had determined it was possible to trace "what touched the springs of his imagination" with a degree of certitude not common among many other writers.

The most important resource for Lowes was a ninety-leaf notebook in the British Museum, written "partly in pencil, partly in ink" between 1795 and 1798, "the years which lead up to and include the magnificent flowering of Coleridge's genius on which his renown as a poet rests." Its value, Lowes asserted, "is incalculable, not only for the understanding of Coleridge, but also as a document in the psychology of genius, and as a key to the secrets of art in the making." The notebook reveals the reach, depth, and comprehension of his subject's reading, and to suggest that Lowes was ebullient about what he had found in it would be something of an understatement:

It is, on the whole, the strangest medley that I know. Milton's Commonplace Book is a severely ordered collectanea of extracts culled from his reading, docketed alphabetically, and methodical as a ledger. Shelley's note books, written upside down, sidewise, and even right side up, with their scribbled marginal sketches of boats and trees and human faces—these battered and stained and happy-go-lucky little volumes are a priceless record of the birth-throes of poetry. But it is chiefly poetry, beating its wings against the bars of words, which they contain. There are few notes of Shelley's reading. The Coleridge Note Book is like neither. It is a catch-all for suggestions jotted down chaotically from Coleridge's absorbing adventures among books. It is a repository of waifs and strays of verse, some destined to find a lodgement later in the poems, others yet lying abandoned where they fell, like drifted leaves. It is a mirror of the fitful and kaleidoscopic moods and a record of the germinal ideas of one of the most supremely gifted and utterly incalculable spirits ever let loose upon the planet.

The single most important question Lowes felt he could ask about his subject, and the italics are his, was this: "*How did Coleridge actually read books?* Few more significant questions can be asked about any man, and about Coleridge probably none." What Lowes found particularly thrilling were the references he found in the notebook that he could then follow from book to book. He was able, for instance, to determine that from a reading of *Botanic Garden* (1791), Coleridge was moved to consult the author Erasmus Darwin's primary sources, most tellingly James Thomson's long, descriptive, philosophical poem in four books, *The Seasons* (1744), and a published report of the mathematician Pierre-Louis Moreau de Maupertuis's 1736 trip to Lapland to measure an arc of the meridian, gleanings of which appear as images in a number of Coleridge's poems. "Darwin, that is to say, sent Coleridge to Thomson; Thomson sent him to Maupertuis, and once more an incorrigible habit of verifying footnotes led the imagination upon fresh adventures." In one of several diverting books about all things bibliophilic— his *Anatomy of Bibliomania* (1930) being one of the all-time great examples of the genre—Holbrook Jackson (1874–1948) offered his take on Coleridge's approach to reading: "One after another vivid bits from what he read dropped into the deep well. And there, below the level of conscious mental processes, they set up their obscure and powerful reaction."

In addition to commenting about what he read in his notebooks, Coleridge also was an inveterate annotator, so much so that he is credited with bringing the word "marginalia" into English usage from the Latin to describe his habitual process of writing in books. The material is of such importance in his case that it is classified as a form of primary manuscript, certainly as important as the material he wrote in his notebooks, and in a league with his correspondence and holographic manuscripts. Some eight thousand notes written in the margins of books by Coleridge have been recovered from about 450 titles by 325 authors, totaling about seven hundred volumes of intensive reading. Scholars know of another seventy books that he annotated, but there is no textual record of the annotations. He also is known to have owned or used no fewer than six hundred and fifty other books, although the total is undoubtedly much higher than that, given the celebrated penchant he had for borrowing whatever interested him from everyone he knew, more often than not failing to return it to the rightful owner, causing consternation among some of his acquaintances, smiling indulgence from others. As part of an ongoing project to publish all of Coleridge's writings in scholarly editions, Princeton University has issued six volumes devoted exclusively to his marginalia. The editor of these writings, Heather Jackson, a professor of English at the University of Toronto, has written that there is "no body of marginalia—in English, or perhaps in any other language—comparable with Coleridge's in range and variety and in the sensitiveness, scope and depth of his reaction to what he was reading."

As a scholar, Jackson's primary interest is in the literary accomplishment of writers. But in 1984, following the death of George Whalley, the first editor of Coleridge's marginal writings, she picked up the task at volume 3, and saw the project through to completion. "My colleagues were incredulous that I was editing somebody's notes in the margins of books," she told me in an interview. "And the truth is, I was asking myself why I was doing this, and how Coleridge's notes in books had come to be perceived as part of his canonical work." But the further she got into it, the more she saw merit in exploring other examples of marginalia, leading her to examine some three thousand books that had been annotated in the English language by various readers over a three-hundred-year period, roughly 1700 to 2000, resulting in two monographs, the aptly titled *Marginalia* published in 2001, and *Romantic Readers*, a companion volume released in the summer of 2005, that considers British readers writing in books from about 1790 to 1830.

The idea to look at marginalia of all forms, not just the lofty scribblings of the brilliant and the famous, came in the most fundamental of ways, one that Jackson recounted first in a scholarly article she wrote for the *University of Toronto Quarterly* in 1992, nine years before *Marginalia* was published by Yale University Press. "It was a student's note that I found in the library stacks, a really rude note that got me going," she said. The book contained a critical essay by the literary critic and scholar Geoffrey Hartman on the structure and use of language of "Yew-Trees," a poem by William Wordsworth. When she turned to the article, she discovered that "a grumpy student" had perused the book before her, and responded to it in a curious way. In his detailed analysis of the poem, Hartman had noted the incidence of *in*, *un*, and *um* sounds, and wrote, "The *in* and *un* struggle to come together as one intense meaning, while *um* presents itself as a stronger or heavier *un*." Next to that statement, the anonymous student had written in the margin, "Long live the Professor of English!" Further on, where Hartman opined that the word *united* was perceived at the same time as *Yew-nited*—an obvious play on yew-trees—the exasperated student had written, to Jackson's amused astonishment, "a pithy *Fuck yew*."

As coarse as the observation may be, it suggested to Jackson, in a jarringly direct way, one reader's response to an author's printed work, stated without any expectation that it would ever be acknowledged by anyone else. It also pointed out, Jackson stressed, "one of the most intriguing qualities of marginalia, the attitude of defiance in which they are often produced," an altogether "elusive but important quality" of the practice. The student who annotated Hartman's essay, she explained, by "pitting the once-unprintable against the published word, is only an extreme case, a marginalist who takes refuge in anonymity and so defies both the author and the educational enterprise in which the author and the public libraries participate." Even more propitious, from Jackson's standpoint, was the startling nature of the discovery. "I thought, 'That was so clever; this is really neat, it's funny, I've got to use it.' I wondered, 'What student would have thought that someone else would ever *read* that? What drove the student to do it?' That was one of those moments where I realized I couldn't just write about Coleridge's marginalia, I had to write about other people's as well." In due course Jackson embarked on the research that resulted in *Marginalia* and *Romantic Readers*.

Because Jackson had to establish a focus, her study was restricted to people writing in books in the English language. Outside of England, notable writers of marginalia include the prolific François-Marie Arouet, the guiding voice of the French Enlightenment who wrote under the pen name Voltaire (1694–1778), and a keen and intelligent reader whose renowned library and all its accoutrements were bought in 1779 by Catherine the Great of Russia for the then-enormous sum of 135,398 *livres*. The 6,814 volumes she acquired were shelved for her by Voltaire's personal librarian and confidant, Jean-Louis Wagnière, in the same order prescribed by their former owner at his chateau in Ferney, and are maintained to this day in the Hermitage Museum in St. Petersburg to the continuing regret of the Bibliothèque nationale in Paris, where the most prominent physical remnant of one of the country's most enduring writers is his desiccated heart, stored like a secular icon inside a statue of the author sculpted from life by Jean-Antoine Houdon.

Some two thousand of the books in the Hermitage contain Voltaire's thoughtful annotations, which themselves have been published in seven volumes as part of an ongoing collaboration among French and Russian scholars. A typical example of Voltaire's celebrated wit appears in his copy of a commentary on the life and philosophy of Claude-Adrien Helvétius (1715–1771), the father of utilitarianism and the author of a 1758 treatise, *De l'esprit*, that was condemned uniformly by the Sorbonne, the Pope, and the Parlement of Paris, and burned by the public executioner. On the half-title page, Voltaire wrote: *Si Dieu n'existait pas il faudrait l'inventer* (If God did not exist, it would be necessary to invent him).

Catherine II acquired the treasure trove from Voltaire's niece a year after his death, fourteen years after she had bought the library of Denis

Diderot (1713–1784), an especially important collection that documented the sources used in the preparation of the *Encyclopédie*, published between 1751 and 1772 in seventeen volumes of text and eleven volumes of engravings. In making the deal with Diderot, the empress proved herself an enterprising negotiator, readily agreeing to the asking price of 15,000 *livres*, with a few stipulations added, the first being that Diderot function as the "depository" for his own books indefinitely, meaning that he keep them for as long as he needed them, and be paid an additional stipend of a hundred *pistoles* a year to serve as her personal "librarian," with five years being paid in advance. "Great Princess," Diderot wrote to Catherine, "I prostrate myself at your feet. I stretch out my arms to you, I would wish to speak, but paralysis grips my soul."

Letters exchanged between the empress and Voltaire demonstrate the great regard she had for the French master, and stress how important she felt it was to possess the books once used and handled by her literary heroes. "I would never have believed that the purchase of a library would bring me so many compliments: everyone is paying me them on my purchase of Monsieur Diderot's," she wrote in 1785, three years before Voltaire's death. "But confess, you, whom humanity should truly compliment for the help you have given to innocence and virtue . . . it would have been cruel and unjust to separate a scholar from his books." Once brought to Russia, the books became a national treasure, perhaps too much so, with researchers denied access to them for decades. Czar Nicholas II made an exception in 1832 for Alexander Pushkin, who was permitted to browse through the library for information he could use in a historical work based on the life of Peter the Great, a work that was left unfinished at his death.

"Books with manuscript annotations have long been the subject of scholarly inquiry," the California bookseller Bernard M. Rosenthal emphasized in the catalog of a collection of 242 books he had assembled privately over thirty-five years and sold en bloc to the Beinecke Rare

Book and Manuscript Library at Yale University in 1995, each one containing the notations of prior owners. Of these books, all but ten were printed before 1600, the earliest from 1474. Most are in Latin, with Greek, Hebrew, Italian, French, and German represented; none were printed in England, and none were annotated in English. The range is eclectic—subject areas include classical authors, patristic and biblical studies, vernacular poetry, Reformation theology—providing insight into how important texts were read in European universities during the Renaissance.

A third-generation bookseller who emigrated to the United States in 1935, Rosenthal wrote in the catalog how books as material artifacts never really came alive for him "until their margins or flyleaves or bindings revealed to us something about the book's life after it left the printer's shop." A superior example in the collection is the sixteenth-century *editio princeps*—the first *printed* edition—of a fourth-century history of the Christian church written by Eusebius Pamphili, Bishop of Cæsarea in Palestine (c. 260–c. 340), which over the centuries had passed through the hands of several scholars. Most prominent among them was Hieronymus Wolf (1516–1580), a "restless, gloomy, superstitious, paranoid and thoroughly unhappy man who, even as a boy, had to suffer from the taunts of his schoolmates and servants because of his obsession with the classics." Wolf acquired the Eusebius in 1550—six years after it was issued from Robert Estienne's famed Paris printing press, possibly even from the printer himself—and wrote some thirteen thousand words of critical observation on 950 of the book's 1,070 pages, which, like the text itself, is mostly in Greek; his later work earned him the distinction of being acclaimed the "father of Byzantinology." The names of other noteworthy owners are represented in the Rosenthal collection—annotations from the brilliant French scholar Joseph Scaliger (1540–1609) and the Dutch classicist Daniel Heinsius (1580–1655) stand out—but the impressions of lesser-known readers are of equal interest to scholars concerned with the history of reading.

But Samuel Taylor Coleridge remains by far the most accomplished practitioner of marginalia profiled by Heather Jackson. Indeed, it was Coleridge who raised the practice to a literary art form, publishing some of his annotations under that title in 1819. Others discussed in her book include Samuel Johnson, Horace Walpole, John Keats, William Blake, the World War I poet Rupert Brooke, T. H. White, the author of *The Once and Future King*, and the popular novelist Graham Greene.

Of merit too is Gabriel Harvey (c. 1545–1630), an English Renaissance figure of some distinction and quite an inveterate annotator, whose activity is of such significance that his life, marginalia, and library have been the subject of an entire monograph. At various times an Oxford don, a professional writer, and a courtier with political ambitions, Harvey's tastes were vast, with readings meticulously recorded in the margins of books reflecting many interests, literature, drama, cosmology, medicine, law, navigation, history, oratory, statesmanship, and the techniques of warfare among them. "His extravagant aim seems to have been to acquire for his own use the sum total of human knowledge—learning, however, not for learning's sake but rather for pragmatic purposes," Virginia F. Stern wrote. Harvey read and annotated his books exhaustively, in most cases signing and dating his comments. Fluent in a number of languages, Harvey's annotations switch easily between Latin, Greek, and English, and when he undertook the study of modern languages, he began recording some observations in Italian, Spanish, and French.

In 1990, another study of Harvey offered a detailed discussion of his repeated reading over a twenty-two-year period of one book, a copy of Titus Livy's *Romanae Historiae Principis, Decades Tres*, familiarly known as his *History of Rome*, printed in Basel in 1555. Written by Anthony Grafton, a Princeton University historian of the Renaissance, and Lisa Jardine, a professor of English at the University of London, the essay is regarded today as one of the foundation studies of the emerging scholarly discipline known as the history of reading. Through careful examination of the text, Grafton and Jardine showed how Harvey returned to the book several times between 1558 and 1590 for reasons other than learning or inspiration, but as a kind of professional reader performing a service for others. In each instance, Harvey recorded the amount of time spent with specific passages and identified other writings he consulted for reference. He also noted the names of people with whom he discussed the history, and set down his changing perceptions of the content. From all this, Grafton and Jardine were able to argue that each reading of Livy was undertaken on behalf of certain people they were able to identify, and to accommodate a pressing intellectual need they had commissioned him to satisfy. The practice of "interpreting, mediating and personalizing texts" on behalf of others, as one scholar has described it, was not uncommon at the time. Indeed, the honorific title itself—*Reader*—is still used in England to designate senior teachers and instructors at universities and at the Inns of Court.

Of equal interest in *Marginalia* is the attention Professor Jackson has extended to those whose names do not echo across the generations. She has a particular affection for Hester Lynch Thrale, later Piozzi (1741–1821), the friend and confidante of Samuel Johnson, a writer in her own right, and hostess of a literary salon that welcomed the likes of Edmund Burke, Frances and Charles Burney, David Garrick, Oliver Goldsmith, and Sir Joshua Reynolds. Of the books she wrote, by far the most popular were two that discussed her friendship with Dr. Johnson: *Anecdotes of the Late Samuel Johnson, LL.D.* (1786) and *Letters to and from the Late Samuel Johnson* (1788). Less successful were her several other published efforts, including a travel memoir, *Observations and Reflections Made in the Course of a Journey through France, Italy and Germany* (1789), but it turns out she was an enthusiastic annotator, especially in her copies of books written by Johnson.

A careful keeper of journals, too, Mrs. Piozzi turned to writing her impressions on the margins of printed pages once she realized that, "far from spoiling them, her marginalia might increase the value of the books they were written in." She even began sending copies of books she had written in as gifts, making them a form of "intimate communication supplementary to and possibly more permanent than letters." In one instance she sent to an acquaintance with a cold a cluster of presents that included "Lozenges for the cough—Books for the Shelf." A copy of Johnson's *Rasselas* that Piozzi annotated for William Augustus Conway, a leading man of the theater and a close friend during the final years of her life, contains tidbits about Johnson that are not found anywhere else. For scholars, Jackson writes, "a great part of the value of Piozzi's notes is the insight they give into the topics of discussion and modes of thought of early-nineteenth-century Britain," enabling today's researchers "by inference to learn something about reading practices in the period."

Jackson's most entertaining profile is her examination of an anonymous eighteenth-century annotator calling himself Scriblerus, a man-about-London whose marginalia in a first-edition copy of Boswell's *Life of Samuel Johnson* make clear that he was quite comfortable moving in privileged circles. Acquired by the British Museum Library from a bookseller in 1839, the book includes various dates, clues, and comments—his gender is disclosed, for example, but not his name—that led Jackson off on an investigation to determine the scribbler's identity. "It is hard to generalize about the content of these marginalia beyond saying that the notes are extraordinarily diverse and uninhibited," she marveled. Of special interest is that Scriblerus gave the *Life* "an alert and minute examination," at times even challenging Boswell's veracity on a few matters, questioning Johnson's observations in others. Where Boswell shows Johnson "preening himself," as Jackson puts it, Scriblerus has written, "Lord Help us all! What a Solomon have you got!—I beg your pardon— have you MADE!" Conducting a painstaking investigation that took in both internal and external evidence, Jackson concluded that the scribbler was one Fulke Greville (1717–1806), grandson of the first Baron Brooke, once Britain's Envoy Extraordinary to Bavaria, and an author in his day of limited repute. "The existence of Fulke Greville's annotated copy of the *Life* makes it possible to flesh out what we know of the career of a minor but not negligible figure in literary circles of the second half of the eighteenth century, and especially to clarify his relationship with Boswell and Johnson—a relationship of which they must have been largely unaware," Jackson concluded.

"The scribbler is presented pseudonymously," Jackson told me. "He concealed his identity, or he tried to conceal his identity, at least, and that's the thing. If it occurs to us at all, most of us think that our books are just going to go on anonymously, and like the student's note I found in the library stacks, nobody is likely to know who wrote it. But that wasn't always the case when people wrote in their books, and if their books were being lent out, and if their notes were being copied, and if heirs were going to be involved, then other considerations come into play. If someone was going to bequeath these books, then someone several hundred years down the road just might be looking into them."

Although numerous people through history have asserted their ability to commune with books, Jackson told me she does not believe there is a genuine dialogue going on between author and reader, that if there is a conversation, it is one-sided. "Erasmus talked about that concept in a letter. There's a long tradition of people thinking about, and talking about, their books as friends and companions, and obviously they *are* ideal companions, because they don't talk back. That's my point. Sometimes readers imagine that they hear the voice of the author in the words of the book, and they *do* talk to it. But it always seems a little bit to me to be like heckling." What Jackson called the "uninhibited nature of marginalia" is in the end a "false conception," because "when we get notes from the past, it is essential that you consider under what conditions they were written, not only the personal circumstances of the reader, but also the social conditions of the time—the taken-for-granted conventions, the assumptions, the attitudes of the time."

For all the books important people are known to have owned, Jackson does not feel knowledge of titles in a person's possession is "good enough" evidence upon which to draw scholarly conclusions unless records, annotations, or marginalia are available to document their influence. "Nobody who owns books will think so either," she added. "But I also think you have to work with the evidence you've got, and the people who write about Emily Dickinson will take a dog-eared book in the family collection as telling them something about her, because they have little else to go on. Coleridge is a very interesting case because we do have lists of his reading, there is a library sale catalog, and people have been working on his collection for a long time. But the books that really were important to him, the ones that he really assimilated, are not necessarily in that collection. You can sometimes work backwards from allusions and quotations in the works to infer something, not only about what the person read, but about how deeply it went with them."

One of the most remarkable collections of books formerly owned and used by a prominent reader—in this instance an entire *family* of prominent readers—may well be the first such library mindfully acquired by an American institution with that justification unquestionably in mind. I am hedging a bit here, since the books of the incomparable James Logan ultimately became a core holding of the Library Company of Philadelphia somewhat earlier, but that library was donated lock, stock, and barrel by terms of a will, not aggressively pursued and purchased, as was the case in 1814 of what is now known as the Mather Family Library. The buyer was Isaiah Thomas (1749–1831), the founder of the American Antiquarian Society in Worcester, Massachusetts, whose passion for collecting everything that had any connection with print culture in what is now the United States is legendary. Indeed, it was a eulogy of Thomas by a grandson declaring the patriot, printer, and publisher to have been "touched early by that gentlest of infirmities, bibliomania," that suggested the title of my first book, *A Gentle Madness*.

In this instance, Thomas acquired the remains of the most consequential private library to have been formed in British North America
prior to the American Revolution, books owned and used successively
by five generations of Mather family members, most notably Richard
Mather (1596–1669), Increase Mather (1639–1723), and Cotton Mather
(1663–1728), determined Massachusetts Puritans one and all, and
exceedingly influential figures of their time. Cotton Mather alone wrote
and published more than four hundred works, with *Magnalia Christi
Americana* (1702), an ecclesiastical history of New England, being his
magnum opus. His *Curiosa Americana* (1712–24) reflected an interest in
science, particularly in various American phenomena, and won him
membership in the Royal Society of London.

How many books the Mathers may have originally owned is a matter
of conjecture, though it is estimated to have been as many as seven thousand volumes, an enormous number for a Colonial library, more substantial even than what Harvard College held at the time. Though most of the
library had been sold off by indifferent descendants or merely taken away
by opportunists, what Isaiah Thomas bought from Hannah Mather
Crocker still amounted to fifteen hundred volumes, most of them containing annotations and marginal writings. Thomas personally went
through his prize cache volume by volume, describing them all in detail,
and writing out a rudimentary catalog on twenty-eight sheets of paper.
Despite the passage of close to two hundred years, a thorough description of the collection has yet to be prepared, though numerous scholars
have worked selectively with the books, most recently Mark Peterson, a
professor of history at the University of Iowa, who is using the collection
for a book he is writing, tentatively titled *The Hub and the Universe:
Boston, New England, and the Making of the Atlantic World.*

"There's some incredible stuff in there," Peterson told me early in 2005.
"Just about everything, of course, was published in Europe, including a
Latin Bible from the 1470s. You can tell by looking at the end pages and fly-

leaves that these books circulated quite a lot, undoubtedly among colleagues and friends of the Mathers. I haven't done a full analysis, but at least a third of the books are in Latin, and almost all are European books. One of the things that surprised me is that about half of them are Continental as opposed to British titles, since we have been led to believe by the scholarship on Puritanism that their reading would be Anglocentric; and there are quite a few in there by Roman Catholics, too, which was another surprise. Using the marginalia, you can specifically determine the things that various people have read; the differences in handwriting are apparent, they're sort of like palimpsests. Cotton Mather spent his whole life in Boston, but Increase Mather made a number of trips to England, and when he was there he bought books like mad. They also had contact with people who would go to book fairs such as Frankfurt, and Boston itself was the biggest book-buying center in America. So they never stopped adding material. The library gave them a lot of the authority that helped their political and cultural position as intellectual leaders. You could safely say that it was their intellectual capital. Without those books, their writings would not have been possible."

Whether annotated or not, the books that important people have owned and are likely to have read are in great demand in research libraries, a circumstance that attracts a modicum of public attention from time to time when transactions involving the acquisition of various archives are reported. In the spring of 2003, the critic and educator Harold Bloom announced that he would be giving his library of twenty-five thousand books and half a century's worth of correspondence with literary figures to a small Roman Catholic college of nineteen hundred students, where he was sure it would all be used and have an impact on future readers. "I intend to give my lifelong accumulation of books to Saint Michael's College, Colchester, Vermont," Bloom wrote simply in his letter of announcement, noting that his 100 percent gift was made partly as a way to "express my admiration for the College's continued upholding of humanistic study, to which I have devoted my career as a teacher, writer and editor." In a later conversation with me, Bloom said one reason why he, a Jewish man with lifelong ties to Yale, chose a small Catholic college with modest resources was partly that "these schools pursue a pure love of literature" in ways that larger institutions with "political agendas" often do not. He also felt that so much of what he had to give would replicate titles already represented among Yale's eleven million–plus volumes, or at New York University, where he also had taught for many years. Bloom's gift followed by several months news that the University of California, Los Angeles, had agreed to pay the novelist and critic Susan Sontag $1.1 million for her library and papers. In 1995 Boston College acquired from the estate of the British novelist Graham Greene an archive comprising sixty thousand items, including three thousand books from his personal library, a good many of them annotated. The books were added to a significant collection of Greene's manuscripts and published works already held by the college.

In the spring of 2004, a subscriber to ExLibris, an online discussion group that serves an international community of librarians, booksellers, and bibliophiles interested in the chitchat and arcana of the rare book world, posed a seemingly innocuous question to the members: "What complete or largely complete personal libraries of important literary persons (i.e., authors of fiction and poetry plus, I guess, some critics) are preserved in research libraries? I suspect the number is fewer than expected." Within hours, replies started coming in from all reaches of the book world. The Bloom, Sontag, and Greene libraries would be mentioned, but they were just part of an extensive list. One of the first respondents noted that the Southern novelist and poet James Dickey's books and papers were at the University of South Carolina, which "makes perfect sense," the curator there wrote, as Dickey had been "Poet-In-Residence and First Carolina Professor of English on staff for over 30 years." Among critics, the personal libraries of Edmund Wilson and Cyril Connolly were reported to be at the University of Tulsa.

On and on it went. Collections at the Library of Congress include books formerly owned by Oliver Wendell Holmes and Ralph Ellison; some two hundred annotated books from the library of Northrop Frye were reported to be at the University of Toronto; Robert Frost's books, it was disclosed, have an agreeable home, complete with their own room, in the Bobst Library at New York University. "I'll see your Frost and raise you a Burton," the bookseller Jay Dillon quipped in response, referring to the 2,500-volume working library of the adventurer, explorer, linguist, scholar, and swordsman Sir Richard Burton (1821–1890) formerly held by the Royal Anthropological Institution in London, and now installed at the Huntington Library in San Marino, California.

Richard W. Oram, librarian of the Harry Ransom Humanities Research Center at the University of Texas, Austin, provided a link to a Web site that itemizes some of the libraries his institution has acquired over the years to complement its powerhouse collections of literary manuscripts, correspondence, and archives. Listed there are details of the libraries of W. H. Auden, E. E. Cummings, J. Frank Dobie, James Joyce, Oliver La Farge, Wyndham Lewis, Sir Compton Mackenzie, Christopher Morley, Ezra Pound, Anne Sexton, and Evelyn Waugh, a good many of them featuring books with marginalia. Melinda Gottesman of Harvard University followed the Texas example by citing a link to a Houghton Library Web site, where a listing of holdings including books formerly owned by authors—"a ton of them," she noted—could be found, Emily Dickinson, T. S. Eliot, Ralph Waldo Emerson, Henry Wadsworth Longfellow, Herman Melville, and Marguerite Yourcenar among them.

A librarian at Emory University in Atlanta, Georgia—another major collector in recent years of choice literary material—noted the acquisition just the previous month by the Robert W. Woodruff Library of six thousand books formerly owned by the late British poet laureate Ted

Hughes, including a number of volumes owned by Hughes and the poet Sylvia Plath during the years of their marriage. These include a study of nightmares that Plath presented to Hughes as a gift, and a copy of Hart Crane's *Complete Poems* that Hughes in turn had inscribed to her. Plath often marked books as she read them, notably D. H. Lawrence's *Kangaroo*, Virginia Woolf's *To the Lighthouse* and *A Writer's Diary*, and Fyodor Dostoyevsky's *Crime and Punishment*. The Hughes books were regarded as an essential complement to the literary archive of his work that Emory had acquired in 1997. Plath's papers and literary manuscripts, meanwhile, are at the Lilly Library of Indiana University, along with one hundred and fifty of her books, including her annotated copy of *The Portable James Joyce*.

William S. Patterson at the University of Maryland advised the ExLibris group that Katherine Anne Porter's library is in the College Park library; he noted further that seven hundred books formerly owned by Flannery O'Connor, many of them annotated and relevant to her writing, are among the prized holdings of her alma mater, the Women's College of Georgia, now known as Georgia College, and that the library of Alfred, Lord Tennyson is at the Tennyson Research Centre in Lincoln, England. Isaac Gewirtz, curator of the Berg Collection at the New York Public Library, reported that he is custodian of the books of the guru of the Beat Generation, Jack Kerouac; also installed there are the books of Vladimir Nabokov. "I hope Dorothy M. Johnson would count," the special collections librarian from the University of Montana in Missoula, wondered. "She wrote *The Man Who Shot Liberty Valance*, *A Man Called Horse*, and a large number of other well-regarded Western stories in the 1950s and '60's. We have her entire library unprocessed in Special Collections here at the Mansfield Library. It came in with her papers which are in Archives."

Mark Samuels Lasner, a senior research fellow at the University of Delaware and a widely respected bibliophile, whose personal collection of books includes many association copies, wrote a thoughtful contribution, noting that "while institutions and private parties may own an 'author's library' they may not possess all the books an author owned during his or her lifetime. Like many of us, authors give books away, lend books to friends who do not return them, sell books (to gain room or cash), and leave books behind when they move. Moreover, heirs of authors do not always keep the inherited books together. Such dispersions—even when large quantities are retained in a particular location—mean that the best way to 'access' an author's library is by way of a 'reconstruction'—should one exist," and he cited in particular the work done on collections once owned by the Brownings and Henry James: "Earlier postings have indicated that Edmund Wilson's library is at the University of Tulsa, that Graham Greene's is at Boston College, and that Thomas Carlyle's is at Carlyle's House in London. Volumes once owned by all three of these writers are also on my shelves—and are no doubt on the shelves of other collectors and institutions."

Just a month before these ExLibris postings got started, and quite apart from that online thread, the estate of the late novelist Iris Murdoch reached a private agreement to sell her library of one thousand books to Kingston University in England, averting the possibility of its being broken up and dispersed. "The collection, which includes books on subjects ranging from philosophy to poetry, as well as makeshift bookmarks and handwritten notes, was put up for sale by her husband, John Bayley, last year," Michelle Pauli reported in the *Guardian*. "He said that, since his remarriage, he no longer had room for the books in his Oxford home, and hoped to use the money raised from the sale to set up a bursary at St. Anne's, Murdoch's former Oxford college. Mr. Bayley faced criticism over his decision to sell the collection amid fears that it would leave the country. There was strong interest from U.S. booksellers, who were prepared to meet the £150,000 asking price." Rachel Lee, the Bristol bookseller who handled the sale—and who was credited with finding a solution involving a public appeal for funds that helped keep the books together—told the newspaper that as soon as she started cataloging the library, she knew "it had to be kept together." For anyone who wants to study Murdoch's fiction, "this helps to piece things together," she said. "It's like a jigsaw. This collection paints a vivid picture of a remarkable woman who was a key figure in English life and letters for a large part of the twentieth century—not only as a novelist, but also as a significant and influential thinker."

In each of these instances, the holdings represent the reading of productive people, writers for the most part, but the collections of scientists, artists, politicians, generals, physicians, and interesting individuals of every conceivable persuasion are fair game as well, as the books of Wilbur Wright (1867–1912) and Orville Wright (1871–1948), the inventors of powered aviation, suggest quite persuasively. Neither man had any formal education beyond high school, and what the brothers were able to accomplish they did through their own intuition and experimentation. I spent a day among the Wright family books maintained at Wright State University in Dayton, Ohio, and also at their former private residence, Hawthorne House, in the summer of 2004, not expecting very much, given the limited time I had available, but looking all the same for a revealing tidbit or two, something that at the very least might suggest an idea that came from a certain book, if not the eureka moment itself.

Happily, there were some titles with a few markings in them, a few actually worth noting. Included among their books is *Progress in Flying Machines* (1894) by Octave Chanute (1832–1910), a Chicago engineer considered the "elder statesman" of aeronautical research and a confidant of the brothers, with a stamp on the title page indicating it is "from the private library of Orville Wright." As his surviving books suggest, Orville was an appreciative reader of eclectic tastes who designed a comfortable reading chair with a lighted tray that could suspend a volume in front of him, a piece of domestic furniture that is still in the library of his elegant house. Two double lines have been penciled alongside several passages in Chanute's book, published nine years before the flight at Kitty Hawk, North Carolina. It is a commentary on *Birdflight as the Basis of Aviation* (1857), by the German Otto Lilienthal (1848–1896), which is also represented in the Wright library in German and English editions: "In the opinion of the writer of these lines," Chanute wrote, "Herr Lilienthal has attacked the most difficult, and perhaps the most important, of the many problems which must be solved before success can be hoped for in navigating the air with flying machines. He has engaged in the effort to work out the maintenance of equilibrium in flight, and to learn the science of the bird. He has made a good beginning, and seems to be in a fair way to accomplish some success in riding the wind."

In the Lilienthal book, a segment that gets an underline and multiple vertical marks offers reasons why "no flying birds exceed some 50 pounds in weight; for small animals must possess more energy in proportion to their size than large ones." One volume that has nothing to do with aviation whatsoever, but which contains multiple marginal notes, is *Introduction to the Study of Philosophy* (1894) by J. H. W. Stuckenberg. Inside the back cover, on the page known as the rear pastedown, someone, presumably Orville, since this book also bears his stamp, wrote this: "What is 'mind?' No matter! What is 'matter?' Never mind!"

On the flip side of all this—some might even say the dark side—are the books once owned and read by people whose influence on history has been anything but salutary. Do we have a reading list, for instance, of Donatien Alphonse François Marquis de Sade (1740–1814)—the author of *Justine* and *The 120 Days of Sodom*, the notorious "Professor Emeritus of Crime," according to the French historian Jules Michelet—and would it help us in any way to explain what are still in many instances the unspeakable proclivities of a disturbed man who gave his surname to the language as a word to connote abhorrent behavior? Two recent biographers of Sade, Maurice Lever and Francine du Plessix Gray, both describe a childhood of voracious reading in the well-stocked library of an aristocratic uncle, the Abbé de Sade, as being so intense that by the age of ten—and here they both cite Sade himself—"he could locate almost any volume with his eyes closed."

Books in the abbé's collection included all the classics from previous centuries and every major text of Enlightenment thought, along with many contemporary works of anthropology and comparative religion that had been banned by the Church and which were all the rage among the French intelligentsia of the period. "The abbé's library, like any accomplished eighteenth-century library, was also rich in erotic literature," Gray wrote, with such salacious titles as *Venus in the Cloister, or the Nun in Her Nightdress* and *The Bordello, or Everyman Debauched* within arm's reach, many of them spiced with illustrations that were equally as lewd. Another book, printed in Amsterdam in 1701 and known to have been in the uncle's library—a fragmentary shelf list has been reconstructed—reads on the title page: *History of the Flagellants, in which the good and the bad uses of flagellation among the Christians are pointed out.* Sade surely knew this book, and many others, both biographers agree. "He knew all the nooks and crannies of the library, even the most secret ones, where the abbé hid his small collection of licentious literature," Lever wrote. "Such books, such images, were an important part of the education Donatien received during the last years he spent with his uncle," Gray concluded, noting that the uncle's nickname—"the sybarite of Saumane"—is revealing, and helpful to scholars in search of evidence that might shed some light on the shaping of a troubled mind.

Karl Marx (1818–1883), German philosopher, economist, socialist, and revolutionary thinker, worked day after day beneath the soaring dome of the Great Reading Room of the British Museum, acquiring his first reading ticket in 1850 and receiving a final renewal card twenty-seven years later. Marx arrived in London in 1849, having been expelled from Belgium, France, and Germany following publication the previous year of *Manifest der Kommunistischen Partei*, the tract he wrote with Friedrich Engels that traumatized Europe with the clarion call, "Workers of the World, Unite!" In 1963, the Printing and the Mind of Man exhibition catalog deemed *The Communist Manifesto* to have been "the most widely read political pamphlet in human history."

Making do in London with periodic freelance writing assignments and occasional largesse from Engels, Marx used the reading room as his base of operations for the next quarter of a century. His custom was to arrive at nine each morning and stay until seven at night, all the while cataloging enormous amounts of information and history for *Das Kapital*, the systematic theory of capitalism that would be issued in three volumes, the first in 1867, and the only one to appear in his lifetime. "Marx lives a very retired life," a friend wrote to Engels in 1851, noting that "his only acquaintances" were the books of the economists John Stewart Mill, Samuel Johns Loyd, and others he was studying with minute care in the library. "The stuff, on which I work, is so damned ramified that despite all efforts one does not succeed in completing it before six to eight weeks," he complained in another letter that year. In an 1868 letter to his daughter Laura, who was sending him additional material from Paris, Marx offered this: "You'll certainly fancy, my dear child, that I am very fond of books, because I trouble you with them at so unseasonable a time. But you would be quite mistaken. I am a machine, condemned to devour them and then, throw them, in a changed form, on the dunghill of history."

Significantly, Marx's "favorite occupation," according to an informal questionnaire he filled out about this time for the amusement of his daughters, was "book-worming." In the same document, Marx listed Shakespeare, Aeschylus, and Goethe as his favorite poets, and Diderot his favorite prose writer. For heroes, he named Spartacus, the Thracian slave who led an armed rebellion against Rome in the first century BC, and the pioneering astronomer Johannes Kepler. As a gesture of gratitude for the many years he was able to read whatever he wanted at one of the finest libraries in the world, Marx presented a first-edition copy of *Das Kapital* to the British Museum in 1871. The first translation of that book into another language appeared the next year in Russian, causing no apprehension for the official censor who approved it for publication. "Few people in Russia will read it," the government functionary wrote in a moment of exquisite understatement and error, "and still fewer will understand it."

Closer to our own time are the books owned by Adolf Hitler (1889–1945), a good number of which were confiscated by American soldiers at the end of World II and turned over to the Library of Congress in Washington, D.C., where they are classified under the general heading of Third Reich Materials. The twelve hundred books shelved in the Jefferson Building represent just a fraction of the books known to have been in the führer's possession, although no systematic inventory was ever kept by him, or if one was, it did not survive the war. Frederick Oechsner, an American journalist who had regular contact with the German chancellor before the onset of hostilities, estimated a collection of 16,300 volumes divided between the chancellery library in Berlin and a country home at Berchtesgaden, and nobody has ever suggested that they were acquired for ostentation. Hitler himself buttressed that point in the second chapter of his book *Mein Kampf*, leaving no doubt in a brief section called "The Art of Reading" as to whether the practice should ever be undertaken for pleasure. "I know people who endlessly 'read' a lot, book after book, letter for letter, yet I would not call them 'well read.' Of course, they possess a wide 'knowledge,' but their intellect does not know how to distribute and register the material gathered." Reading, Hitler emphasized, "is not a purpose in itself, but a means to an end," one meant to "give a general picture of the world," and in his view best done selectively. "When studying a book, a magazine, or a pamphlet, those who master this art of reading will immediately pick out that which in their opinion is suitable for them—because it serves their purposes or is generally worth knowing—and therefore to be remembered forever."

A number of scholars have taken a careful look at Hitler's books, two of them, Philipp Gassert, a professor of history at the University of Heidelberg, and Daniel Mattern, senior editor at the German Historical Institute, in Washington, D.C., for purposes of compiling a bibliographical reconstruction, *The Hitler Library*, which was published in 2001. Their 550-page effort includes basic publication information—title, author, date, number of pages—but does not enumerate marginalia, which was the central concern of Timothy W. Ryback, director of the Salzburg Seminar in Salzburg, Austria, in an essay written for the *Atlantic Monthly* two years later, "Hitler's Forgotten Library: The Man, His Books, and His Search for God."

The books were discovered by soldiers of the 101st Airborne Division in the spring of 1945 stored in a salt mine near Berchtesgaden, loosely packed in wooden crates with the Reich Chancellery address written on them. Brought to the United States and largely forgotten—most of the titles to this day have not been cataloged by the Library of Congress—the books have been ignored because of a long-held belief that few of them were ever perused by Hitler, much less read. Ryback did not find evidence of extensive annotation, but he did see handwritten marks inserted for emphasis in a number of the volumes, and through them discovered what he called a Hitler he "had not anticipated," a man betraying what appeared to be "a sustained interest in spirituality," with more than 130 books on religious subjects, ranging from Occidental occultism to Eastern mysticism to the teachings of Jesus Christ. In an eight-volume set of the complete works of the nineteenth-century German philosopher Johann Gottlieb Fichte—a rare first edition, no less—Ryback encountered "a veritable blizzard of underlines, question marks, exclamation points, and marginal strikes that sweeps across a hundred printed pages of dense theological prose." As he traced the penciled notations, Ryback concluded that Hitler "was seeking a path to the divine that led to just one place. Fichte asked, 'Where did Jesus derive the power that has held his followers for all eternity?' Hitler drew a dense line beneath the answer: 'Through his absolute identification with God.' " In another section, "Hitler not only underlined the entire passage but placed a thick vertical line in the margin, and added an exclamation point for good measure."

Elsewhere, Ryback found further evidence of Hitler's fascination with the subject. "One leather-bound tome—with *WORTE CHRISTI*, or 'Word of Christ,' embossed in gold on the cover—was well worn, the silky, supple leather peeling upward in gentle curls along the edges. Human hands had obviously spent a lot of time with this book. The inside cover bore a dedication: 'To our beloved Führer with gratitude and profound respect, Clara von Behl, born von Jansen von den Osten. Christmas 1935.' " A close examination found no marginalia, just one penciled line next to an aphorism entreating the faithful to *love your neighbor as you would love yourself.* "Given Hitler's legendary disdain for organized religion in general and Christianity in particular, I didn't expect him to have devoted much time to the teachings of Christ, let alone to have marked this quintessential Christian virtue," he wrote. "Had this in fact been made by the pencil of Hitler's younger sister, Paula, who occasionally visited her brother at the Berghof and remained a devout Catholic until her dying day? Might some other Berghof guest have responded to this holy Scripture?"

After a lengthy analysis, Ryback concluded otherwise, quoting reliable contemporary observers who had perceived in Hitler's final months a desperate drift toward a belief in divine providence. In his *Atlantic* essay, Ryback quoted a confidential psychological report prepared during the war that supported this claim: "A survey of all the evidence forces us to conclude that Hitler believes himself destined to become an Immortal Hitler, chosen by God to be the New Deliverer of Germany and the Founder of a new social order for the world. He firmly believes this and is certain that in spite of all the trials and tribulations through which he must pass he will finally attain that goal. The one condition is that he follow the dictates of the inner voice that have guided and protected him in the past."

In his 1942 book *This Is the Enemy*, the correspondent Frederick Oechsner wrote that Hitler's books were evenly divided between the chancellery residence in Berlin and the country retreat on the Obersalzberg at Berchtesgaden. Of these, he determined that 1,500 dealt with architecture, theater, painting, and sculpture, with another 800 or so mere "popular fiction, many of them pure trash in anybody's language." By far the largest concentration, according to Oechsner, were some 7,000 books devoted to "the campaigns of Napoleon, the Prussian kings; the lives of all German and Prussian potentates who ever played a military role; and books on virtually all the well-known military campaigns in recorded history." Most of them have been scattered to the four winds, a good many probably confiscated by the Russians, others taken as trophies by soldiers, and from the slice of Hitler's library that remains intact in Washington, it is obvious that only a fragmentary picture of Hitler's supposed reading is possible.

Still, volumes with his distinctive bookplate—an eagle in profile, a swastika, and the name Adolf Hitler underneath—are to be found in numerous collections both public and private. One of the bibliophiles I profiled in my 1995 book, *A Gentle Madness*, the late Walter Pforzheimer of Washington, D.C.—a former Central Intelligence Agency senior officer who created the world's preeminent "spy collection," as he called it—described for me how he had made off with five of these books in 1945 while serving with the U.S. Army. "I was in the Reich Chancellery, and there they were," he told me. "I didn't think the Führer was going to be needing them anymore. I gave one to the guy who cut my orders for Berlin, I gave one to the Grolier Club, I gave one to Yale, and I kept the other two," both of which he showed to me in his Watergate apartment library.

I was reminded of that conversation during an interview I had for this book with Breon Mitchell, director of the Lilly Library at Indiana University and a lifelong bibliophile, when he showed me one of his prize possessions, and told me the story of how he had acquired it in 1965 while studying at Oxford University as a Rhodes scholar. Mitchell recalled a day four decades earlier when he was in London browsing through the German section in Maggs Brothers Ltd. in Berkeley Square, one of the world's leading purveyors of rare books, and spotted a copy of Thomas Carlyle's famous biography of Frederick the Great. "It had a blue leather binding—it was pretty—and I pulled it out to see what it was." Inside was Hitler's bookplate, along with a typewritten note explaining how Maggs had acquired the item in 1945 from one of the first soldiers to have entered Hitler's mountain retreat in the Bavarian Alps shortly after the fall of Berlin. "The book had been on Maggs's shelves for twenty years, apparently nobody back then was much interested in the German section," Mitchell speculated. The price, penciled in, was £5. Next to that book on the shelf was a three-volume edition of Shakespeare, also in German, also bearing Hitler's bookplate, and priced at £25. "The short of it all is that I had enough money to buy the Carlyle, but to my everlasting regret I could not afford the Shakespeare."

Returning to his rooms at Oxford, Mitchell went immediately to Hugh Trevor-Roper's best-selling history of 1947, *The Last Days of Hitler*, and checked to see what he could find in the index that might bear on this extraordinary find. "Well, right away I saw, 'Carlyle, Thomas, *Life of Frederick the Great*, Hitler's favorite book, page so and so.' I turned to the page and there Trevor-Roper says, 'Hitler's favorite book was Carlyle's *Frederick the Great*, because Hitler identified with Frederick— how he was surrounded by enemies and so forth. In fact he loved the book so much that Dr. Goebbels reports in his diary that in the last days in the bunker, he read aloud to Hitler from a copy of the *Life of Frederick the Great*, and the tears stood in the Führer's eyes." The fingerprints of many people were on this volume, a circumstance that prompted Mitchell to write Trevor-Roper, who was teaching a course at Oxford at the time, and tell him about the acquisition.

"He wrote me back promptly and said, 'Yes, it definitely was a favorite book of Hitler, would you like to come by for tea? I would very much like to see it.' He wanted to see, obviously, if it had annotations. There are no annotations, I had checked that out by then, I was a young scholar, and that would have interested me greatly too. The only thing I could tell was that Hitler—or someone—had read the book carefully, because the ribbon, with the top edge, is gilded, and you can see that it had been moved all the way through, and it had made marks all the way through. It had been read from beginning to end. You can tell that."

The history of reading is a fairly recent endeavor, with major contributions appearing in print with increasing frequency, a cousin of sorts to *histoire du livre*, or the social history of the book, which was developed in France in the years following World War II. A basic premise each follows is the idea that it is readers, not just authors, who give meaning to texts, and that there is value in knowing how individuals through history respond to them. A few recent examples are instructive. In *Reading Revolutions*, the British historian Kevin Sharpe centered an exhaustive study of reading and politics in early modern England—roughly all of the seventeenth century, but with particular emphasis in this case on the time of the English Civil War, the execution of King Charles I in 1649, the Commonwealth, and the Restoration—on the reading practices of one person, Sir William Drake (1606–1669). Lawyer, aristocrat, landowner, opportunist, and most assuredly a man of his period and place who read often and with purpose over four eventful decades, Drake recorded his impressions in no fewer than fifty-four commonplace books and numerous annotated books.

An epitaph on a monument erected in Drake's memory reports him to have been a "promoter and patron of letters," a person who "collected from every quarter the best editions," one who "sought especially Latin writers who taught true wisdom and common sense." Given Drake's willingness to adapt himself to the vicissitudes of the times, it is not surprising to learn that his favorite work was Machiavelli's *The Prince*, and that he found wisdom to be gleaned from its teachings. With access to all of these materials, Sharpe wrote that he had been presented with a "unique opportunity to observe an early Stuart gentleman reading, reflecting, organizing a programme of study to equip himself for personal gain and considered action in the public sphere," validating a conviction he holds that how people read "is an essential component of how they experienced and perceived society and politics."

Another monograph published in 2000 took an entirely different approach by focusing on the cultural impact one book had on thousands of readers in the fifteen years preceding the publication in 1859 of Charles Darwin's *On the Origin of Species by Means of Natural Selection*, a work that "shattered notions of humanity, morality, and truth" and removed "at a single stroke any intellectual justification for God's role in nature." Praise it or condemn it, the Cambridge University scholar James A. Secord asserts in *Victorian Sensation*, Darwin's *Origin* remains "the secular Bible that made the modern world." Making these circumstances all the more striking—and it is at the heart of Secord's thesis—is that "the *Origin*'s main novelty, natural selection, was rejected by almost all readers for the first seventy-five years after publication," and one of the reasons he cited was the enormous impact of an earlier book, *Vestiges of the Natural History of Creation*, and the many controversies that swirled around it.

Published anonymously in England in 1844, *Vestiges* contained a little bit of everything. Secord classified it as an "evolutionary epic" that was as "readable as a romance, based on the latest findings of science," ranging "from the formation of the solar system to reflections on the destiny of the human race," a work more controversial "than any other philosophical or scientific work of its time," a "hugely ambitious synthesis that combined astronomy, geology, physiology, psychology, anthropology, and theology in what amounted to a general theory of creation." Indeed, it suggested that the planets had originated "in a blazing Fire-mist, that life could be created in the laboratory, that humans had evolved from apes."

And it took Great Britain by storm, more popular in its time than the early novels of Charles Dickens, read variously by Queen Victoria, Alfred Tennyson, Florence Nightingale, William Ewart Gladstone, Thomas De Quincey, Thomas Carlyle, even Charles Darwin (1809–1882) himself, whose own reading habits—which are fairly well documented by books of his that are now at Cambridge University, and in a memoir by a son, Francis Darwin—are discussed at some length by Secord. Curiously, when he wanted to be entertained or amused by fiction or light history, Darwin's custom was to have his wife, Emma, read to him aloud; books and pamphlets that held any scientific interest for him, on the other hand, were engaged directly, often split apart and the relevant contents physically removed, while others were marked up and coded for future reference. Darwin read *Vestiges* in the British Library, taking copious notes, dismissing some assertions out of hand while reminding himself to avoid certain expressions in his own work, words such as "higher" and "lower," preferring instead to write of certain organisms as being "more complicated" than others. He also took steps to distance himself from *Vestiges* and to avoid structural elements that would draw comparisons between the two. "No one would accuse the *Origin* of reading like a novel."

Vestiges was mentioned in thousands of letters and diaries in its time, according to Secord, "denounced and praised in pulpits, discussed on railway journeys, and annotated on an Alabama River steamboat." Equally intriguing was the identity of the author, and as the book went through printing after printing, speculation as to who wrote it raged through Britain, with authorship finally acknowledged forty years after the fact by Robert Chambers, a prominent Scottish writer and publisher. Looking closely at the reception accorded this single work in "all its uses and manifestations," Secord suggested an approach to history that takes in "the role of the printed word in forging new senses of identity in the industrial age."

Among other works in the history of reading, special mention must be made of *The Reading Nation in the Romantic Period* (2004), a mammoth attempt to determine which books people actually read in the English-speaking world, from about 1790 to 1830. To do this, William St. Clair, a senior research fellow at Trinity College, Cambridge, employed a quantitative approach that began by examining publishing records to determine how many copies of certain titles were printed and the prices that were charged. He then investigated how books were marketed and sold, and looked at tariffs that were in place to monitor the importation of printed matter. Other factors he took into account were copyright laws, piracy practices, the cost of admission tickets to readings, census figures, literacy rates—a whole plethora of considerations—and all supported by 270 pages of fascinating appendices.

"The contemporaneous canon was a judgment of literary value, not a list of bestselling authors," St. Clair stressed, making clear that his goal was to determine what books people actually were reading. "As every author knows, reputation does not mean readers, and print runs are not sales." Since almost all copies of books manufactured during this period appear to have been sold, and because sales records survive, St. Clair was able to draw some conclusions. "The author whose verse works were sold in the largest numbers during the romantic period was, by far, Walter Scott. By 1836, four years after Scott's death, at least 180,000 copies of his long romantic poems had been printed, more than 200,000 counting the less famous works, and they were still being reprinted in ever larger print runs. After Scott, the poet whose works were produced in the largest numbers was Byron."

Elsewhere, St. Clair offered this: "Of all the literary works written during the romantic period, *Frankenstein* is the one whose continuing presence is most obvious." Mary Godwin—later Mary Shelley—was eighteen years old when she put pen to paper, created the character of Victor Frankenstein, and wrote the words, "It was on a dreary night of November that I beheld the accomplishment of my toils." Rejected by many of the major publishers in London, the novel—deemed a piece of "unnatural disgusting fiction" by Thomas Carlyle, and the "foulest Toadstool that has yet sprung from the reeking dunghill of present times" by William Beckford—was issued in 1818 in a pricey first printing of five hundred copies. Too expensive for most people to own, the book soon fell out of print and was largely forgotten for the next forty years. By 1880, when copyright restrictions had lapsed, inexpensive reprints were being produced, and by the turn of the century, the dark tale was "accessible to the whole reading nation," and because the idea of manufactured monsters had struck an uneasy nerve in the Victorian mind, sales figures began to soar.

With each of these books—*Reading Revolutions, Victorian Sensation,* and *The Reading Nation in the Romantic Period*—it is the reader that is at the heart of the discourse, although all rely heavily on principles embodied by *histoire du livre*, a parallel discipline that has been around a bit longer, and one that takes a more concrete approach. *Histoire du livre* is concerned fundamentally with the book as material object, its physical makeup as an artifact, its production, distribution, and circulation, extending down to the quality of the paper that is used, the number of pages, what typeface was chosen, the composition of the binding—is it leather or is it cloth?—the presence or absence of illustrations, indices, and bibliographical devices such as footnotes and appendices, the cost, certainly, as price can determine the nature of the audience—all of these factors are taken into account—but rarely does it try to evaluate reading in personal terms, one of the problems being the nature of personal information that for the most part is anecdotal, and thus largely subjective.

In *The Printing Press as an Agent of Change* (1979), Elizabeth Eisenstein, professor emerita at the University of Michigan, concentrated on the years immediately following the introduction of movable type in Europe, roughly 1450 to 1550, to show how the sudden availability of a technology that made rapid communication widely available served as the handmaiden, not just the witness, to history, and how the Protestant Reformation in particular was shaped in large measure by the widespread dissemination of ideas and arguments. The 1520 tract of Martin Luther—*To the Christian Nobility of the German Nation Concerning the Reformation of the Christian Commonwealth*—was published in Wittenberg in August 1520, three months after a Bull of Excommunication had been issued against him in Rome. Within two weeks of its release, four thousand copies were sold; another seventeen editions would appear over the next eighty years.

Was the French Revolution of the late eighteenth century a product of the printing press? No historian of any stature will say for certain one way or other, though knowledge of what was read, sold, and distributed—both legally on the open market and clandestinely "under the cloak" (*sous le manteau*) by street peddlers—has been scrutinized for more than thirty years by Robert Darnton, professor of European history at Princeton University and one of the world's leading authorities in early modern French history, an area that he has probed in exhaustive detail using the principles of *histoire du livre* in half a dozen pathbreaking books. In *The Business of Enlightenment: A Publishing History of the Encyclopedie*, Darnton fashioned a profile of Denis Diderot's masterpiece by looking at records he located that shed light on publishers, bookshops, binders, and transportation systems.

"Why bother to identify a corpus of literature that has been forgotten for two hundred years," he asked in *The Forbidden Best-Sellers of Pre-Revolutionary France*, a compilation of works that were legally forbidden, but read with great enthusiasm all the same. "Why pore over the texts of best-sellers from the eighteenth century when the best-sellers of our own day seem so trivial? What is at stake in all this scholarship?" His answer was unequivocal: that the history of books as a new discipline within the "human sciences" has made it possible to "gain a broader view of literature and cultural history in general," and that by documenting such details as which books were published, how many were distributed, what they cost, and who read them, it is possible to glean some sense as to whether or not they "shaped reality itself and helped determine the course of events."

6.

Paving the Way

✾ ✾

Perhaps the sentiments contained in the following pages are not yet suf-
ficiently fashionable to procure them general favor; a long habit of not
thinking a thing wrong, *gives it a superficial appearance of being*
right, *and raises at first a formidable outcry in defence of custom. But*
the tumult soon subsides. Time makes more converts than reason.
—Thomas Paine, *Common Sense* (1776)

✾ ✾

Few numerals from the past can claim the allure of 1776, four digits immediately recognizable as the year of American independence, and everything that implies. There are other dates that carry historical weight by their mere mention—1066 and the Norman Conquest of England, 1492 and the European arrival in the New World, 1588 and the sinking of the Spanish Armada—and there are individual days that have the power to evoke feelings and memories, December 7, 1941, and November 22, 1963, coming immediately to mind. Taking on an almost iconic aspect of its own in a very short period of time is September 11, 2001—known throughout the world simply as 9/11—and the horrific events of a single morning seared forever in the consciousness of those who watched what was by far the most witnessed news event in the annals of humanity. But 1776 remains a year of extraordinary consequence, not only for Americans but for students of human endeavor everywhere.

"It was also a very big year for books," the historian and biographer David McCullough reminded me one morning when we met at the Massachusetts Historical Society in Boston for a wide-ranging conversation that took in significant people, defining events, and the myriad ways that important writings have figured into the shaping of history and into the making of his own books, a series of studies that have included penetrating cultural histories of the construction of the Panama Canal and the building of the Brooklyn Bridge, and magisterial biographies of Harry S. Truman and John Adams. McCullough was spending time among the Boston collections that day, tying up the loose ends of a book he was then finishing, a narrative history, aptly enough, about the year 1776, and aspects of America's inexorable drive toward creation of a new nation. I had asked him specifically about Thomas Paine, and whether events would have played out differently had there been no *Common Sense*, had there been no fiery essays collectively called *The Crisis*. Questions such as this have been asked often about other key moments in Western history—most notably the function of the printing press in the spread of conflicting religious views during the time of Martin Luther, the impact of pamphleteers during the period of the English Civil War, and the role of print in setting the stage for the French Revolution, as discussed in the previous chapter—but the issue here was the writing of a single individual, and whether its influence could be detected in any meaningful way.

"Paine's importance is phenomenal and can't really be overemphasized," McCullough said. "*Common Sense* was, I guess, hands down our first bestseller, and it wasn't just how many people read it, but *who* read it, and *who* was influenced by it, including George Washington. Many people were holding back their support until *Common Sense* came along, and it was still touch-and-go right up until July whether Congress would declare to vote independence. Had there been no book *Common Sense*, I don't think it would have happened, not that summer anyway, and probably it wouldn't have happened at all because the fortunes of war went so against us after that summer of '76 and all through the rest of the year, it's very doubtful that Congress ever would have done anything so rash as independence."

Published anonymously on January 10, 1776—indeed, *Common Sense* was attributed at first to the pen of "an Englishman"—its authorship was quickly known on both sides of the Atlantic, with Paine himself claiming before the year was out that 150,000 copies had been circulated. Then, on Christmas Day of that year, with his dispirited army in disarray and the future of their bold enterprise very much in doubt, Washington instructed his officers to read to their troops an essay by Paine that had been printed in Philadelphia just six days earlier. Titled *The American Crisis*, it began with the stirring words,

These are the times that try men's souls: The summer soldier and the sunshine patriot will, in this crisis, shrink from the service of his country; but he that stands it NOW, deserves the love and thanks of man and woman. Tyranny, like hell, is not easily conquered; yet we have the consolation with us, that the harder the conflict, the more glorious the triumph.

Later that day, Washington's ragged troops would cross the Delaware River in open boats, march on Trenton, and achieve one of the most improbable—and one of the most critical—victories of the entire rebellion. But as McCullough stressed, other forces were at work in Europe and contributing to the nature of a discourse that had heated up and was approaching a boil. Also appearing in print in 1776 was *An Inquiry Into the Nature and Causes of the Wealth of Nations* by the Scottish economist Adam Smith (1723–1790), who strongly disapproved of excessive regulation of colonial trade, and who saw futility in England's furtherance of established policies he regarded as failed. It was observations like the following that gave people in power pause to reflect about events that were taking place in the Crown Colonies:

> At first sight, no doubt, the monopoly of the great commerce of America naturally seems to be an acquisition of the highest value. To the undiscerning eye of giddy ambition, it naturally presents itself amidst the confused scramble of politics and war, as a very dazzling object to fight for. The dazzling splendour of the object, however the immense greatness of the commerce, is the very quality which renders the monopoly of it hurtful, or which makes one employment, in its own nature necessarily less advantageous to the country than the greater part of other employments, absorb a much greater proportion of the capital of the country than what would otherwise have gone to it.

Before the year had ended, a friend and admirer of Smith, Edward Gibbon, saw the first volume of his own magnum opus, *The History of the Decline and Fall of the Roman Empire*, ushered through the press, and the similarities perceived between the collapse of a powerful nation from antiquity and the challenges being mounted against a dominant state of the Enlightenment were not lost on attentive readers. The curators of the Printing and the Mind of Man exhibition singled out the *Decline and Fall* as the only historical narrative written before the works of Thomas Babington, Lord Macaulay (1800–1859) "which continues to be reprinted and actually read."

In a memoir of his youth written in 1930, Winston Churchill recalled discovering Gibbon and Macaulay while serving with the British Army in India, an interlude he called "the university of my life" for more reasons than one, most pointedly because he had bypassed a college education to serve in the military. When Churchill arrived on the Indian subcontinent in the winter of 1896 at the age of twenty-two, he found himself increasingly anxious to learn whatever he could about philosophy, history, politics, and economics, and wrote his mother in England asking for help. "She responded with alacrity, and every month the mail brought me a substantial package," he recalled. Fittingly, Churchill began his course of self-instruction with Gibbon, and was "immediately dominated" by both the story and the style.

"All through the long glistening middle hours of the Indian day, from when we quitted stables till the evening shadows proclaimed the hour of Polo, I devoured Gibbon," he wrote. "I rode triumphantly through it from end to end and enjoyed it all. I scribbled all my opinions on the margins of the pages, and very soon found myself a vehement partisan of the author against the disparagement of his pompous-pious editor. I was not even estranged by his naughty footnotes." The books Churchill consumed over the next two years of his posting easily equaled the reading list of what he might have read at Oxford or Cambridge, had he gone to either institution, prompting the future prime minister to dedicate *My Early Life* "to a new generation," along with a bit of advice: "It is a good thing for an uneducated man to read books of quotations. Bartlett's *Familiar Quotations* is an admirable book and I studied it intently. The quotations when engraved upon the memory give you good thoughts. They also make you anxious to read the authors and look for more." As for Gibbon, Churchill read the *Decline and Fall* in its entirety, one volume after the other.

Neither Adam Smith nor Edward Gibbon set the stage for the American Revolution in 1776, of course, but as David McCullough had emphasized in his conversation with me, it was quite a year for books all the same, and books had roles to play in the course of events. "When Thomas Jefferson sat down to write the Declaration of Independence, he acknowledged later that there was nothing new in what he was saying, that everything he was saying there he had taken from what he had read,"

McCullough said. "That's literally true—and his sense, as so many people of the eighteenth century also felt, that the world of the mind was to be found in books. *Ideas* were to be found in books, and there was nothing a person could not learn from them."

As Pauline Maier wrote in *American Scripture*, a meticulous account of the making of the Declaration of Independence, the generative document of the new nation benefited from the contributions of no fewer than five Founding Fathers, but it was Jefferson who did most of the writing, and when under mounting pressure to produce hard copy, he turned to what he knew for inspiration. "He was no Moses receiving the Ten Commandments from the hand of God," Maier wrote, "but a man who had to prepare a written text with little time to waste, and who, like others in similar circumstances, drew on earlier documents of his own and other people's creation, acting within the rhetorical and ethical standards of his time, and producing a draft that revealed both splendid artistry and signs of haste." With the exception of the seventeenth-century British philosopher John Locke, whose widely known treatises on government enjoyed enormous respect, historians are vague on which specific works were helpful, though they cite no less an authority than Jefferson himself as to his mode of composition. In 1823, just three years before his death, Jefferson wrote to James Madison that he "did not consider it part of my charge to invent new ideas altogether, and to offer no sentiment which had ever been expressed before." But one question lingered then as it does now: Did he draw directly from his vast store of reading material to produce the document, or from his acute memory of the sources? Jefferson had an answer. "I do not know," he frankly admitted forty-seven years after the fact. "I know only that I turned to neither book nor pamphlet while writing it."

The "world of the mind," as McCullough phrased it, is a fundamental quality that he, as a greatly admired writer of American history, has studied closely, especially in the cases of John Adams and Harry Truman, presidents he profiled in biographies that each has received the Pulitzer Prize as well as numerous other prestigious awards. In the instance of Adams, McCullough is credited with marshaling renewed attention on a figure who had fallen into the shadows of neglect over the decades, and restoring him to public prominence. One of the most startling assertions McCullough has made is that Adams was probably the most assiduous American reader of his generation, stronger, in his opinion, than Jefferson, a legendary bibliophile who once asserted, "I cannot live without books," and Benjamin Franklin, an intellect respected on both sides of the Atlantic whose private library was among the most sophisticated of its era. "Adams's reading was not only broader, it was deeper than Jefferson's," McCullough told me. "He was more eclectic than Jefferson, and his reading was more passionate, as he was a more passionate kind of person. I think we are what we read to a very large degree, and I don't think it's very easy or possible to understand any particular generation, or certainly that generation of the Founding Fathers, without reading what they read."

McCullough's research was enriched by the vast body of correspondence that has been preserved at the Massachusetts Historical Society, an archive that maintains more than seven thousand Adams family letters, fifteen hundred of them between John Adams and his wife, Abigail Smith Adams. For McCullough, this material was the mother lode, providing unparalleled access to his subject's thoughts and emotions, but of great significance too was the 3,200-volume library of Adams's books, which has been installed in the Boston Public Library since 1893. Not only was Adams an eclectic reader, he was an enthusiastic reader as well, as the many annotations he wrote in the margins attest. "He would argue with the author of the book he was reading, and he loved to read authors whose opinions were different from his," McCullough said. "There are books where it's almost as if he wrote more in the margins than the author wrote in the book. And they are sometimes quite funny, and they sometimes are quite pertinent, and sometimes, in my view, quite convincing." One example McCullough found riveting involved Mary Wollstonecraft's *An Historical and Moral*

View of the Origin and Progress of the French Revolution, which Adams read at least twice, and in which he wrote marginal notes totaling some twelve thousand words. "He was an ambitious reader, and there was nothing he would not undertake," McCullough said. "I think he was seventy-five years old when he undertook the reading of a sixteen-volume French history—in French." There is a letter from Abigail Adams to John Quincy Adams, written in 1816, in which the following observation is made: "Your father's zeal for books will be one of the last desires which will quit him."

The catalog of the John Adams Library issued by the Boston Public Library in 1917, itself considered a collector's item today, documents a wide spectrum of intellectual interests, with books by Jean-Jacques Rousseau and the mathematician Marquis de Condorcet sharing shelf space with Adam Smith and Joseph Priestley. A schoolteacher in his youth, Adams "never stopped reading, never stopped growing intellectually," McCullough made clear. "In his eighties Adams could still be seen out in his hayfields at Quincy, swinging a scythe. He saw no contradiction between reading Thucydides at lunchtime and making hay in the afternoon." Eleven years before the outbreak of the Revolution, when he was twenty-nine years old, Adams exhorted his countrymen to action: "Let us dare to read, think, speak, write. Let every sluice of knowledge be open and set flowing."

Like most cultured men of the eighteenth century, Adams was fluent in the classics, and he often made reference to favored passages from his reading without directly citing the source, an accepted convention of the period. In one letter written to his wife during a dark hour of the Revolution, Adams wrote a passage that McCullough said "nearly lifted me out of my chair" when he first read it. "We cannot insure success," Adams declared, "but we can deserve it." It was the kind of remarkably gritty statement that gave McCullough unexpected insight into the character of the man, suggesting a conviction that while the outcome of the war might be in God's hands, how mortals acquitted themselves in the effort was entirely up to them. Not long after reading that, McCullough ran across virtually the same sentiment, expressed in almost the very same words, in a letter written by George Washington, and he began to wonder if "maybe they were quoting somebody." A determined search of *Bartlett's Familiar Quotations* turned up a line from *Cato*, a tragedy written in 1713 by the British dramatist, poet, and essayist Joseph Addison based on the life of the Roman statesman Cato the Younger. "'Tis not in mortals to command success," the line in question goes, "But we'll do more . . . We'll deserve it." General Washington had a particular fondness for the play, seeing it on the stage numerous times throughout his life, once having it performed for his troops at Valley Forge. "It was a play they all knew," McCullough concluded, "a line they all knew."

Further inquiries turned up similar examples. "The last words we are told that were uttered by Nathan Hale as he was about to be executed—'I only regret that I have but one life to lose for my country'—is another line from *Cato*," McCullough said, the realization of which prompted him to speculate that Hale was paraphrasing a familiar line from an English play to a group of English officers who were about to hang him, "throwing it right back at them," as it were, "because he knew that they knew the line too." Getting a sense of nuances like these is part of the work McCullough does as a historian whose job is to discern how certain things happen: "We can't understand the people of that distant time without understanding the culture. You have to read what they read, not just what they wrote."

McCullough applied a somewhat different twist on this approach to his study of the year 1776, which was still a work in progress when we spoke in Boston in the summer of 2004. "Two of the most interesting figures in this book, Nathaniel Greene and Henry Knox, became high-ranking officers at the very start of the Revolutionary War without having had any experience in the military. None. All that they knew, all that they knew about being officers, about armament, about drill, about military tactics and strategy, they had gotten from their reading. All they knew was what they had read in books. But they lived at a time when that was not considered an unusual way to learn something. This was a very good way to learn things. Through a close study of books there was no limit to what one could learn. And Nathaniel Greene was made a general when he was thirty-three years old. He was a general and he had never commanded any troops of any kind, and had never seen warfare first-hand, or had any schooling in warfare. And he turned out to be the best general we had. By the end of the war I think one can safely, quite accurately, fairly say that Nathaniel Greene was the most brilliant general we had."

Exactly how it was that Greene had access to these books is yet another story of interest. A native of Rhode Island, Greene was a neighbor of Ezra Stiles, a noted theologian and educator who became president of Yale in 1778, and conducted the first experiments with electricity at the university with equipment donated by Benjamin Franklin. Along with the fortuitous circumstance of having a brilliant mentor, Greene had independent means and the wherewithal to buy the books he wanted to read. For these, he traveled to Boston and patronized the London Bookshop, a store run by Henry Knox. "Henry Knox was a bookseller, and part of his stock-in-trade was military books published mostly in England," McCullough said. "Greene could afford those books, and he would talk with his friend the bookseller, Knox, about military matters, and they became quite good friends. Knox, meanwhile, became Washington's head of all the artillery while in his twenties, and all *he* had ever known about these matters was what he had read in books. Now it is hugely to Washington's credit, it seems to me, that he spotted the talent in these two young men and gave them their head as leaders, but of course Washington himself was an uneducated man; he had very little formal education, not even completing what we might call grade school. He did not know Latin or Greek as any educated man of the time did, so I'm sure he saw some of himself in these two young men. And he read the same military treatises they did. So part of the language of the profession, if you will, that they had in common were the books they had read. We are not only the product of what we read, we are in association with others who have read the same things."

The circumstance of Knox and Greene learning their military skills from their reading brings to mind the memorable line uttered by the late actor George C. Scott in his Academy Award–winning role as General George S. Patton in the 1970 film *Patton*, when in the immediate aftermath of a decisive victory over German forces under the command of Field Marshal Erwin Rommel in North Africa, he shouts, "Rommel, you magnificent bastard, I read your book!" A keen student of military history, Patton, according to his biographers, did indeed read *Infanterie Greift An: Erlebnisse und Erfahrungen*—Infantry Attacks—as did many other influential people of the period, not least among them Adolf Hitler, who gave Rommel his first in a series of high-profile commands a year after the book was published in 1938. What presumably impressed Hitler most about Rommel's account was that the man destined to be known as the Desert Fox drew on his own exemplary record in World War I to write about tactics, and did not bemoan or dwell on Germany's humiliating defeat in that war.

For all the exceptional qualities that made John Adams a true Founding Father of the American Republic, McCullough said he is most impressed by the man's unquenchable curiosity and lifelong drive to learn and know more. "There is no end to his journey of the mind and of the soul, and a lot of that is in his reading. And there's no end to his growth, his evolving, nor his love of life, and love of the language." These attributes are especially apparent in a letter Adams wrote to his son John Quincy Adams when the lad was a student in the Netherlands, encouraging him to think openly, and to enrich himself by dipping into works of the imagination:

Read somewhat in the English poets every day. You will find them elegant, entertaining, and constructive companions through your whole life. In all the disquisitions you have heard concerning the happiness of life, has it ever been recommended to you to read poetry?

And having asked his precocious son that salient question, he offered one more bit of fatherly advice: "You will never be alone with a poet in your pocket." For all the depth and sophistication of John Adams, it is John Quincy Adams, in McCullough's view, who was quite possibly the brightest person to ever serve as president of the United States, with a level of brilliance that even his parents occasionally had to put in perspective. Once, when living in England with her husband after the war, Abigail Adams was advised by one of her sisters back home that John Quincy was beginning to have something of an inflated opinion of himself. She promptly wrote a letter to her son with the following piece of advice:

If you are so conscious to yourself that you possess more knowledge upon some subjects than others of your standing, reflect that you have had greater opportunities of seeing the world, and obtaining a knowledge of mankind than any of your contemporaries. That you have never wanted a book but it has been supplied to you, that your whole time has been spent in the company of men of literature and science. How unpardonable would it have been in you to have been a blockhead.

The lifelong commitment to reading is apparent in yet another letter, written from France by John Adams, explaining why he was embarked on a mission that had kept him so long away from his family and neglecting his responsibilities as father and provider.

I must study politics and war that my sons might have the liberty to study mathematics and philosophy. My sons ought to study mathematics and philosophy, geography, natural history, naval architecture, navigation, commerce and agriculture in order to give their children a right to study paintings, poetry, music, architecture, statuary, tapestry, and porcelain.

Before immersing himself in the life of John Adams, McCullough spent an equal amount of time absorbed in the life of Harry S. Truman, the last president of the United States not to have earned a college degree, "a beautiful example of an unlettered man who never stopped reading," he said. "Truman loved history and biography, and that's mostly what he read. I'm not sure that he ever read a novel, I don't know that he read a novel, he certainly never talked about one, that I know of. Unlike Adams, a book to Truman was very precious, he didn't even like to pull down the corner of a page to mark where he'd stopped reading because that would damage the book. Adams as we know wrote furiously in the margins of his books. Truman did not acquire a great library. He loved the work of Douglas Southall Freeman, the biographer of Robert E. Lee and Lee's lieutenants, and also the biographer of George Washington. He was very fond of those books. He never stopped reading. Nor did Kennedy, for that matter."

Theodore Roosevelt carried a portable library with him on all his journeys, whether it was to Africa for big game hunting or to Cuba with the Rough Riders. Jimmy Carter's reading rate was clocked at two thousand words a minute, possibly a record among chief executives. Bill Clinton, a Rhodes scholar in the 1960s, admitted in his 2004 memoir that he ran out of space in the White House to shelve books. When it comes to reading among presidents, the most striking pair of contrasts involves Abraham Lincoln, the sixteenth chief executive, and Thomas Jefferson, the third. Aptly, the speeches and writings of both men were chosen by the Library of America for publication in uniform editions. Tutored early at home and later as a boarder in schools taught by Anglican clergymen, Jefferson entered the College of William and Mary at the age of sixteen, concentrating on philosophy. When the young scholar arrived on the campus in Williamsburg, Virginia, he was already reading Greek and Latin authors in their original languages, a practice he continued throughout his life. He was instructed in physics, metaphysics, mathematics, rhetoric, logic, and ethics. Jefferson showed keen interest in all fields, sometimes studying fifteen hours a day. It was not uncommon for him to "tear himself away from his dearest friends" and "fly to his studies," his closest college friend, John Page, reported. "The Sage of Monticello," as Jefferson's greatest biographer, Dumas Malone, called him, possessed a devotion to books that is legendary, with his greatest memorial, perhaps, not so much the beautiful temple on the banks of the Tidal Basin in the nation's capital but the Library of Congress, where his personal library of 6,700 volumes—in his words, "the choicest editions" in the United States at the time—established the universal tone of the great national repository that endures today.

Most of the books Jefferson turned over to the nation in 1815 were destroyed by a fire that engulfed the Capitol in 1851, but a catalog survived, along with a document bearing manuscript corrections in his hand meant to restore the original classification scheme he had adapted from Sir Francis Bacon's *Advancement of Learning*. Bacon (1561–1626) had organized all knowledge into three categories, Memory, Reason, and Imagination, each of which were divided into subsections. Jefferson had renamed the main categories History, Philosophy, and the Fine Arts, and added forty-four sections he called chapters, which included subjects such as chemistry that did not exist as such when Bacon was formulating his scheme in the early years of the seventeenth century. "One of the most systematic of men, he was in character as a cataloguer," Dumas Malone wrote of Jefferson. The value of knowing what books Jefferson read, even if most of the copies he owned have not survived, is not lost on historians. "Since his library was the product of extraordinary devotion, and, as he said, 'handpicked,' it is a valuable index to his intellectual attachments," Adrienne Koch wrote in her monograph, *The Philosophy of Thomas Jefferson.* As a bicentennial project undertaken in 2000, the Library of Congress began replacing titles of the same editions that were lost, with the hope of replicating the entire collection. In one instance, the University of Virginia donated a copy of Constantin-François Volney's *The Ruins: Or a Survey of the Revolutions of Empires,* a translation from the French of *Les Ruines, ou Méditations sur les Révolutions des Empires,* published in 1796 by William A. Davis in New York, the same edition as the copy Jefferson had sold to Congress.

Lincoln, by contrast, had a formal education that went no further than the second grade; almost entirely self-educated, he taught himself to write and express himself through home instruction. The story of how he walked from his family's home in New Salem, Illinois, to a farmhouse twelve miles away for the single purpose of bartering hard labor for a copy of Thomas Kirkham's *English Grammar* is well documented, and the book itself—in its time one of the most popular language manuals in the United States—went through 105 editions between 1823 and 1853. In an autobiographical sketch written in 1860 for use in his first presidential campaign, Lincoln described his lifelong attempts to improve himself. Speaking of himself in the third person, Lincoln wrote that "the aggregate of all his schooling did not amount to one year," and described his method of learning:

> He was never in college or Academy as a student; and never inside of a college or accademy building till since he had a law-license. What he has in the way of education, he has picked up. After he was twentythree, he had separated from his father, he studied English grammar, imperfectly of course, but so as to speak and write as well

as he now does. He studied and nearly mastered the Six-books of Euclid since he was a member of Congress. He regrets his want of education, and does what he can to supply the want.

Lincoln received some help in New Salem from Mentor Graham, a schoolmaster who told him where to find that copy of Kirkham's *Grammar*, now a prized possession of the Library of Congress, and also from a man named Bill Greene. Another neighbor, Jack Kelso, introduced Lincoln to history and literature. Lincoln paid special emphasis to the works of Shakespeare, Robert Burns, and Lord Byron, many of whose poems and passages he committed to memory. His law partner in Springfield, Illinois, William H. Herndon, recalled that Lincoln enjoyed reading favorite verses aloud, even in the office, claiming that hearing the words helped him retain them. "When he was young he read the Bible," Herndon recalled, "and when of age he read Shakespeare." Herndon wrote that when Lincoln was a boy in New Salem, he always had a book in hand. "Wherever he was and whenever he could do so the book was brought into use. He carried it with him in his rambles through the woods and his walks to the river. When night came he read it by the aid of any friendly light he could find. Frequently he went down to the cooper's shop and kindled a fire out of the waste material lying about, and by the light it afforded read until far into the night." Biographers agree that Lincoln turned to Shakespeare in his most pressing moments of crisis, seeking solace and wisdom in the plays. "To some indeterminable extent and in some intuitive way, Lincoln seems to have assimilated the substance of the plays into his own experience and deepening sense of tragedy," the Lincoln scholar Don E. Fehrenbacher wrote.

The discussion of presidents and their reading prompted me to ask McCullough if he recalled what was reported to be Bill Clinton's one piece of advice for George W. Bush as the latter was about to take his place in the Oval Office in 2001, namely, that he would urge Bush to read David Herbert Donald's 1996 biography of Abraham Lincoln. What, I wondered, might Clinton have wanted his successor to learn from that one book? McCullough's response was immediate. "I think he probably wanted him to realize how difficult it is to be president of the United States," he said. "The more I know about the presidency, the more I know people who have been or are president, the more understanding I feel about how hard that job is. There is no one human being who can handle that job, no matter how much they protest to the contrary. Imagine trying to go to sleep at night with all the worries that any president has, and I think it's a miracle that any of them has had time to sit down and read a book, to take their mind off their immediate problems. And my guess is that President Clinton also wanted President Bush to have a sense of how heavy the burden has been in times past. Truman probably knew more about the presidency from having read books about the presidency than any president up to his time. I think that the value of reading for people in high public positions is that they get a sense of cause and effect." McCullough pointed out that one of Lincoln's favorite passages of poetry was two stanzas from Thomas Gray's "Elegy Written in a Country Churchyard," which he recited for me from memory:

> *Let not ambition mock their useful toil,*
> *Their homely joys, and destiny obscure;*
> *Nor grandeur hear with a disdainful smile*
> *The short and simple annals of the poor.*
>
> *The boast of heraldry, the pomp of power,*
> *And all that beauty, all that wealth e'er gave,*
> *Awaits alike the inevitable hour:—*
> *The paths of glory lead but to the grave.*

"Lincoln, as we know, had a very dark view of life, he was melancholy, very down and blue, and he loved that poem. My guess is because he comes out of that sentiment. He is of that world. And he loved the poetry. What is so interesting about Lincoln is that his phenomenal gift of using language doesn't show up until he becomes president," an example, McCullough said, of a person "rising to the occasion" against nearly insuperable odds. "We never know what we can do. And you can never predict who is going to be a great president. There is no curriculum vitae that says this guy has what it takes to be a great president. If your résumé was the blueprint for your presidency, then Herbert Hoover would easily have been one of the best presidents we ever had. He'd led a fabulous life, he was good in everything he'd ever done, he was a superb executive, a great American, splendidly well read, but he was the wrong man for the time. Who would ever have thought that Harry Truman would in retrospect be seen as one of the stronger, more effective and important presidents of all?"

As the Clinton administration was coming to an end in 2001, Harold Evans, the former president of Random House and author of *The American Century* (1998), wrote an essay for the *New York Times Book Review* that attempted a classification of the presidents on the basis of their reading, with twenty-two of the forty-two men to have occupied the Oval Office up to that time being judged by decidedly unorthodox means to have been bibliophiles. Evans explained that he was moved to write the piece on the strength of a single burning question: "Does history suggest any correlation between a passion for serious reading and an ability to inspire and manage the nation?" Unable to come up with a comprehensive answer in a 1,400-word piece, Evans offered a few telling observations based on an informal survey of presidential biographies he consulted to determine whether former chief executives read with any consistency. He then compared the list he had made with a study compiled in 1994 by the Siena Research Institute, which asked academic historians and political scientists to rank chief executives in order of excellence. The presidents Evans determined to have been bibliophiles—see endnote for the complete list—"turned out to trail clouds of glory," while the "nonreaders" by and large "flop," though a few *not* known for a keen interest in reading—Andrew Jackson, William McKinley, and Lyndon Johnson in particular—are "regarded favorably" all the same, making clear that there are few hard-and-fast rules.

At the opposite end of the spectrum, Evans could just as easily have noted an anomaly involving Herbert Hoover, whose single term in office is regarded by most historians to have been a failure. In addition to being "splendidly well read," as David McCullough pointed out, Hoover also loved books as artifacts and assembled a personal library of one thousand volumes in the fields of mining, mathematics, astronomy, alchemy, natural history, and geology while traveling the world in the early 1900s as a consulting engineer. Presented to Claremont College in 1970 by Herbert Hoover III, the Herbert Clark Hoover Collection of Mining & Metallurgy, also known as *Bibliotheca De Re Metallica*, boasts many important items, including Euclid's *Elementa Geometriae* (1482); William Gilbert's pioneering study on the magnet, *De Magnete* (1600); an *editio princeps* of a geography by Strabo printed in Venice in 1472; and Alvaro Alonzo Barba's *Arte de los Metales* (1770), as well as notable works by Conrad Gesner, Giovanni Alfonso Borelli, and James D. Dana. One item of particular note is the Claremont College copy of *De Re Metallica* (On the Nature of Metals), by the German physician and scientist Georgius Agricola, also known as Georg Bauer, printed in Basel in 1556, but not available in English until the publication in 1912 of a translation from the Latin by the future president and his wife, Lou Henry Hoover.

Along with the translation, Hoover wrote a number of books, including a three-volume autobiography, one of thirteen American presidents through 2005 to have done so, though how many actually wrote their life stories themselves, or relied on ghost writers, is arguable in some cases. It is certainly not arguable in the instance of Ulysses S. Grant, whose *Personal Memoirs* (1885) are by common consent far and away the best, distinctive for their candor, honesty, and incisive thought. "Although frequently urged by friends to write my memoirs," Grant wrote in his preface, "I had determined never to do so, nor to write anything for publication," and then explained why he changed his mind:

> At the age of nearly sixty-two I received an injury from a fall, which confined me closely to the house while it did not apparently affect my general health. This made study a pleasant pastime. Shortly after, the rascality of a business partner developed itself by the announcement of failure. This was followed soon after by universal depression of all securities, which seemed to threaten the extinction of a good part of the income still retained, and for which I am indebted to the kindly act of friends. At this juncture the editor of the *Century Magazine* asked me to write a few articles for him. I consented for the money it gave me; for at that moment I was living upon borrowed money. The work I found congenial and I determined to continue it. The event is an important one for me, for good or evil; I hope for the former.

The editor and publisher of the memoirs was Mark Twain, whose selfless dedication to Grant and his welfare was extraordinary. Suffering grievously from throat cancer, Grant toiled on the book for eleven months, turning out in some instances ten thousand words in a single day, a level of production that amazed everyone who read his copy. On July 19, 1885, Grant dictated the final words, his voice barely a whisper. A few hours after declaring he had finished, Grant wrote a letter to John Hancock Douglas, the doctor who had been treating him through the ordeal, declaring his readiness to die. "I first wanted so many days to work on my book so the authorship would be clearly mine," he announced with obvious relief. Four days later, he died; published posthumously, *Personal Memoirs* sold 300,000 copies in less than two years. In *Patriotic Gore*, a landmark work of literary history (see chapter 9), Edmund Wilson wrote that "this record of Grant's campaigns may well rank, as Mark Twain believed, as the most remarkable work of its kind since the *Commentaries* of Julius Caesar. It is also, in its way—like Herndon's *Lincoln* or like *Walden* or *Leaves of Grass*—a unique expression of the American character."

The most prolific author by far among chief executives was Theodore Roosevelt, who proved himself an authentic man of letters outside of politics, writing more than a thousand magazine articles and twenty-six books that included such disparate works as *The Naval War of 1812* (1882), *Ranch Life and the Hunting-Trail* (1896), *The Rough Riders* (1899), and *African Game Trails* (1910). "Theodore Roosevelt would have prescribed print for the recently embattled president," Harold Evans wrote in his *New York Times* piece of Bill Clinton, then about to leave office after surviving an embarrassing impeachment proceeding brought on by a scandalous liaison with a White House intern, since it was the first Roosevelt who said, "I find it a great comfort to like all kinds of books, and to be able to get half an hour or an hour's complete rest and complete detachment from the fighting of the moment." But T. R. also had it in him to get "fired up" from his reading, an immersion in Admiral Alfred Thayer Mahan's *Sea Power* (1890) being one instance of where a work had "inflamed his imperial passions." Other books written by the naturalists John James Audubon and Spencer Fullerton Baird "hardened his determination to resist the ravagers of America's natural beauties." The former Princeton University educator Woodrow Wilson, on the other hand, developed a "fatal contempt for Congress" on the strength of his having read negative accounts on the British ways of organizing government. Evans continued:

But perhaps more important than the number of books presidents read is what they get from them. Ronald Reagan, not a bibliophile, was stimulated to support the Star Wars missile system by science fiction and the comics. John Kennedy had a passion for Ian Fleming's espionage thrillers. After the Bay of Pigs fiasco, he said ruefully, "It would have been better if we had left it to James Bond." On the other hand, his reputed attempts to get Castro to extinguish himself with either an exploding cigar or a poison pen may have owed all too much to Bond.

The suggestion by Evans that these colossal missteps in twentieth-century American history may have resulted in part from a misreading of a particular book brings to mind the allegation of Thomas Hobbes that writings from antiquity had contributed to the English Civil War fought between 1640 and 1651. Hobbes singled out seven groups in his *Behemoth* (1668) for having "corrupted" and "seduced" a populace that had been so loyal to the crown for six hundred years into dissolving the monarchy and executing King Charles I; one of the most influential consisted of an "exceeding great number" of university-educated members of Parliament who had "read the books written by famous men of the ancient Grecian and Roman commonwealths" in which "the popular government was extolled by that glorious name of liberty, and monarchy disgraced by the name of tyranny." It was these men, Hobbes believed, who "by advantage of their eloquence, were always able to sway the rest."

Many leaders through history, in fact, have made books an intimate part of their lives. Alexander the Great carried a copy of Homer with him throughout his campaigns; Julius Caesar, Napoleon Bonaparte, and William Gladstone were voracious readers. Winston Churchill, a prolific author who won a Nobel Prize for literature, had a private library containing thousands of volumes. King Henry VIII, according to a recent monograph, was one of the most intelligent and widely read monarchs of the Renaissance, "a collector *par excellence*" who "stocked his palaces as grandly as he could," and when he died had more than sixty residences at his disposal. His books were not acquired for ostentation, but for use, according to James P. Carley, who tracked the king's reading of materials that supported his plans to break with the Catholic Church in Rome, justified his divorce from Catherine of Aragon, and permitted his marriage to Anne Boleyn, herself a reader of considerable consequence. "When a book interested him, Henry was a compulsive annotator, and his copies of Erasmus's works are deeply scored (usually positively), as are his copies of Luther (negatively)," Carley wrote. "Henry actively engaged with texts which furthered his own desires or whims at any given time." During the crisis brought on by the alleged adultery of his fifth wife, Catherine Howard, "Henry annotated his copy of the books of Solomon in the translation by Miles Coverdale. In his marginalia, probably all made in one sitting, he was particularly attentive to passages relating to salvation and judgment, kingship, wisdom, riches, and marriage."

Elizabeth I (1533–1603), the daughter of Henry VIII and Anne Boleyn, was an enthusiastic reader in her own right. As a girl growing up with an uncertain future—her mother, after all, had been executed on the orders of her father, her half-siblings, Edward VI, and Mary, who detested and imprisoned her, had both preceded her to the throne— Elizabeth developed a delight in learning under the general supervision of Henry's last wife, Katherine Parr. The precocious princess was fluent in six languages, as noted by the brilliant Cambridge humanist Roger Ascham (1515–1568), who tutored Elizabeth for two years while she was a teenager, and later served as her Latin secretary. "She talks French and Italian as well as she does English," he marveled of her linguistic skills, "and has often talked to me readily and well in Latin, moderately in Greek."

Throughout her forty-five-year reign, Elizabeth followed a regimen that set aside three hours of each day for reading. In 1593, she tried her hand at translation, choosing the *De Consolatione Philosophiae* (*The Consolation of Philosophy*), an eloquent meditation on life and purpose written in the sixth century by the imprisoned Roman statesman-philosopher Boethius (c. 480–524) as he awaited execution in Pavia on trumped-up charges of political conspiracy. Denied access to his beloved books, Boethius drew on a lifetime of reading to compose a series of thirty-nine dialogues in verse between himself and a female personification of philosophy. The work has provided comfort for many people over the centuries, including Dante Alighieri, who placed Boethius in the Fourth Heaven of his *Paradiso*. "Boethius's influence in the Middle Ages was immense," the British historian of philosophy John Marenbon wrote. "Only Aquinas and Augustine had so great a direct influence over so wide a range of intellectual life."

In an essay published in *Medieval English Studies*, two scholars suggested that Elizabeth may have translated Boethius as a veiled commentary on her own experience with intrigue and survival at the highest levels. "The text deals with treason, uses and abuses of the law, imprisonment, and deeply felt responses by a person of considerable intellect to the forces of fate that act upon him," John Morris Jackson and Noel Harold Kaylor Jr. wrote. "By this thirty-fifth year of her reign, Elizabeth herself had lain in prison under possible accusation of treason and she had imprisoned many accused of treachery against her person." It is noteworthy, too, that Sir Thomas More—condemned by Henry VIII—turned to Boethius as he awaited his own execution in the Tower of London in 1535.

The first version of the *Consolation* to appear in the language of the Anglo-Saxons was translated by King Alfred the Great (871–900) in the ninth century; a Middle English version by Geoffrey Chaucer (c. 1342–1400) appeared in the fourteenth. King Alfred, in particular, committed himself to raising the level of literacy throughout England during his reign. Part of that effort included making available what he called a "handful of books" from antiquity he thought it "most needful" for his subjects to know. As an aside to the text, Alfred had this observation: "I may say that it has ever been my desire to live honorably while I was alive, and after my death to leave to them that should come after me my memory in good works." True to his word, an important literary work rendered into the language of his people became part of Alfred's legacy.

7.

A TERRIBLE BEAUTY

One of the cornerstone principles of *histoire du livre*, the scholarly discipline introduced in France in the 1950s that looks at the innumerable ways books influence society and culture, is that "new readers make new texts," and that "their new meanings are a

function of their new forms." Put another way, what this approach suggests is that words set down on paper may be fixed indefinitely there in
immutable form, but the reception given to writings acclaimed over time as
canonical—and, indeed, the impact they might have on successive waves of
readers—is subject to periodic interpretation. This is not an issue for writings that have short shelf lives, of course, but it becomes relevant with
works from antiquity that were composed in what some people might
regard flippantly today as "dead languages," and have made their way
through the centuries by way of translations that are constantly being tailored to the tastes and standards of their particular audience. The fact that
new generations of readers approach venerable texts differently is one reason why there will never be a "definitive" rendering of any important work,
regardless of how faithful or luminous it may be at the time it appears
between hard covers, a belief put forth by such formidable critics as Samuel
Johnson in the eighteenth century, Matthew Arnold in the nineteenth, and
Walter Benjamin in the twentieth. Robert Fagles, a translator whose rendi-
tions of *The Iliad* and *The Odyssey* of Homer, the three Theban plays,
Antigone, *Oedipus the King*, and *Oedipus at Colonus*, by Sophocles, and *The
Oresteia*, by Aeschylus, have had combined sales of more than two million
copies—a heady circumstance that has astounded people whose business it
is to assess trends in publishing—could not agree more, and had some
thoughts to share on why he believes that to be the case.

"A translation, if it is a really serious translation, becomes a new
work of art in its own right, because it is a transplant in many ways,"
Fagles told me. "It can be a new interpretation, an adaptation, a revision,
sometimes drastic, sometimes very slight, but it is always being carried
over into a new language, a new time, a new culture, and I think that
means invariably that it's never the same as the original. What I'm saying in essence is that the original, in a way, becomes the translation. How
many of us speak ancient Greek or Latin? Or in the case of Seamus
Heaney's brilliant translation of *Beowulf*, how many of us speak Old

English? Fewer still. To me, by the way, that is a far more astounding success than anything I or anyone else has done, because the *Odyssey* and the *Iliad* have always been familiar companions, whereas *Beowulf* has remained a little snarly and distant. But Seamus truly brought it home, and one of the reasons for its tremendous success as a work of art, in my view, is that Seamus is a remarkable poet who, through his own creative work, is in perfect tune with the idiom of today." In the citation he received on the occasion of accepting the Nobel Prize for Literature in 1995, Heaney was recognized for producing "works of lyrical beauty and ethical depth, which exalt everyday miracles and the living past," an observation that applied perfectly to his work on the Anglo-Saxon epic believed composed around the tenth century, and regarded as the first work in the long history of English literature that could be regarded as being "great."

Fagles entered Amherst College in Amherst, Massachusetts, in 1951 with the idea of pursuing a career in medicine, "but there was a radical switch for me halfway through," he said. "My love of language, my love of literature, caught up with me and wouldn't be put down. When I entered my junior year, I began to learn Greek, I began to learn Latin; I came to those ancient languages late, but I went with what Coach Vince Lombardi of the Green Bay Packers called *desire*. I had a lot of it. I had never had much exposure to classical literature when I was in senior high school; my first exposure came in the first years at Amherst, where we had a Great Books sequence in the curriculum, and that was my introduction, through translation." The first *Iliad* that Fagles read was the Richmond Lattimore translation of 1951, the first *Odyssey* version one in prose by E. V. Rieu that had appeared in 1949, "an old Penguin standby," and he was "totally entranced" by what he read.

"I fell in love with these things through excellent translations, and I thought how wonderful it would be to get the beauty of it *hot*, to go back to the source itself. I don't think I went at it with the intention of becoming a translator, I didn't know that at the time, but I simply wanted to get as close as I possibly could to Homer's *Iliad* and *Odyssey*, to Virgil's *Aeneid*. That was my goal at that point. And it wasn't until a little later, when I was a graduate student in English at Yale, that it began to cross my mind, wouldn't it be challenging to *try* to re-embody these things in my own language? That would be the strongest demonstration of my affection for them, my affiliation with them, my feeling toward them."

The first translation he attempted that ultimately made its way into print was of the choral odes by Bacchylides, a Greek lyric poet from the fifth century BC, whose mere survival is a product of "sheer dumb luck," the sole papyrus text of his work having been found in a clay pot in the Nile River Delta in 1896; Fagles's version was published by Yale University Press in 1961. "I did this strictly for myself and the desk drawer, since I had no clue as to how to share these things. I had no notion if I could do it in the first place, and it wasn't until a little later that I got up the gumption, some outrageous gumption, to give it a try. I went at it for the very simple reason that I had fallen in love with the poetry in Greek, and wanted to see if I could turn it into English. My translations from Homer begin, as a matter of fact, with my mother's death. She died in 1976, and it fell to me, as it falls to many of us, to put together a program of readings for our friends and relatives, and my first thought was of that marvelous scene in the eleventh book of the *Odyssey*, where Odysseus confronts the ghost of his mother, tries to embrace her three times, fails, and it breaks his heart. That's the text that came to mind first. I hadn't translated it myself, and I was too unnerved at that point to try my hand at it, so I went to Robert Fitzgerald's superb version, and read that aloud for the occasion. But then in the few weeks following, as I began to gather myself again, I tried my own hand at it, and that is when and where I began to translate Homer."

By that time, Fagles had been teaching for sixteen years in the Princeton University English Department. From 1975 to 1994 he served as founding chairman of the Department of Comparative Literature, and retired from teaching in 2002 to devote his full attention to his wife, his daughters, and his translations. When we first met in Cambridge, Massachusetts, in 1997, he was on tour promoting his rendering of the *Odyssey*, which had just been released to widespread acclaim; one of the highlights of that interview was to hear him speak aloud an excerpt in the original Greek, a melodic, beautiful riff that offered dramatic proof of the oral roots of the poem. When we talked again in the summer of 2004, he was approaching the end of his work on the *Aeneid* after wrestling with the original Latin for seven years, or about as long as it took the poet Virgil to write the great Roman epic in the first century BC. "The *Aeneid* is a cautionary tale. It is one we need to read today," Fagles said, amplifying his oft-stated conviction that readers of every generation need enduring works from the distant past available to them in their own idiom, freshly imbued with new vitality and insight. The *Aeneid*, in particular, he stressed, "speaks of the terrible price of victory in war, for Virgil knew that victory is finally impossible, that it always lies out of reach. He saw the unforeseen aftermath, the way war could all go wrong, whether from poor planning or because of the gods on high. He knew the sheer accumulation of death, the destruction, the pain we inflict when we use force to create empire. Even though in Virgil, as in Homer, you find great reservoirs of memory. You find the restorative power of love set against a world of violence. There is still an overriding sadness in the poem. There are countless losses. War rages on too long. The majority of books in the *Aeneid* end with certain death. Aeneas reaches out to the ghosts of those he loved, always beyond his grasp."

Fagles described for me the process of translation as unremitting and often unrewarding, with successful days at times marked by the selection of a single word. "If you hit it right, it's worth it; if you miss, it lays you low," he said. As an example, he cited his decision to use the word "rage" to open his version of the *Iliad*, a choice that consumed hours of thought and rumination. "How you start one of the founding poems of Western civilization is not a matter to be taken lightly," he said. "I had to struggle with that one, because this is a case in which the translator has a few options. The first word of the *Iliad*, in Greek, is *menin*, from which we get *mania* or *rage*, even *wrath*. In English, rather than in Greek, that word can become a noun or it can become an imperative, and I use it both ways in the first word of that poem. The first line as I translated it goes like this: *Rage—Goddess, sing the rage of Peleus' son Achilles*. So what you do here is you let *rage* be your subject, and then, if it pleases you, you can go ahead and *rage* at the same time. That way it's both an imperative verb and a noun. It is not that in Homeric Greek, but it is in English, and I thought that was the only way I could do it." By contrast, the greatly respected Richmond Lattimore translation of 1951 follows another tack entirely in its opening line: *Sing, goddess, the anger of Peleus' son Achilleus*.

A published poet in his own right, Fagles said that he likes to keep an open ear and an alert eye to work being produced by contemporaries he admires, as a way of staying in touch with prevailing usage. "On the desk in front of me I keep two big books. Let us say that the first big book is the text of Homer or the text of Virgil, with all the lexicons, and the commentaries, and on the other hand—and I mean the right hand—will be a big book of modern verse, English verse, and I try to keep the two in tandem, because I've got a dual responsibility. One is to the ancient text and the other is to the modern reader. They don't always work in balance, but I do the best I can." Among modern poets he turns to while working on a classical text, Fagles mentioned C. K. Williams, Paul Muldoon, Derek Walcott, and Seamus Heaney in particular. Though a great admirer and reader of Shakespeare, Fagles said he will not consult any of the great bard's works for inspiration while doing a translation. "As a translator I regard him as a dangerous poet, and by dangerous I mean he is someone you don't want to get too close to because you just might end up trying to imitate him and fall flat on your face. So I've always given Shakespeare a wide berth when it comes to writing. As a reader, I read him all the time."

On whether a work of poetry or fiction can be *dangerous* in a literal sense, Fagles said that he believes it can. "I think there is no question about it," he said, quoting a line from William Blake: "The Classics! It is the Classics, that desolate Europe with Wars." Fagles said he believes Blake "meant something very specific" in that remark. "There are certain poems that tend to let loose sources of human energy which are often ungovernable. When I say that, I think first and foremost of Homer's *Iliad*. That is a truly dangerous poem, unless you read it all, and I don't mean only all twenty-four books; I mean if you respond to every aspect of the poem, because if you do, then you begin to feel that, while it is a relentlessly cruel poem, it is also a very compassionate one. In fact there must be some symbiosis going on between the ferocity of the poetry and the feeling of compassion that it often rouses in people. That's an old paradox, which I think is always with us. There is a refrain in Yeats's "Easter 1916" that goes, *All changed, changed utterly: / A terrible beauty is born*. That phrase, 'terrible beauty,' summarizes it all, I think. The *Iliad*, like Helen in the old men's eyes, is a terrible beauty, though whether both are equal forces, I'm not sure. But one gives rise to the other."

Fagles outlined for me a routine of work that goes through several phases. "Once I get a working draft, that's when the hard hammering really begins," he said, noting that the transition from one language to another is only the first step in a process that leads to publication, and that several steps in between involve a few people he regards as his "readers of first resort," the most notable of whom is Bernard Knox, one of the leading classical scholars in the world, and his teacher in the 1950s at Yale. Indeed, the relationship Fagles and Knox share is quite extraordinary in that the instructor and mentor of a major scholar has continued to work with the student for decades. For the three Theban plays, the *Iliad*, and the *Odyssey*, Knox not only read the manuscripts for Fagles but wrote the introductions and prepared the notes, a collaboration they have continued with the *Aeneid*. "One of the beauties of having Bernard as a reader is that he knows the Greek text, and the Latin text, by heart. He also knows modern literature by heart and what the demands of modern English are. It is an absolute blessing. My working relationship—my friendship—with Bernard is one of the great privileges in my life."

Others whom Fagles regards as "main readers" include his wife, Lynne ("the muse herself"), and their two adult daughters, Nina, a physician, and Katya, in marketing research; both are eclectic readers "in the truest sense" who devour books voraciously and with great insight, but not as specialists in any particular genre. "That is very important, because for me the ideal reader of what I write is somebody interested in a given story and alert to the kind of life you are trying to lend it. I used to think that a great deal depended on educational or even sociological background, but the more I see the way the *Iliad* and the *Odyssey* have caught on in many younger grades throughout the country, the less convinced I am that the audience has to be that elite or that selective. So for all the hand-wringing we have had about the state of reading in America, I for one am much encouraged by the literacy of the Republic. I think it is a lot broader, a lot healthier, a lot more inquisitive than many people have thought."

Even though Homer is the national poet of Greece, it is Fagles's conviction that the *Iliad* and *Odyssey* have become, in the hands of fine translators in the past, "great English poems" in their own right, on a level with John Milton's *Paradise Lost* and Edmund Spenser's *Faerie Queene*. "Thanks to John Dryden's translation of the *Aeneid* and Alexander Pope's *Iliad*," he said, "we have two great, sturdy English poems. Our mode of translation is much less radical than Pope's or Dryden's, and we have an appreciation and respect for historicity, the accuracy of Homer's portrayal, not of his time, but a time about five hundred years before him.

These days we stand much closer to the text, if we are translators. If we are bold adapters like James Joyce, we can stand beside the text of Homer, as he did with his *Ulysses*, and place Edwardian Dublin on an equal footing with Homer's Ithaca. But that's another kind of translation altogether, and a momentous one."

In an essay for the *New Yorker*, Garry Wills declared Fagles to be "the best living translator of ancient Greek drama, lyric poetry, and epic into modern English," placing him firmly in a tradition that extends back to the sixteenth century, beginning with George Chapman (c. 1559–1634), a dramatist whose best-known theatrical work was *Eastward Ho* (1605), a collaboration with Ben Jonson and John Marston that got all three of them thrown in prison for an unflattering reference to Scottish royalty, a slip of the pen that did not amuse the recently installed British monarch King James I, also known as James VI of Scotland. Educated at Oxford, Chapman called on his skills as a classical scholar to complete the narrative poem *Hero and Leander*, left unfinished in 1592 with the untimely death of Christopher Marlowe, who was stabbed to death at the age of twenty-nine in a tavern brawl.

The first seven books of Chapman's version of the *Iliad* appeared in 1598, the completion thirteen years later; his *Odyssey* was finished in 1616, at which time both volumes were released together. Acclaimed by several generations as the standard English version of the epics, the translations bear the unmistakable hand of a poet, with moments of power and beauty. Reading it straight through one night in the company of a friend, John Keats was inspired to write one of his great sonnets, "On First Looking Into Chapman's Homer." The critic George Saintsbury (1845–1933) wrote that for more than two centuries, Chapman's translations were "far nearer Homer than any modern translator in any modern language," going so far as to assert that they were the "resort of all who, unable to read Greek, wished to know what Greek was."

The cartographer and printer John Ogilby (1600–1676), the philosopher Thomas Hobbes (1588–1679), and the great man of letters Alexander Pope (1688–1744) produced versions that were widely admired. Pope unapologetically wrote for his time, prompting the critic and chronicler of Romanticism Hugh Honour to quip in a 1977 monograph that "his Achilles sometimes seems to be on the point of taking snuff." For Samuel Johnson, on the other hand, Pope's Homer was a "poetical wonder," a "performance which no age or nation can pretend to equal." The poet John Dryden (1631–1700), a literary critic of such stature that Samuel Johnson declared him the "Father of English criticism," also tried his hand at Homer, though he was best known as a translator from the Latin of Virgil's *Aeneid* and Ovid's *Metamorphoses*.

In the preface to his translations of the Greek epics, Thomas Hobbes confided that he had turned to the classics basically out of boredom, and took on the task of offering a new version because he had "nothing else to do." Given the fact that he was eighty-six years old at the time, and already renowned for his philosophical treatises, he could be forgiven for coming forth with a seventeenth-century version that reflected his philosophical views; not one to ascribe much influence to divine intervention, for instance, he marginalized the role of the gods, and indulged in occasional anachronisms, picturing at one point a petulant Achilles playing a guitar two thousand years before the instrument was invented in Spain.

Popular as many of these translations were, they spoke directly for their times. For those whose goal it was to get as close to the source as possible, the only alternative then was to access the masterpieces in their original language. That, certainly, was the course taken by William Blake (1757–1827), the great Romantic poet and artist, who taught himself Hebrew, Italian, French, Latin, and Greek so that he could engage directly with the masterworks that interested him in their primary languages, acquiring knowledge and insights that he could apply to the engravings he prepared of scenes from the Bible and Dante's *Divine Comedy* according to his own artistic vision. One of the enduring triumphs of Blake is that he was self-educated, a circumstance that elevates this accomplishment to the realm of the extraordinary.

Just as dazzling was the determination of James Joyce (1882-1941) to master the languages of his heroes, beginning while the budding novelist was still a teenager. In 1900, Joyce received a postcard from the Norwegian playwright Henrik Ibsen containing praise for an essay he had written for the *Fortnightly Review,* a literary journal. Overwhelmed by the recognition, Joyce sent a letter to Ibsen's English translator expressing his joy: "I am a young Irishman, eighteen years old, and the words of Ibsen I shall keep in my heart all my life." It was then, according to Richard Ellmann, his biographer, that Joyce "set himself to master languages and literatures, and read so widely that it is hard to say definitely of any important creative work published in the late nineteenth century that Joyce had not read." With limited financial support from his father, Joyce bought "foreign books whether or not the family had enough money to eat." In addition to tackling Norwegian—he was determined to read in the original the plays of Ibsen, who he had flatly declared was superior to Shakespeare—Joyce taught himself French, Russian, German, Latin, and Italian, reading the works of Tolstoy, Verlaine, Horace, and Dante, an interest in the latter so pronounced that an acquaintance called him "the Dante of Dublin." Given that his best-known work was an adaptation of the *Odyssey,* it is curious indeed to learn that Joyce was not conversant with Greek, an "ignorance" he lamented, but one that did not hinder him from the great task at hand. "Just think," he told a friend, "isn't that a world *I* am peculiarly fitted to enter?" And indeed, as Ellmann pointed out, Joyce's "imperfect acquaintance with the language served the useful purpose . . . of making him wild and daring in etymological speculation."

Of more recent vintage, the American writer and critic William H. Gass translated a major work of Rainer Maria Rilke (1875–1926), the cycle of ten elegiac poems known as the *Duino Elegies,* as a challenge to himself, one that combined a deeper reading of a favored work with a determined attempt to savor the act of literary translation itself. The winner of numerous prestigious awards for works of fiction and nonfiction that include the novels *Omensetter's Luck* (1966) and *The Tunnel* (1995), the story collections *In the Heart of the Heart of the Country* (1969) and *Cartesian Sonata: And Other Novellas* (1998), and several volumes of essays, Gass took on the task after a lifetime of reading Rilke's masterwork in the renderings of others, and finding so many of them wanting. "In a translation, one language, and one particular user of the language, reads another," Gass wrote in the book that emerged, aptly titled *Reading Rilke*, noting a few pages later that "translation is a form of betrayal," a "traduction, a reconstitution made of sacrifice and revision. One bails to keep the boat afloat." Not contenting himself with a translation in and of itself, Gass peppered the book with biography, commentary, and comparisons with the versions of fourteen others who had worked at giving the German of Rilke an audience in English. He was not impressed. "Most of the hands here hold the right cards," he wrote of his rivals, "but few know how to play them."

I had occasion to spend a morning with Gass among the thousands of books in his St. Louis, Missouri, home on April 23, 2005—Shakespeare's 441st birthday—with the topic of literature and translation occupying our full attention. "I would say that almost all of my writing emerges from my reading," Gass told me, "which is why I am a great accumulator of books. I am at home with my books, and I have arrived at a point in my life where almost everything I need is within reach." Indeed, he said that the 652-page novel that took him twenty-six years to write, *The Tunnel*, "draws almost entirely on my reading—not all of it, there's a bit of autobiography in there—but it's overwhelmingly material that bounces off what I have read over the course of a lifetime."

Located just off the campus of Washington University, where he taught philosophy for many years before retiring in 1999, Gass's house contains about twelve thousand volumes, with rooms designated by the nature of their content, the German, French, art, and literature rooms being the most richly stocked. In the German room, Gass indicated the row of books that had prompted him to become a translator. "Each is a version of Rilke," he said, "and I was not happy with any of them. Because I was teaching Rilke at the university, that circumstance alone forced me to start translating him. I felt it was the only way to bring out more of the philosophical elements in his work that I wanted to emphasize with my students." It also happened that the narrator of *The Tunnel*, the middle-aged professor William Frederick Kohler, is a historian of German, and also a translator. "I have an invocation of a hundred pages in the novel where my narrator invokes the muses, and calls on his books," Gass said. "His muses *are* his books, and that's the same with me. But I had a practical problem with him as well; I had to translate some Rilke poems the way my narrator would have translated him. So in doing this myself, I felt liberated, and suddenly, instead of trying to be totally faithful to the original poem, I found that I could sort of play around with it in ways that suited my purposes."

Gass said his favorite consideration of the phenomenon in which great literary works take on entirely new lives of their own in translation is to be found in the Jorge Luis Borges short story, "Pierre Menard, Author of the *Quixote*" (1939), in which the following observation is made of the fictional author Pierre Menard:

Those who have insinuated that Menard devoted his life to writing a contemporary *Quixote* besmirch his illustrious memory. Pierre Menard did not want to compose *another* Quixote, which surely is easy enough—he wanted to compose *the* Quixote. Nor, surely, need one have to say that his goal was never a mechanical transcription of the original; he had no intention of *copying* it. His admirable intention was to produce a number of pages which coincided—word for word and line for line—with those of Miguel de Cervantes.

What has been described by Harold Bloom and others as quite possibly the "greatest novel of the twentieth century," greater even than James Joyce's *Ulysses*, comes to English-speaking readers by way of several translations, each a variation of its predecessor. The first English translation of Marcel Proust's three-thousand-page magnum opus, *A la Recherche du Temps Perdu* (1922–1931), by C. K. Scott Moncrieff, was judged by F. Scott Fitzgerald to be "a masterpiece in itself." Revised by Terence Kilmartin in 1982, it is still available under the title *Remembrance of Things Past*, though that clear echo of a Shakespeare sonnet displeased Proust when it appeared, and today bears the more accurate title *In Search of Lost Time*. By far the translation of choice of Proust into English, it was updated by Kilmartin on the basis of the new French Pléiade edition of 1954, and further touched up by D. J. Enright, who used an updated 1987 Pléiade edition of the opus, which had originally been published in thirteen volumes. Several other translations have appeared in English, one, by Andreas Mayor, using yet another alternate title, *The Past Recaptured*.

In *Proust's Way*, a most useful "field guide" to reading the novel, the National Book Award–winning scholar Roger Shattuck began by discussing in what language the book should be approached. "Anyone who can comfortably read Balzac, Tocqueville or Camus in the original should tackle the *Search* in French," he made clear. "The translation will not turn out to be much easier, and one should at least make the attempt." On the matter of how many pages a casual reader should consider engaging, Shattuck had some frank advice. "With great profit as a boy, I read *Don Quixote* and *Robinson Crusoe*, *Arabian Nights*, and *Gulliver's Travels* in truncated children's editions. Shall we be offered one day a pocket Proust? *In Search of Lost Time* in three hundred pages? The prospect is not utterly unthinkable. As in the classics mentioned above, there is in Proust a deep universal element, an aesthetic consciousness, that may one day reach many more people than can read the novel."

Proust was most comfortable, of course, in French, his native language, but he did have occasion early in his career to take up the writing of the great Victorian art critic John Ruskin (1819–1900), and did so with such enthusiasm that he was moved to learn English so that he could translate two of his works, *The Bible of Amiens* (1884) and *Sesame and Lilies* (1865), into French; *La Bible d'Amiens*, Ruskin's passionate account of Gothic cathedrals of Amiens and Abbeville, appeared in 1900; *Sésame et les Lys*, a classic nineteenth-century statement on the natures and duties of men and women, was published in 1906. What had moved the young novelist most deeply was Ruskin's "religion of beauty," especially his notion that the artist must submit totally to the work of art within him. Toward the end of *Recherche*, Proust's narrator remarks that the one "essential book" that each person carries within is not a work of invention, but translation, going so far as to state that the "duty and task of the writer are those of a translator." Proust expanded on this thought in the two remarkable prefaces and notes he wrote to the studies, both of which were translated into English and published in one volume by Yale University Press in 1987 with the title *On Reading Ruskin*. Proust's preface to *Sésame et les Lys* is called "On Reading," and is movingly eloquent on the subject, not just as it applies to Ruskin in particular but to the act of reading itself. "A tragedy by Racine, a book of memoirs by Saint-Simon, resemble beautiful things that are no longer made," he offered toward the end. "The language in which they have been sculpted by great artists with a freedom that makes their sweetness shine and their native force stand out, moves us like the sight of certain marbles, unused today, which the works of the past used. No doubt in those old buildings the stone has faithfully kept the thought of the sculptor, but also, thanks to the sculptor, the stone, of a kind unknown today, has been preserved for us, adorned with all the colors he knew how to obtain from it, to bring out, to harmonize."

While Proust's mammoth undertaking may well endure as the masterpiece of the twentieth century, the greatest novel of them all from *any* century remains the first example of the genre, Miguel de Cervantes's *Don Quixote de la Mancha*, one of those exquisite circumstances from history where such a judgment can be made, the Gutenberg Bible and the Declaration of Independence being two others that come to mind, the Gutenberg the first—and arguably the most outstanding—printed book ever produced, and the Declaration also the first—and by far the most eloquently phrased—official document issued to date by the United States of America acting as a political entity.

"I believe that my obligation as a literary translator is to recreate for the reader in English the experience of the reader in Spanish," the American translator Edith Grossman wrote in the preface to her version of the novel, which was published to considerable critical approbation in the fall of 2003. Grossman's strategy was to render the seventeenth-century text into contemporary English, a task she asserted was not nearly as difficult as it might sound, since Cervantes wrote in a "crackling, up-to-date Spanish that was an intrinsic part of his time," a "modern language that both reflected and helped to shape the way people experienced the world." For all the twenty-first-century nuances she worked in, Grossman nevertheless felt that her greatest responsibility was to maintain the integrity of the original text. The prospect of translating the novel was "stupefying," she confessed, and the stakes were enormous. "The extraordinary significance and influence of this novel were reaffirmed, once again, in 2002, when one hundred major writers from fifty-four countries voted *Don Quixote* the best work of fiction in the world."

Don Quixote was written in two parts, the first appearing in 1605, an immediate sensation that went into ten Spanish editions before Cervantes died on April 23, 1616, the same date—but because of different calendars, not the same precise day—as Shakespeare. Three authorized Spanish editions, along with numerous others that were pirated, appeared in print the first year alone. By the time the second volume was published ten years later, translations had been printed in England, France, and Italy. And the novel traveled far and wide, in some cases to the exasperation of the Spanish Inquisition, which had issued royal decrees in 1531 and 1543 prohibiting the importation of fictional literature to the New World. In *Books of the Brave*, the late Irving A. Leonard scrutinized hundreds of old archives, diaries, ship manifests, and logs to determine which works were carried to America by the conquistadores for their own amusement, and for the edification of settlers in the Spanish colonies. In some instances, copies of *Don Quixote* were taken from the cargo holds and read on the ships before they had crossed the Atlantic, helping the "cramped and weary voyagers" endure the tedium of the voyage. The first copy sent to Peru arrived in the year of publication, and was read aloud to the viceroy on his deathbed, "too ill to read the novel which came so highly recommended." In 1606, six more copies arrived from Spain "and passed into the possession of aristocratic personages" living in the capital, followed by six dozen more that same year.

Leonard documented similar patterns throughout Spanish America, the enthusiasm for the novel so intense that even people who were illiterate were able to enjoy it by way of a venerable practice that Cervantes was pleased to acknowledge in the voice of an innkeeper in chapter 32 of the First Part of *Don Quixote*, who told about the enthusiasm for works of chivalry that crossed all social barriers. At harvest time, the innkeeper tells Don Quixote and Sancho Panza—who himself is illiterate—how many of the itinerant reapers "gather during their time off, and there's always a few who know how to read, and one of them takes down one of those books, and more than thirty of us sit around him and listen to him read with so much pleasure that it saves us a thousand gray hairs; I can tell you that when I hear about those furious, terrible blows struck by the knights, it makes me want to do the same, and I'd be happy to keep hearing about them for days and nights on end." A point made in the Printing and the Mind of Man catalog is pertinent in this regard: "*Don Quixote* is one of those universal works which are read by all ages at all times, and there are very few who have not at one time or another felt themselves to be Don Quixote confronting the windmills or Sancho Panza at the inn."

The appearance in 1726 of *Gulliver's Travels* gave the author Jonathan Swift "an immortality beyond temporary fame," and it too has managed to capture readers of all ages—adults with a ready willingness to engage hundreds of pages of sophisticated humor, children who have delighted for decades in the scores of abridgments prepared for their delectation—bringing him "a different and far wider readership than he had ever envisaged." By no means restricted to English-language readers, Lemuel Gulliver's extraordinary travels among Lilliputians and Brobdingnagians have been enjoyed in many languages, not least of them French, courtesy of Pierre François Guyot Desfontaines, whose translation appeared just a year after the book had taken England by storm, and remained the most popular version on the continent for more than two centuries, evoking commentary from such notables as Voltaire.

But what the French read was a severely bowdlerized rendition of the work, with many of the racier parts toned down measurably, with no apologies whatsoever offered by the translator. He went on record as asserting that a complete version "would have revolted the good taste which reigns in France" during the early eighteenth century. The influence of *Voyages du Gulliver* in France has been the subject of a research project undertaken by Benoit Léger, a professor of translation studies at Concordia University in Montreal. "We forget the role that Desfontaines played as introducer of *Gulliver's Travels* into the French world at a time when such a text was highly problematic because of the sexual, scatological, political and religious satire that is to be found in it," Léger has pointed out. "Knowing this, how can we ignore that this text played a major role in France, was read by adults and children for two hundred years, and not acknowledge that this text belongs to French literature—in the version by Desfontaines?"

Breon Mitchell's day job since 2001 has been director of the Lilly Library at Indiana University, but he brings to the task the background, education, and temperament of a scholar. Before assuming responsibility as custodian of one of the strongest research collections of rare books and manuscripts in the United States, he was a professor of Germanic studies and comparative literature, a position he still holds. Mitchell began translating literary works from the German into English during his sophomore year at the University of Kansas in 1961, motivated, he told me, "just out of love, actually," for the "glowing language" of Hugo von Hofmannsthal's *Death and the Fool*, which he fashioned into blank verse with a classmate. "We just did it for fun because we were both learning German, but neither of us had any German in our background. From there we started a bilingual German-English literary magazine called *Versuch*, which means *attempt*, or *trial*."

The journal thrived, appearing twice a year and attracting contributions from many sources, continuing on as a publication for some twenty-five years. In 1964 Mitchell went to Oxford University to study philosophy on a Rhodes scholarship. "I wound up doing some comparative literature and writing on James Joyce's *Ulysses* and its impact on the German novel." Mitchell began teaching at Indiana University in 1968, and continued translating works on what is best described as a recreational basis. An introduction to James Laughlin, the owner of New Directions publishing, a small press that from its inception has concentrated on publishing works of enduring literary merit, including the works of the playwright Tennessee Williams, occasioned an invitation to do some professional translating for his imprint.

Among the works Mitchell has translated into English is Franz Kafka's novel *The Trial*. "Kafka is by far the most famous author I've translated," he said. "If you would have told me, you can translate any book from German literature you want to, that's ever been written, I would have picked *The Trial* to translate, and I was asked to do it. That's a dream that not many people have come true." Mitchell said he was commissioned to do the translation because a new critical edition of the original German text had been done, occasioning the need for a new version in English. "The translation I did was very close and faithful in the sense that for every sentence in the German, there's one sentence in the English. For every paragraph in the German, there's one paragraph in the English. All punctuation for the most part for sentences almost stays the same. And that is generally not the case in translation. Generally, German sentences, because they're long, often are broken up into shorter sentences. The paragraphing is changed. This translation I did is a very unusual translation in this respect. But that is what I was asked to do, and I am happy with it because I was requested to do it closely and faithfully. I was happy to do that because it accurately reflects the new critical edition of the German text, and the reader can be sure in English that they're getting something very close to the original. Of course I also tried to make it so that everyone understood what the German meant, and to make it faithful in the sense that it was powerful as a text, because *The Trial* is extremely powerful. But I could do it again. And I could do it very differently."

If he were to translate the same book again, Mitchell said he would adopt an approach that, in his words, is looser. "I would try to do the text with paragraphing and sentences closer to the normal English. In other words, how Kafka might have written the text, or what he might have done with it, had he been writing in English. Now that's a little bit different. If I were doing it again in this freer way, I would change the paragraphing because paragraphing in English is a different sort of thing than in German, and I think that there would be certain ways it could be quite effective. The other thing is that Kafka's *Trial* is done from a manuscript. It was never published during his lifetime. Therefore we don't know for sure that the paragraphing is the paragraphing that he would have used. Nor do we know for sure that he wouldn't have revised sentences or broken them up."

Regardless of what approach he might take with a Kafka manuscript, Mitchell said that the final product would still be a document of its time. "One of the great mysteries of art is that the original somehow retains its freshness over decades and even over centuries, that we return to it and read it with great pleasure and great joy. Translations, by contrast, age very quickly. If you don't have a new translation every twenty years, the translation is dated in a way that somehow the original text seems to be able to avoid. So that if I read a translation that was done of Kafka in the 1930s, it may in many ways be a great translation, but it's clearly 1930s British English. It's not Kafka 1915, it's 1930s British English. My translation is, let's say 1990s; it's not American English really, because I avoided Americanisms, but basically it's the language of the 1990s, as effective as I could make it. But it's a different translation. And if it's translated in the year 2010 by someone else, or 2020, it'll have a different cast to it, without a doubt."

A few weeks before I sat down with Mitchell in his office at the Lilly Library in April 2004, I had, quite by coincidence, picked up a heavy volume that had been waiting in my "must read" cabinet for the better part of seven years, not a record for me by any means, but a long haul all the same, seducing me finally to pick it up not by the melodious title, *Le Ton Beau de Marot* (The Sweet Tone of Marot), or even because of the great regard that I have for its author, Douglas R. Hofstadter, whose *Gödel, Escher, Bach* is one of the most stimulating works of nonfiction to be published in the past quarter century. Actually, it was his subtitle, *In Praise of the Music of Language*, and the premise he put forth early in the introduction, that the work was "all about translation," and that it would involve eighty-eight different renderings of the same obscure poem done in some instances by friends, students, and colleagues, in others by established poets and translators, each one different, each one contributing to a larger whole, all taking into careful account such seemingly mundane details as "line-breaks, page-breaks, hyphenations, widows, orphans, density of word spacing within lines, fine-grained intercharacter spacing ('kerning') and so forth and so on—things that most people are usually unaware of and simply leave to their publisher or word processor."

If there is "one metaphor for the unpredictable evolution of this book," wrote Hofstadter—who is a professor of cognitive science at Indiana University, and a faculty colleague of Mitchell—"it is the idea of designing a multi-leveled mosaic." What he was saying, in essence, is that everyone brings something different to the same text, in this instance "A une damoyselle malade" (To a Sick Damsel), a charming poem of twenty-eight lines, each line consisting of just three syllables, by Clément Marot (1496–1544), poet of the French Renaissance whose experimental use of the forms and imagery of Latin poetry was tremendously influential in its time. The results of Hofstadter's project—conceived as a tribute to his wife, who died in 1993, and presented beautifully in the book with accompanying essays—are striking for their individuality, and had a particular resonance for me when Mitchell offered yet another impression of his literary calling. "The interesting thing to me about translation," he said, "is that the translation is not only a reading—*every* translation is a close reading of the text—but every translation is a *different* reading of the text, too. If the same text is translated by three different people, it's going to be three different readings of that text." And not only is the translator a mediator of the text, he said, the translator is a "filter and a conveyor" of the work. "It's inevitable that the translation is the translator's reaction to a text and language, and the other interesting side of it, to me, is that the translator in some sense is the ideal reader. When Joyce wrote *Finnegans Wake*, he said, you know, I spent seventeen years writing this novel, and I expect somebody to spend an equivalent time reading it. Somebody who writes a novel cares about every sentence, and has paid attention to every sentence. But the only reader who *ever* reads a novel and looks at every sentence, how it's constructed and what it means and why it's there, is the translator. Nobody ever reads as closely as a translator does. When I translate a novel, I've read that novel not once, but many times. I've looked at and thought about every sentence and how it's put together, and why it's put together and how it could be transported into another language effectively."

In a 1921 essay, the German critic Walter Benjamin (1892–1940) offered the opinion that "all great texts contain their potential translation between the lines," and suggested that the "task of the translator" is to straddle a region that lies "midway between poetry and theory" in order to find it. In offering this view, Benjamin asked a seemingly elementary question: "Is a translation meant for readers who do not understand the original?" His answer is appropriate in this context: "This would seem to explain adequately the fact that the translation and original have very different standing in the realm of art. Moreover, it seems to be the only conceivable reason for saying 'the same thing' over again."

8.

Gospel Truth

In the beginning was the word.
—John 1:1–3

The Princeton University historian of religion Elaine Pagels
enjoys the rare distinction of having written several works of
serious scholarship that have become international bestsellers,
quite an accomplishment for a woman who spends much of her time
absorbed in texts written in languages that are two thousand years old,
sometimes reading from the earliest surviving copies themselves. It was
from her translation of a number of ancient writings found near Nag
Hammadi in Egypt that Pagels came to write *The Gnostic Gospels*, a
widely read book that paid careful attention to material that up until then
had been dismissed as marginal curiosities from the formative years of
the Christian era, paving the way for other studies to demonstrate how
sharply divided the church was in its earliest years of formation, when the
movement was very much a work in progress.

An academic who specializes in a period of history scholars call late
antiquity, Pagels has written several other carefully researched books
with the general reader in mind. In 1988, she explored the creation myth
and the development of sexual attitudes in *Adam, Eve, and the Serpent*; in

1996 she examined Christian and Jewish concepts of evil in *The Origin of Satan*. When I met with her in her office in the summer of 2004 on the Princeton campus, her most recent effort, *Beyond Belief*, had just finished a long run on the national bestseller lists. All of her writing, she told me, begins with a fundamental premise. "They all work out questions that I find I have to deal with. *The Gnostic Gospels* was directed to people like me who are interested in questions about religion and spirituality, but who are disaffected from institutions. These texts gave me a way to talk about them, and about that issue."

Pagels was raised in Northern California in what she has called a "nominally Protestant" family. At Stanford University, where her father was a plant biologist, Pagels earned a bachelor's degree in history in 1964, followed by a master's degree in the classics. After a brief interlude in New York City studying dance at the Martha Graham studio, she enrolled in a doctoral program at Harvard University in 1965 with the intention of studying the history of Christianity. It was then that she learned about the fifty-two papyrus manuscripts known collectively as the Nag Hammadi Library that had been unearthed twenty years earlier in the desert.

"I had no idea that there were all these secret documents; they hadn't been published yet, they were still in Coptic, and access to them had been severely restricted," Pagels told me. Having mastered Greek and Latin while earning her MA, and already reading French, Italian, and German, Pagels set about learning Coptic, which is idiomatic Egyptian written with the Greek alphabet and a few other characters, and Hebrew, which she felt would be essential. When a batch of mimeographed transcriptions of the ancient documents arrived at Harvard in 1968, she was eager to proceed. "Nobody had any inkling about what it was," Pagels said. "To tell you the truth, very few people thought very much of these texts at all, including my Harvard professors. I was told they were blasphemous and strange, they were heretical, that nobody knew anything about who wrote them or when they were written, they didn't make sense at all, they were pretty much garbled, they were a kind of magical nonsense. Well, I was totally hooked by them; I was just amazed by what I saw."

Pagels laughed as she recalled a casual conversation just a few weeks earlier with a biblical scholar she had studied under at Harvard. "He told me, 'Elaine, before you wrote about them, we just thought these texts were weird.' That was his word—'weird.'" After completing her doctoral dissertation in 1970—the subject was the controversy that had flared between gnostic and orthodox Christianity—Pagels took a teaching position at Barnard College, Columbia University, and continued to work with the material. In 1975, she visited the Coptic Museum in Cairo to examine the papyrus documents firsthand, describing the twelve hundred sheets mounted in sturdy Plexiglas sheaths she handled there as resembling cured tobacco leaves, with the black calligraphic letters inscribed on their golden-brown surfaces making them beautiful objects to behold. From these persistent inquiries she wrote *The Gnostic Gospels*, a sensation when it appeared in 1979, and winner of the National Book Award and the National Book Critics Circle Award; in due course she would receive Rockefeller, Guggenheim, and MacArthur grants to continue her work.

Beyond the compelling artifacts she had pored over in a cramped room in Cairo, of course, was the content, and what she had gleaned from her reading was convincing evidence that numerous factions had competed for control of the church in its earliest years, that there was diversity in the ranks, and that women had roles that went well beyond subservience. Why so much of this history had been lost over the centuries was a story unto itself, which Pagels sought to put into perspective in her book. What she learned was that as the church moved toward becoming an orthodox body, complete with canon, rites, and clergy, writings that she would come to call the Gnostic Gospels were suppressed, ordered destroyed, and largely forgotten, though some mentions of these curious writings did turn up from time to time over the centuries; but until a farmer digging for fertilizer nitrates stumbled across a huge clay pot containing the leather-bound books known as codices in 1945, no texts from the movement were known to have survived in any form.

"These texts were found near an ancient monastery, they were probably copied by monks," Pagels said. "They were copied by somebody who put in the beginning of Codex 1 a prayer attributed to the apostle Paul, and the prayer is for understanding and for insight and for wisdom and inspiration. So these were written and copied and loved and read by Coptic monks, probably from that monastery, and they were there in the library when the archbishop sent out an order in about the year 320 telling the monks to get rid of them—not to hide them, but to destroy them—because they were leading people astray, and they should not be disseminated." The literature is clear on this point, and documentation abounds, Pagels has made clear in her books and stressed again in her conversation with me. Convinced that the survival of Christianity depended on a unified doctrine and structure, and that contrary views were not only unproductive, they were heretical, opposition to them that had been building steadily went into action.

Around the year 180, Bishop Irenaeus, an orthodox theologian based in Lyons, had written a five-volume tract titled *The Destruction and Overthrow of Falsely So-called Knowledge* in which he denounced a number of these conflicting views, admonishing his followers to "urge all those with whom you are connected to avoid such an abyss of madness and of blasphemy against Christ." He described these works as "secret and illegitimate writings, which they themselves have forged, to bewilder the minds of foolish people, who are ignorant of the true scriptures." When the emperor Constantine converted to Christianity and made the religion the official faith of the realm about one hundred and forty years later, what had been an admonition suddenly had the force of a command. In the year 367, Athanasius, the bishop of Alexandria and a great admirer of Irenaeus, sent out an Easter letter in which he demanded that Egyptian monks destroy every writing that was not "acceptable" or "canonical," and he issued a list of what basically became the New Testament. Books that were denounced as heretical were ordered burned and destroyed, Pagels wrote in the *Gnostic Gospels*. One way to justify the banning of contrary works was to assert that the accepted gospels of Matthew, Mark, Luke, and John had been divinely ordained, making all others profane and sacrilegious. With the discovery of the Nag Hammadi texts, some Christians have been forced to reconsider their roots, and voices once condemned as heretical are now being heard after centuries of silence. That they remain controversial is underscored by some of the issues the texts raise anew, the virgin birth and conflicting versions of Jesus rising from the dead not least among them. Indeed, some of the discovered texts assert that the Resurrection was not a physical event at all, but a symbol of how the spirit of Christ could continue to be felt in the present and in the future.

"Who was it that disobeyed the order and buried these texts in a clay pot?" Pagels said, repeating my question. "I think the obvious answer is that they were monks from the monastery. Maybe they had participated in copying the texts. Copying is very hard, long labor, and it may be they were aghast at the order to destroy what they clearly regarded as precious. We knew there were people who were called Holy Ones who lived out on the desert and were particularly devout. But did we know they had a library? Not at all." She picked up a facsimile copy of a Nag Hammadi text she had been working on, and explained that it is a dialogue between a father and a son. "This is a teacher here—*abba* is a teacher—talking about how one goes into the higher state of being, and becomes enlightened in an ecstatic way. This discourse is quite wonderful, but it's not the kind of thing orthodox bishops want people doing or even trying."

In 1982, Pagels left Barnard College in New York for Princeton University in New Jersey to become a professor of religion, focusing on early Christian history. That same year, there arrived in her life a moment that in another context might be described as an epiphany. Two days after learning that her two-and-a-half-year-old son Mark was dying slowly from pulmonary hypertension, Pagels stopped for a break at the Church of the Heavenly Rest in Manhattan while out jogging on a cold Sunday morning. "Since I had not been in church for a long time, I was startled by the response to the worship in progress—the soaring harmonies of the choir singing with the congregation; and the priest, a woman in bright gold and white vestments, proclaiming the prayers in a clear, resonant voice," she wrote of the experience. "As I stood watching, a thought came to me: Here is a family that knows how to face death." The emotional pull of the moment was clear, but there was also an intellectual element. "I am a historian of religion, and so, as I visited that church, I wondered when and how being a Christian became virtually synonymous with accepting a certain set of beliefs. From historical reading, I knew that Christianity had survived brutal persecution and flourished for generations—even centuries—*before* Christians formulated what they believed into creeds."

Thus began another round of inquiries that would result in the publication twenty-one years later of the aptly titled *Beyond Belief.* The loss of her son Mark in 1987 from his illness, and the death of her husband fifteen months after that in a Colorado hiking accident, left her devastated, but in time sharpened her resolve to deal with the twin tragedies in a meaningful way, and after seeing *The Origin of Satan* and *Adam, Eve, and the Serpent* through the press, she turned her attention to a focused reading of just one of the Nag Hammadi texts, a book known as the Gospel of Thomas. "A lot of people think you get religious when you grieve, but I wasn't one of them," she said. "In my experience, that sort of response just didn't make any sense."

Pagels said she chose Thomas because it bears a number of similarities to Matthew, Mark, Luke, and John—which she suggests became the authorized gospels of the New Testament some fifty years after the conversion of Constantine—and also for some crucial differences, especially with John, which may have been written to counter Thomas, believed to have been written sometime between AD 50 and 100, which would mean that it predates the official gospels. It is no coincidence, Pagels said, that only John among the evangelists portrays Thomas as ignorant and faithless, and only John calls him "doubting Thomas" for failing to accept at first that Jesus has returned from the dead.

"That was the greatest surprise of all for me, to suddenly realize that the Gospel of John was written as a rebuttal to the teachings of Thomas," Pagels told me. "To tell you the truth, I was stunned with the realization." The fundamental difference between the two, in her view, is that Thomas has a profound respect for people, while John's opinion of human nature is low. "John is quite clear that Jesus is a divine being, that the world is lost in sin and evil, that salvation comes only through repentance and the belief that Jesus alone grants access to God." But in the Gospel of Thomas, Jesus directs each believer to discover the light within, and Pagels cited a key phrase: "Within a person of light, there is light."

That books like *The Gnostic Gospels* and *Beyond Belief* are bestsellers is unusual enough; that they deal with matters of spirituality, particularly as they pertain to controversial interpretations of the Bible, makes it doubly significant, especially at a time when a condition of "biblical illiteracy" is being decried as endemic throughout the United States, even among people who regard themselves as people of profound faith. While it may be true that most households in the United States own copies of the Bible, it is also true that very few people are literally conversant with its contents, while fewer still read it with any regularity, a situation that has caused increasing anxiety among religious groups, as various Web sites make abundantly clear. "Americans revere the Bible—but, by and large, they don't read it," the pollster George Gallup and religion writer

Jim Castelli concluded in *The People's Religion*, a comprehensive survey of American religious beliefs compiled in the 1980s, and reaffirmed in a study conducted by the same polling organization and released in 1999. "And because they don't read it, they have become a nation of biblical illiterates."

At the other extreme there is, paradoxically, a plethora of books *about* the Bible and the events it recounts that fascinate contemporary readers, especially when they are shaped into entertaining works of the imagination, as with Dan Brown's blockbuster novel of 2003, *The Da Vinci Code*. In Brown's scenario, the origins of the early church are brought into question amid hints that Jesus may have been married to Mary Magdalene, the plot driven by a premise that a conspiracy was concocted centuries ago to obscure the truth. When I asked Elaine Pagels to comment on this apparent anomaly—biblical illiteracy on the one hand, blockbuster novels on the other—she agreed that fewer Americans actually read the Bible today than they used to, "and I think that's true of our students, too, but there is a tremendous interest in *issues* about religion and spirituality, as these cases you cite indicate. I am reminded of Alexis de Tocqueville, who said that something can be wildly religious, and still true. A lot of people who wouldn't necessarily read the Bible will look at a book like *The Da Vinci Code*, because what that book is suggesting is that there are things that have been left out of the tradition that we don't know about. That is an accurate statement, and that of course is what I write about in my books. This is all very intriguing to people. They probably do know that these books that are in the Bible were chosen by *somebody* to be there—they do sort of know that, I think, but so many people stop their thinking about religion when they are five or six years old; whatever they learned when they were children is pretty much what stays with them." And it is texts like the Gospel of Thomas, she has maintained, that reveal a more diverse early Christian landscape than was ever imagined.

While it is certainly possible to read some of this material in transla-tion, Pagels said she regards reading original texts as essential to what she does. "Otherwise you are dealing with somebody else's interpretation. And even when you read these texts in Coptic or Greek, you're still deal-ing with your own English—I am translating the Coptic and the Greek into *my* English." Many religions have their texts, Pagels agreed, but they are not necessarily foundation texts. "The Buddhists have their sutras, but as you say, they were orally transmitted for hundreds of years before they were written down, so I think textual transmission is certainly much more the case for Western religions. In antiquity there were many reli-gions that were based on ritual practice, celebrating games, honoring the gods, that sort of thing. It was not about texts at all."

The same year that *Beyond Belief* appeared, two other books touching on the same premise were published. Bart D. Ehrman of the University of North Carolina, the author of both works, put them in perspective: "The New Testament did not emerge as an established and complete set of books after the death of Jesus. Many years passed before Christians agreed concerning which books should comprise their sacred scriptures, with debates over the contour of the 'canon' (that is, the collection of sacred texts) that were long, hard, and sometimes harsh." In *Lost Scriptures: Books That Did Not Make It Into the New Testament*, Ehrman gathered texts that were at one time considered as authorities for Christian faith and practice, but were not included among the twenty-seven books that finally won out over the others; his second book, *Lost Christianities: The Battles for Scripture and the Faiths We Never Knew*, pro-vided commentary and context. None of the texts he included or described were among those found at Nag Hammadi and discussed by Pagels in her books. Though Ehrman called the early Christian texts he wrote about "lost," he allowed that a more accurate term might have been "forgotten," since a good deal of the discarded texts he wrote about were simply ignored and left untouched in monasteries and libraries in the Middle East and Europe for centuries, though a few were discovered in archaeological digs. The important distinction to make, particularly in reference to the gnostic texts, is that the writings found at Nag Hammadi were ordered destroyed, and their survival came about only because some monks refused to comply.

These examinations come at a time when biblical scholars are embarked on a decidedly rigorous approach that focuses on the *writing* of the Old Testament and New Testament, and their transformation over time into "sacred" texts. "The Bible is a book," William M. Schniedewind emphasized in the opening paragraph of a searching monograph, an assertion, he readily acknowledged, that "seems like an obvious statement, but it is also a profound development in religion. We may take books for granted, but the ancients did not. The fact that a sacred, written text emerged from a pastoral, agricultural, and oral society is a watershed of Western civilization."

The central thrust of Schniedewind's work is expressed quite succinctly by its title, *How the Bible Became a Book*, and his analysis pays close attention to recent archaeological evidence suggesting that much of the Hebrew Bible began to be written down as early as the eighth century BC and continued for about two hundred years, roughly between the time of the prophets Isaiah and Jeremiah. With the transformation from an oral tradition to a scriptural one being his central concern, Schniedewind's argument involves a seeming paradox, that once recorded, the canonized manuscripts that would become known as the Bible were not subject to substantive change, though the interpretation constantly evolved. While the reader as such is not central to Schniedewind's study, he does touch lightly on a school of thought that holds that the "interpretive community" of a text—the audience, in other words—is "ultimately more important than the author" because the reader "ultimately defines the meaning of a text." To support this contention, he compared the Hebrew

Bible to the U.S. Constitution, a document constantly being consulted for nuances and meanings appropriate to the period in which it is being defined by the federal judiciary. The "meaning" of the Constitution, he emphasized, "keeps changing along with the changing generations of its readers." Although the intention of the framers is central to the discussion, it is the "historical moment" when American society reads the articles set down in the document that shapes its interpretation. "In the same way, biblical meaning has reflected its readers more than its writers."

As an example, Schniedewind cited *Brown v. Board of Education*, the 1954 Supreme Court decision that overturned "separate, but equal" provisions mandated fifty-eight years earlier in *Plessy v. Ferguson* on the basis that the earlier ruling violated "equal protection of the laws" guarantees of the Fourteenth Amendment. "The different interpretations of the Constitution in 1896 and 1954 reflected the changing social context of the interpreters. The text had not changed, but the readers and the social context had. Similarly, the meaning of the Bible will be imbedded in the history of the people who wrote it, read it, passed it on, rewrote it, and read it again. It is closely tied to when the traditions were collected, written down, edited, rewritten, and finally coalesced into the book we call the Bible."

The Yale historian Jaroslav Pelikan, a noted authority on the Christian tradition, devoted an entire study to parallels apparent in the interpretation of the New Testament and the Constitution. "Both texts are centuries old by now, whether two or twenty, and both are 'venerable' and even venerated and enshrined," he wrote, explaining his rationale to pair the two. "Every official action of the community thus has had the obligation of conforming to it, or at any rate of not violating it, and of demonstrating that conformity when challenged to do so; and members of the community are under the strictest possible obligation to obey it. Therefore its words and phrases have for centuries called forth meticulous and sophisticated—and sometimes painfully convoluted—interpretation, as well as continual reinterpretation." Yet for all that fluctuation, the words themselves remain fixed, and the text "does not itself prescribe the method of such interpretation."

A civil constitution, according to this argument, is a form of secular scripture, a great, enduring code meant to arbitrate in situations that its framers could never have imagined, with interpretation being at the core of its viability. It is no coincidence, he pointed out, that each of the three great religions that claim descent from Abraham, Judaism, Christianity, and Islam, "accept the authority of a historical revelation" as set down in a sacred book. "In all three religions, therefore, is as well a special relation between the sacred book as written revelation and the idea of a written constitution, also by contrast with cultures that do not possess either one even though they have an unwritten 'constitution.' " In *People of the Book*, Moshe Halbertal, professor of Jewish thought and philosophy at the Hebrew University in Jerusalem, makes something of a parallel claim with his assertion that the most effective way to appreciate the coherence of Jewish life through history is by understanding what he calls its "text-centered tradition." He gets the reader's attention quickly by making the bold claim that "in the beginning was the text," and that it was "the shared commitment to certain texts and their role in shaping many aspects of Jewish life" that endowed the tradition with coherence. The "canon," in other words, goes well beyond defining spiritual matters involving "life after death," but, more directly, impacts "life on earth."

Most readers of the Bible fail to engage these texts as literature and history, a circumstance that the historian of religion Donald Harman Akenson has found unfortunate. "To a remarkable degree, the scriptures tell us how to read the scriptures, although these self-contained instructions are now out of fashion among biblical scholars," he wrote. "The Hebrew Bible is a book of puns, of irony, and the occasional joke, and these, while not the heart of the text, are like a set of stage directions: read the solemn part solemnly, but know also that almost every word can have a second or third meaning and that word-play is the analgesic we have been given to keep the heavy parts of the scriptures from becoming more of a load than we can bear." Akenson's advice to readers, basically, was to lighten up, and to "read the scriptures *as if* they were history. That is how the book tells us to read the book. Taken collectively, the Hebrew and Christian scriptures, the Apocrypha, the Pseudepigrapha, are a vast set of historical investigations, wonderful in their quality, surprising in their character. They cry out to be read as many things—as poetry, romance, law—but first, they are history, because they attempt to situate sequences of events along the skein of time."

For all the "biblical illiteracy" that is decried as being so rampant, no comparable state of affairs can be said to prevail among Muslims. If there is any irony to the expression introduced in the sixth century to identify the Jews as "people of the book"—people, in other words, who had received earlier revelations—it is that the description appeared in the holy book of Islam, the Qur'an (also called the Koran). "The Qur'an is the supreme authority in Islam," M. A. S. Abdel Haleem stated in a recent translation of the book believed by its adherents to be the absolute word of God as revealed to the Prophet Muhammad. "The Qur'an was the starting point for all the Islamic sciences: Arabic grammar was developed to serve the Qur'an, the study of Arab phonetics was pursued in order to determine the exact pronunciation of Qur'anic words, the science of Arabic rhetoric was developed in order to describe the features of the inimitable style of the Qur'an, the art of Arabic calligraphy was cultivated through writing down the Qur'an, the Qur'an is the basis of Islamic law and theology; indeed, as the celebrated fifteenth-century scholar and author Suyuti said, 'Everything is based on the Qur'an.'" Muslim children memorize portions of the Qur'an as part of their formal schooling. A person capable of reciting the entire text is known as a *hafiz*, continuing a tradition that began during the lifetime of the Prophet Muhammad in the sixth century.

According to tradition, Muhammad, a successful businessman who lived in Mecca, began to receive revelations from the archangel Gabriel in the year 610 when he was forty years old, and continued to receive them over the remaining twenty-two years of his life. The very first word the prophet received came in the form of a command: "Read in the name of your Lord." Replying that he was unable to read—indeed, that he was illiterate—Muhammad was told twice more to *read*, at which point the first two lines of the Qur'an were recited to him. The word *qur'an* itself literally means "reading" and "reciting," and came to identify "the text which is read and recited." Those first words passed on to Muhammad now appear at the beginning of chapter 96, known as a *sura*, and were followed with yet another explicit injunction: "Read! Your Lord is the Most Bountiful one who taught by the pen, who taught man what he did not know." Although Muhammad's first revelation is said to have taken place when he was alone in a cave, others were witnessed by members of a band of followers, whose task it became to record precisely the words that he relayed to them. According to some accounts, twenty-nine scribes were given the assignment. As each new *sura* was transmitted, Gabriel is said to have told Muhammad where each one should be placed in the final book.

In October 2004, a dozen Muslim intellectuals gathered in Cairo for a seminar called Islam and Reform in which questions once thought unthinkable were raised, with some scholars calling for adjustments to the Qur'an itself. In an interview with the *New York Times*, one of the participants, Muhammad Shahrour, a Syrian layman who writes extensively about Islam, suggested that the only way Muslims can separate their faith from violence that is being committed around the world in its name is by reappraising their sacred texts. Shahrour singled out the ninth chapter of the Qur'an as the source of many verses used to validate extremist attacks. Known as the "Sura of Repentance," the chapter describes a failed attempt by the Prophet Muhammad to form a state on the Arabian Peninsula, and contains such lines as "slay the pagans where you find them." Shahrour said that these verses are inflammatory and should be isolated to their original context; he described other sayings attributed to Muhammad as "ridiculously archaic," and long overdue for reappraisal. "It is like this now because for centuries Muslims have been told that Islam was spread by the sword, that all Arab countries and even Spain were captured by the sword and we are proud of that," he said. "In the minds of ordinary people, people on the street, the religion of Islam is the religion of the sword. This is the culture, and we have to change it." Ten recommendations emerged from the seminar, one calling for a new interpretation of some Islamic tenets, though the event was marred by demonstrations mounted by opponents, with some religious conservatives calling the speakers "liars" and "infidels."

The reliance on a sacred text to legitimize various religious beliefs goes well beyond the major faiths, of course, and guiding documents do not necessarily have to date from antiquity in order to be revered by their adherents. Among the works selected by the Grolier Club in 1946 as being among the one hundred most influential books published in North America prior to 1900 were *The Book of Mormon*, which in its first printed edition of 1830 bore on the title page the credit "Joseph Smith, Junior, Author and Proprietor," and a preface that also identified Smith as the author. Only a thousand copies of this version of the 275,000-word tract made it into print; all later editions dropped the preface and identified Smith as "translator," a modification of no small import, since the content by then was being described as conceived by God and delivered to a modern-day prophet.

Smith asserted that he had found the plates in 1827 and spent several months translating them behind a screen, dictating to his wife, Emma, and her brother a truly amazing narrative that claimed to explain the divine origins of the American land and people. They took down his every syllable, and were aided by several other scribes expressly recruited for the effort. Whether or not this twenty-five-year-old farm boy penned the text that gave rise to what has become an extraordinarily powerful religious group, the Church of Latter-day Saints, or actually found it as he so fervently insisted inscribed on sheets of gold plate buried on a hill in upstate New York—and which were later reclaimed by the mediating angel—are not issues to be explored here. What is relevant is the claim itself, that a text of surpassing importance was found in the ground with the help of a divining stone, transcribed from a script vaguely described as "Reformed Egyptian" characters into crude English, and delivered to a growing corps of believers as the sacred word of God.

Another book included in the Grolier 100 list—one that also made it into the 1963 Printing and the Mind of Man exhibition in London—is of more recent vintage, and also gets a good deal of its currency from suggestions that it was divinely inspired. *Science and Health* was published in 1875 in an edition of one thousand copies, and offered for sale at $2.50 a copy. When the author, Mary Baker Glover, an impoverished widow of fifty-five who married again and became known as Mary Baker Eddy, died at the age of eighty-nine, her book was known to many thousands of readers, and the Boston-based movement it engendered, the First Church of Christ, Scientist, enjoyed an influence well beyond anything anyone could have imagined when she started. A sickly woman whose quest for health led her to consultation with Dr. Phineas Parkhurst Quimby, of Portland, Maine, Eddy became a disciple of the man's philosophy, and using one of his manuscripts as a text, began teaching his methods, and formulating her own manifesto. She claimed to have been divinely inspired for the title of the book she came to write, though some critics suggest she drew on the name by which Quimby called his system of faith healing, "The Science of Health."

Regardless of where the title came from, her creation—arguably the most influential religious movement to be introduced *anywhere* by a woman—is of considerable interest for several reasons, as Eddy's most recent biographer, Gillian Gill, makes clear: "One of the most salient features of *Science and Health* as a foundational religious text is that from 1875 to 1907 Mary Baker Eddy was engaged in a virtually daily revision of the book. Thus the text of 1875 and the text of 1907, the one Christian Scientists read today, are radically different. Mrs. Eddy saw this work of revision as being a progressive clarification of a divinely revealed message, which was in essence unchanged but which she needed to labor to understand for herself and find the words to express so that others could understand it too." Given the assertion that the text was divinely inspired—and thus a model of unassailable perfection—it is of more than cursory interest to point out that the first appearance of *Science and Health* was rife with errors, many of them obviously the result of clumsy writing on the part of the self-educated author, others the fault of shoddy printing by the compositors. Indeed, it could be argued that this is the only book to have engendered a religious movement of consequence that was issued in its first printing with two pages of errata inserted at the back. "Our next printer," the then Mrs. Glover wrote to an associate, "should have a proof reader who is *responsible* for this." The organizers of Printing and the Mind of Man took these glitches into account. "In spite of the mechanical faults of her book and the controversial nature of many of her teachings," they wrote, "Mary Baker Eddy was far ahead of her time in the emphasis she placed upon positive thinking, a force which modern psychology was belated in recognizing."

According to figures furnished by the Church of Christ, Scientist, about eleven million copies of the book have been sold since its publication in 1875, a million of them since 1996 alone. It is available in sixteen languages, including an edition in English Braille, and is sold in some eighty countries. When its copyright ran out in the 1970s—an unusual enough circumstance for a work claiming to be divinely inspired—*Science and Health* entered the public domain, though it is still published primarily by the Mother Church, and sold in its reading rooms around the world and through authorized agents.

9.

Harvest of Riches

*For we are apt to forget, reading, as we tend to do, only the master-
pieces of a bygone age, how great a power the body of literature pos-
sesses to impose itself; how it will not suffer itself to be read passively,
but takes us and reads us; flouts our preconceptions; questions principles
which we had got into the habit of taking for granted, and, in fact,
splits us into two parts as we read, making us, even as we enjoy, yield
our ground or stick to our guns.*
— Virginia Woolf, "Notes on an Elizabethan Play" (1925)

Toward the end of a full day spent in the company of Matthew J.
Bruccoli at the University of South Carolina, I asked this man
whose vast range of literary interests goes beyond teaching,
writing, and publishing to seeking out and securing rare and important
artifacts that document the lives and work of twentieth-century American authors, what pursuit, above all others, shines brightest in his constel-
lation of professional endeavors. "I am a bookman," he said simply.
"Everything I do, everything I write, everything I buy, everything I collect, has to do with the role of the book in American culture and the profession of authorship."

Described in a front-page article of the *New York Times* as the "senior

pack rat of American letters" for his tenacious pursuit of literary artifacts, Bruccoli regards himself as a conservative man when it comes to
assessing evidence. "I don't like guesswork," he insisted, "I require evidence," an operational mandate drilled into him many years earlier at the
University of Virginia, where he pursued his graduate studies under the
tutelage of two people, rare books curator John Cook Wyllie, and
Fredson Bowers, the noted bibliographer who was faculty adviser for
his doctoral dissertation, a detailed examination of the composition of
F. Scott Fitzgerald's 1934 novel, *Tender Is the Night*. "John Cook Wyllie
is the one person above all others who made me a bookman," Bruccoli
said, "and Fredson Bowers was the greatest bibliographical theorist who
ever lived." After receiving his Ph.D. in 1961, Bruccoli (pronounced
brook-lee) supervised preparation of the Centennial Edition of the works
of Nathaniel Hawthorne at the Ohio State University Center for Textual
Studies for eight years before accepting a position at the University of
South Carolina, where he has lived and worked contentedly ever since.
Although he has always collected books for his own scholarly uses,
Bruccoli's efforts to bring major research collections to the library began
in earnest in the 1980s, when he secured the enthusiastic backing of the
university's administration to acquire collections and archives in its
behalf. George Terry, the late library dean at South Carolina credited
with giving the green light to Bruccoli's far-flung forays in search of literary material, once called him "the most unique man" he had ever met,
the only person he had ever known who would fly to Australia for the
sole purpose of buying books, and then return immediately to the United
States. "He really loves books that much," Terry said, and the ultimate
beneficiary of the symbiotic relationship has been the university, which
now maintains one of the premier research collections of twentieth-
century American fiction in the United States, with success begetting
success. "All of my collections—and I've formed, what, maybe twenty
collections?—have always had the rationale of documenting the profes-

sion of authorship," Bruccoli told me. "That, in fact, is what the room in which we are standing right now does."

The room in which we were standing, identified by a brass nameplate outside the door as the Matthew J. and Arlyn Bruccoli Collection of F. Scott Fitzgerald, occupies a prime location in the Thomas Cooper Library on the campus of the university. While the three thousand printed books and eleven thousand or so documents and artifacts relevant to Fitzgerald are certainly impressive, it is the scope and nature of the holdings that make them supremely important to students. Gathered over a span of fifty years by Bruccoli, the contents became the property of the university in 1994 when he agreed to sell them for less than half their market value, pegged then at just under $2 million, and undoubtedly worth much more today. If not unique among collectors of books and literary significa, Bruccoli is in a class by himself in that every undertaking is pursued with a zeal that has become anything but mellow with the passage of time, his seventy-third birthday in the offing when he showed me the fruits of his labors early in 2004 notwithstanding. While it is true that Bruccoli has gathered this material with the single-minded enthusiasm of the most ardent of bibliomaniacs, there is a reward for him that extends well beyond the exhilaration of victory, one that actually involves the purposeful reading of the material itself, deriving insights that are not possible from writings known only from the standard printed versions. "My collections always have the rationale of documenting the profession of authorship, and in the case of Fitzgerald, that is what this room does," he emphasized.

My introduction to the Fitzgerald Room was preceded by a tour of the treasure vault, a high-security enclosure where the most valuable materials in the university's collections are kept locked behind a steel door, a good number of them related to the life and works of F. Scott Fitzgerald (1896–1940). One item in particular Bruccoli wanted me to see was a decidedly nonliterary artifact that he had acquired serendipitously in 1973 at a Sotheby's sale in New York, a perfect example of what is prized today in research libraries as a "material artifact," an item that is not a manuscript by any means, but a tangible object that offers unexpected insight into artistic expression. In this instance, we were looking at a brown leather briefcase, obviously of another era and heavily worn, secured by two straps at the center. "Fitzgerald had this with him when he was in Hollywood," Bruccoli explained, an interesting biographical detail, to be sure, but hardly deserving of a favored place in a major research collection in and of itself. "If you notice the gold stamping, it says 'F. Scott Fitzgerald, 597 5th Avenue, New York.' Well, that's the Scribner Building. Fitzgerald didn't have a home, much less one on Fifth Avenue in Manhattan; Fitzgerald's home *was* the Scribner Building. What does that tell you about the man who wrote *The Great Gatsby*?"

Knowing everything he can about the man who wrote what is arguably *the* Great American Novel of the twentieth century, and documenting whatever he can about the creation of lasting literature in general, is central to the mission Bruccoli has fashioned for himself, an endeavor that has resulted in the release of more than sixty works of literary biography and bibliography, a good number of them published by Bruccoli Clark, an imprint he established in 1962 with C. E. Frazer Clark Jr., another bibliophile whose interest in Nathaniel Hawthorne resulted in the compilation of several bibliographical treatments of the New England author's works. Known since 1976 as Bruccoli Clark Layman, the company produces works of scholarly nonfiction, most notably the *Dictionary of Literary Biography*, at 370 volumes the largest reference series published to date in the English language. The initial concept envisioned by Bruccoli and Clark was to publish limited editions of literary works they had collected, several of them versions of texts that Bruccoli was able to "restore" to what he determined were the original intentions of the authors, with the brunt of the documentation coming from the materials he had acquired. Some of these he bought from established antiquarian booksellers and in the major auction galleries;

others he turned up in basements, attics, junk shops, and barns, all pursued with an enthusiasm that showed no signs of ebbing when he spoke with me early in 2004. Just two months after we met, the *New York Times* reported on its front-page news of Bruccoli's acquisition for the University of South Carolina of a rich collection of movie scripts written by Fitzgerald over an eighteen-month period in 1937 and 1938 for the Metro-Goldwyn-Mayer studio. Comprising some two thousand pages of original material, the archive includes sketches, drafts, and rewrites of movie treatments, much of it written out in longhand with a soft pencil, and provides evidence, in Bruccoli's opinion, of Fitzgerald's seriousness as a screenwriter, a resolve that has been a matter of some contention over the years.

"I regard book collecting as the obligatory and mandatory occupation of a scholar," Bruccoli made clear in his conversation with me, adding frankly his dismissal of people "claiming to be scholars" who disdain "access to the great books" in their fields. "I think most of the teaching of literature today is flawed because the author is ignored. All of this non-sense about postmodernism—the idea that the author is dead—actually injures the work, and it certainly injures the students." Access, in Bruccoli's view, means consulting every available version of a favored author's writings, which is why the catalog of his Fitzgerald collection lists one hundred and forty-eight entries for *The Great Gatsby* alone, another sixty-five for *Tender Is the Night*, thirty-nine for *The Beautiful and Damned*, fifty-four for *This Side of Paradise*, even four for *Fie! Fie! Fi-Fi!*, a musical comedy presented by the Triangle Club at Princeton University in 1914, with lyrics written by Fitzgerald when he was a college freshman. "He wrote for every publication at Princeton with the exception of the *Daily Princetonian*, and he wrote three Triangle Club shows, his first one as a freshman. He claimed that he wrote whole issues of the *Princeton Tiger* overnight. He wrote serious short stories and a great deal of poetry. When he was at Princeton he wasn't sure whether he wanted to be a novelist or a poet. So this section here"—Bruccoli indicated bulging shelves—"has all of his Princetoniana." What this wealth of material confirms for Bruccoli is that Fitzgerald "was not the uneducated man that many critics would have. Sure, he was probably the worst student that Princeton ever had, but that doesn't signify anything. Fitzgerald knew there was nothing in the chemistry classrooms and the math classrooms at Princeton he needed, that he could possibly use; he flunked out because he neglected the required courses."

The youthful Fitzgerald is represented in the Bruccoli collection by even earlier material, most strikingly *The St. Paul Academy Now and Then* for the period between 1908 and 1911, when Fitzgerald was a student at the academy, a day school in St. Paul, Minnesota, and publishing his earliest fictional works. "There are two sets of these in the world," Bruccoli said. "St. Paul Academy has one, this is the other." How Bruccoli managed to find his set is a story unto itself. "I got hold of a Minneapolis phone book and a St. Paul phone book, and I wrote to every name that had a Fitzgerald connection, and I wrote and I wrote and I wrote, and finally, somebody said, 'Yes, I've got one.'" A similar strategy helped him locate his copies of the college theatrical productions written by Fitzgerald, including *Fie! Fie! Fi-Fi!* "I wrote to every surviving member of the classes of 1917, 1916, 1915, and 1914, saying that I would not presume to offer you money, but if you have any material relating to the Triangle Club productions for 1914, '15, and '16, I would be very happy to make a generous donation to Princeton University in your name. It worked."

When, I wondered, did Bruccoli realize that he was acquiring books that had cultural value that extended beyond the texts that are contained between the hard covers of these various titles? "The week of my graduation from Yale, in Whitlock's, a textbook store in New Haven that sold used books in the basement, I found two Fitzgeralds, one for $5, the other

$7.50; they were the first books I bought strictly for their bibliophilic appeal." Later, when he was a graduate student at the University of Virginia, he found a magnificent copy of *The Great Gatsby*, which remains a centerpiece holding in his collection. "This copy is worth about one hundred and fifty thousand dollars today, the first printing in dust jacket. I bought it from Henry Wenning for thirty dollars, and I didn't have the thirty dollars. I paid it off five dollars at a time. Something like that is easy, because if you want one of these, and if you are willing to spend one hundred and fifty thousand dollars, you can get one, no problem. But try and find one of *these*," he said, pulling out another volume. "Here is the second printing, with the corrected J [on Jay Gatsby's name on the back of the dust jacket], and here is the third printing with the blurb [excerpting favorable reviews] on the jacket. It gets even better; here is the first English edition, using the American dust jacket."

At this point I jumped into the conversation, trying to ask what in the world curiosities like this had to do with the reading experience and the importance of the text itself, but Bruccoli would have none of my interruptions. "Wait," he said. "It's going to get better. Now—here it is— look at *this*—a copy they couldn't sell at all; they couldn't *give* it away in London. This is a remaindered copy. They priced it originally at seven shillings, only nobody wanted it, so they offered it at two and six. Then they couldn't sell it at that price, so they reduced it to two shillings. They knocked off six pence. Here it is, and nobody else has a copy." What evidence like this documents, better than any yellowed press clippings from the period, is the apathy that greeted Fitzgerald's earliest professional writings in the marketplace. "Again, if *The Great Gatsby* is the great American novel, then anything that documents the reception and reputation is meaningful as literary history. It is meaningful that *The Great Gatsby* was a flop in England and a relative failure here in the United States when it was published," a gloomy circumstance borne out by the fact that copies of the second printing were still in a warehouse when Fitzgerald died in 1940, fifteen years after it first appeared in print, with no immediate prospects apparent for a rush on orders.

All quite fascinating, I agreed—and I was totally charmed by Bruccoli's acumen as a collector—but what, I asked, does all this have to do with understanding the text? "The enemy of literary history, the enemy of literary biography, is talk," he replied. "This substitutes evidence for chitchat." Evidence is one thing, though, and *reading* is something else again, a point that I pressed. "This is an item of supreme value," Bruccoli said, choosing to answer by way of example, selecting a unique set of galley proofs with the word *Trimalchio* appearing at the top of each galley sheet as a running title. The work had been ordered set into type late in 1924 by Maxwell E. Perkins, the legendary editor at Scribner's whose authors included Ernest Hemingway and Thomas Wolfe, and who had been championing the work of F. Scott Fitzgerald. The *Trimalchio* galleys had been set from the manuscript of a novel Fitzgerald had titled after the name of an ostentatious party-giver in the *Satyricon* of Petronius, a freed slave who became wealthy and hosted a lavish banquet. In translations of Petronius, the chapter is usually called "The Party at Trimalchio's" or "Trimalchio's Feast." When Fitzgerald read the *Satyricon* is not known, but just the choice of the name Trimalchio itself—and the parallels between that character from antiquity and Jay Gatsby's own mysterious rise to affluence—is germane to any discussion that might involve Fitzgerald's work as it progressed toward publication.

Typically, the making of galleys represents the penultimate stage in the publishing process, with alterations often being made by authors, but only of a rudimentary and factual nature or to correct spellings. Revisions were costly to make, and were meant to be kept to a minimum. In this instance, however, not only was the title changed—it became *The Great Gatsby*, a reference to Jay Gatsby, the central character—but Fitzgerald worked painstakingly to improve the writing, using two sets of the galley proofs to cut and paste one final, heavily edited version together, which Scribner's published on April 10, 1925, to warm reviews, but disappointing sales. The cut-and-paste set of the galley proofs is with the Fitzgerald archives at Princeton University.

Bruccoli is renowned for his tenacity in pursuit of literary materials, and the hard-nosed, sometimes salty propensity he has for not taking fools lightly. He enjoys telling how he acquired the *Trimalchio* proofs at auction in 1971 for what even then was the ridiculously meager sum of $2,500. "It's got to be worth a quarter of a million today," he said, suggesting that his competition did not yet understand the value of galley proofs. "At that time collectors only wanted high spots." And what does reading such a document do? "It gives my students and me a chance to see how a genius took something that was brilliant and turned it into a masterpiece." Bruccoli said he accomplishes such scrutiny by having his students read the published *Gatsby* while he reads aloud from the actual galleys, which he brings with him into the classroom. "We stop, and we argue about all the important revisions, and in this way we appreciate how a great work comes into being." Since 2000, the *Trimalchio* text has been available in a facsimile edition to streamline the procedure even more. "But I have the real thing right on the table. It's good for them to be near a great literary artifact. And with any luck, the good ones can hear it talking to them. I can hear books talking. Can't you?" In an afterword to the facsimile, Bruccoli identified the sources for the novel's characters and setting, discussed various aspects of Fitzgerald's revisions, and detailed the correspondence between Perkins and Fitzgerald about the novel's structure and character development. Comparing the final text of *The Great Gatsby* with the *Trimalchio* galleys, Bruccoli was able to reconstruct Fitzgerald's work during the winter of 1924–1925, which included a substantial restructuring of chapters 6, 7, and 8.

The driving point in all this, Bruccoli said, is his wish to establish what was once referred to in bibliographical circles as the "definitive" edition of an author's work—a text, in other words, that best reflects the artistic vision of the author, and not the intrusions or modifications imposed by others—and known today as a "critical" edition. "I am talking about the book as an expression of a genius's mind. And since I was trained by Fredson Bowers, I was trained in the methods of recovering the author's intention. And so therefore I have done definitive editions of *Gatsby*, *Tender Is the Night*, and *The Last Tycoon*, for which I recovered Fitzgerald's title, *Love of the Last Tycoon*, which was published as *The Last Tycoon* posthumously because Edmund Wilson, who did the salvage job, didn't like *Love of the Last Tycoon*, and he called it something else. The word 'definitive' has become cheapened and meaningless, so I prefer to use the phrase 'critical edition.' A critical edition is based on all of the drafts and prepublication material, as well as any alterations and revisions the author may have made in the book postpublication. And something like that is impossible to do without the material you see around you in this room. If there was a single reason for building this collection, it was so I could do critical editions of F. Scott Fitzgerald." Bruccoli has also produced critical editions of other works, most spectacularly the 2000 release of *O Lost: A Story of the Buried Life*, comprising the original text of Thomas Wolfe's great coming-of-age novel before Maxwell Perkins edited out 66,000 of the 294,000 words that had been submitted, including a 21,000-word opening sequence, and changed the title to *Look Homeward, Angel*.

Bruccoli does not deny that he is passionate about his work, perhaps even obsessed by the chase, but for him the prize is always defined by a work of scholarship that emerges from the materials he is able to locate and scrutinize, "otherwise it is a meaningless exercise." And while Fitzgerald without question represents the jewel in Bruccoli's crown, his ambitious outings in search of extraordinary materials have resulted in the assembly of other research collections that illumine the life and works of Ernest Hemingway, Joseph Heller, James Gould Cozzens, John O'Hara,

Historian and biographer David McCullough at the Massachusetts Historical Society in Boston.

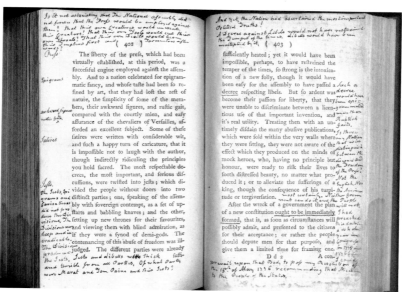

The marginalia of President John Adams is everywhere apparent in his copy of Mary Wollstonecraft's *Historical and Moral View of the Origin and Progress of the French Revolution*, 1794. (*Courtesy of the Boston Public Library*)

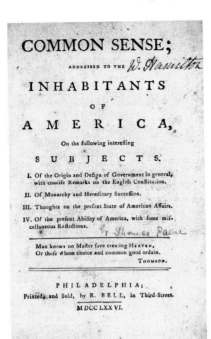

Thomas Paine's *Common Sense* openly called for separation of the American colonies from England and is believed by many historians to have contributed directly to the Declaration of Independence. *(Courtesy of the Lilly Library, Indiana University)*

AN

INQUIRY

INTO THE

Nature and Causes

OF THE

WEALTH OF NATIONS.

By ADAM SMITH, LL. D. and F. R. S.
Formerly Professor of Moral Philosophy in the University of GLASGOW;

IN TWO VOLUMES.

VOL. I.

LONDON:
PRINTED FOR W. STRAHAN; AND T. CADELL, IN THE STRAND,
MDCCLXXVI.

Volume 1 of Adam Smith's *Wealth of Nations*, published in 1776. *(Courtesy of the Lilly Library, Indiana University)*

THE

HISTORY

OF THE

DECLINE AND FALL

OF THE

ROMAN EMPIRE.

By EDWARD GIBBON, Esq;

VOLUME THE FIRST.

Jam provideo animo, velut qui, proximis littori vadis indutti, mare pedibus ingredi-
untur, quicquid progredior, in vastiorem me altitudinem, ac velut profundum inveht ; et
crescere pene opus, quod primâ quâque perficiendo minui videbatur.

LONDON:
PRINTED FOR W. STRAHAN; AND T. CADELL, IN THE STRAND.
MDCCLXXVI.

Volume 1 of Edward Gibbon's *Decline and Fall of the Roman Empire*, one of several influential books issued in 1776, a "banner year for books," according to David McCullough. *(Courtesy of the Lilly Library, Indiana University)*

Critic, author, and educator Harold Bloom: "I don't pretend to be a canon maker. I simply say that this is the best that I can make on the basis of what I've read twice."

Helen Vendler, "the finest close line reader in the world" of poetry, according to the Nobel laureate Seamus Heaney.

Author and critic Christopher Ricks: "The trouble with the word canon is that it sells the past."

Robert Fagles, translator of *The Iliad* and *The Odyssey*: "A really serious translation becomes a new work of art in its own right." *(Courtesy of Mary Cross)*

William H. Gass, author and translator of Rainer Maria Rilke's *Duino Elegies*.

Breon Mitchell, scholar, director of the Lilly Library of Indiana University, and translator of Franz Kafka's *The Trial*.

Elaine Pagels, translator of ancient Coptic texts and author of *The Gnostic Gospels* and *Beyond Belief*.

Engraved portrait of Ulysses S. Grant, used as frontispiece of his *Personal Memoirs*, published posthumously in 1885 and arguably the outstanding American presidential autobiography.

UNCLE TOM'S CABIN;

OR,

LIFE AMONG THE LOWLY.

BY

HARRIET BEECHER STOWE.

VOL. I.

BOSTON:
JOHN P. JEWETT & COMPANY.
CLEVELAND, OHIO:
JEWETT, PROCTOR & WORTHINGTON.
1852.

Title page of Harriet Beecher Stowe's 1852 abolitionist novel, *Uncle Tom's Cabin*, an enormously influential work in the years leading up to the American Civil War.

Rachel Carson's *Silent Spring* ushered in the environmental protection movement.

Silent

Spring

by Rachel Carson

Drawings by Lois and Louis Darling

HOUGHTON MIFFLIN COMPANY BOSTON

The Riverside Press Cambridge

1962

The Communist Manifesto, published in London in 1848. *(Courtesy of the Lilly Library, Indiana University)*

The Matthew J. and Arlyn F. Bruccoli Collection of F. Scott Fitzgerald.
(Courtesy of the Thomas Cooper Library, University of South Carolina)

Matthew J. Bruccoli: "Everything I do, everything I write, everything I buy, everything I collect, has to do with the role of the book in American culture and the profession of authorship."

Daniel Aaron, founding president of the Library of America: "To tell you the truth, I don't like the word canon."

A page from Daniel Aaron's commonplace book.

Top shelf: James Agee's *Let Us Now Praise Famous Men* (1941), a now legendary work that "began as a book with no audience," according to Robert Coles, and Walker Percy's trenchant novel *The Moviegoer* (1961), issued in a first printing of fifteen hundred copies and winner of a National Book Award.

Pulitzer Prize–winning author and psychiatrist Dr. Robert Coles: "My mother preached that everyone needs stories they can live their lives by."

Dr. Sherwin B. Nuland, author of numerous books on medicine, including the National Book Award–winning *How We Die*: "Dickens's only advice to writers was to make them *see* it."

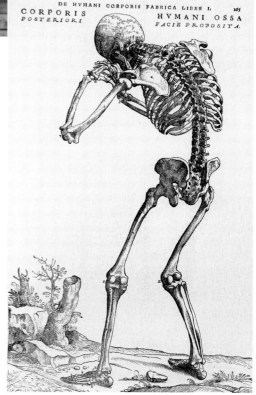

A drawing included in *De Humani Corporis Fabrica Libri Septem* (On the Fabric of the Human Body), 1543, by Andreas Vesalius, celebrated as "the most famous series of anatomical illustrations ever published." *(Courtesy of the Lilly Library, Indiana University)*

Boston pediatrician and author Dr. Perri Klass, medical director and president of Reach Out and Read.

Perri Klass: "One of the things I have come to understand working with this program is just what an impressive thing it is—what a hard job it is—that we have learned to read."

University of Massachusetts English professor Robert Waxler congratulates a graduate of his alternative sentencing reading program for criminal offenders, Changing Lives Through Literature.

The personal library of inventor Thomas A. Edison, West Orange, New Jersey, circa 1920.
(*Courtesy of the Thomas A. Edison Papers, Rutgers University*)

Woodside Villa July 16 1885

I find on waking up this morning that I went to bed last night with the curtains up in my room= glad the family next door retire early — I blushed retroactively to think of it — Slept well — weather clear — warm. Thermometer prolongatively progressive — day so fine that barometer anaethized — breakfasted — Diaried a lot of nonsense — Read some of Longfellows Hyperon, read to where he tells about a statue of a saint that was attacked with somnambulism and went around nights with a lantern repairing roofs, especially that of a widow woman who neglected her family to pray all day in the church   Read account of two murders in morning Herald to keep up my interest in human affairs — Built an air castle or two — Took my new shoes out on a trial trip — Read some of Miss Clevelands book where she goes for George Eliot for not having a heavenly streak of imaginative Twaddle in her poetry — The girls assisted by myself trimmed the Elizabeth collars on twelve dasies, inked eyes nose & mouth on the yellow part which gave them a quaint human look, paper dresses were put on them

Thomas Edison's diary entry for July 16, 1885, in which he discusses his reading of the previous day. (*Courtesy of the Thomas A. Edison Papers, Rutgers University*)

A reading chair designed
and built by aviation
pioneer Orville Wright
for use in his Dayton,
Ohio, study.

A first printing of the German edition of Otto
Lilienthal's *Birdflight as the Basis of Aviation*,
1889, from the library of Orville Wright.

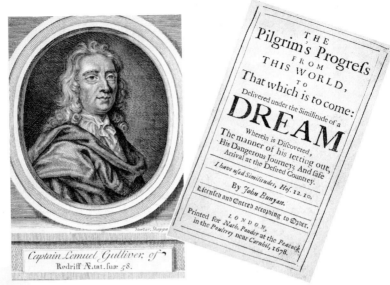

Fanciful portrait of
Lemuel Gulliver,
the purported
author of Jonathan
Swift's satire
Gulliver's Travels,
1776, included
in the Printing and
the Mind of Man
exhibition of 1963.
*(Courtesy of the
Lilly Library,
Indiana University)*

John Bunyan's *Pilgrim's Progress*,
1678, described by the curators
of the Printing and the Mind of
Man exhibition as one of the
"foundation texts of the English
working-class movement."
*(Courtesy of the Lilly Library,
Indiana University)*

Florence Nightingale's 1858
critique of British medical
practices during the Crimean
War, which led to sweeping
reforms. *(Courtesy of the Lilly
Library, Indiana University)*

Sigmund Freud's
monumental treatise
on the interpreta-
tion of dreams, 1900.
*(Courtesy of the Lilly
Library, Indiana
University.)*

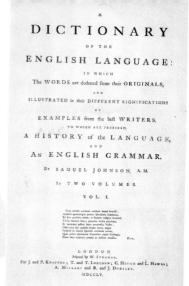

Science and Health by Mary Baker Glover (Eddy), the generative text of the Church of Christ, Scientist. *(Courtesy of the Lilly Library, Indiana University)*

Samuel Johnson's *Dictionary of the English Language*, 1755, according to Lord Macaulay "the first dictionary which could be read with pleasure." *(Courtesy of the Lilly Library, Indiana University)*

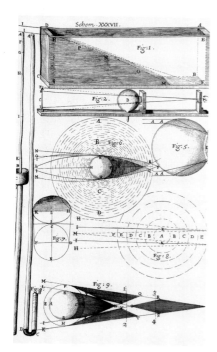

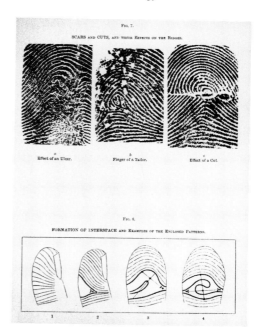

Robert Hooke, sometimes described as England's Leonardo, introduced the world of microscopy in *Micrographia* (1665). *(Courtesy of the Lilly Library, Indiana University)*

Francis Galton's *Finger Prints* (1892) revolutionized forensic investigations and changed forever the way people are positively identified. *(Courtesy of the Lilly Library, Indiana University)*

Cabinet in the American Antiquarian Society, Worcester, Massachusetts, containing many annotated
books gathered in the seventeenth and eighteenth centuries by five generations of
the Mather family, acquired for the institution in 1814 by Isaiah Thomas.

James Dickey, Ring Lardner, H. L. Mencken, Thomas Wolfe, Budd Schulberg, Maxwell Perkins, and others. "Everything connects," Bruccoli repeats as a mantra. "Research begets research. Books beget books."

Another interest includes two collections of British and American posters, literary works, sheet music, broadsides, manuscripts, ephemera, movies, photographs, anything relating to World War I, both named in honor of Bruccoli's father, Joseph M. Bruccoli, a veteran of the war. The first collection was installed in the University of Virginia; the second was created after he had moved to South Carolina. "When I was a child, my father used to take me to Armistice Day parades every November 11, with his medals pinned to my jacket. My father was very proud of his war record. He came back from France with a metal plate in his head. And when he died in 1965, I went to Mr. Wyllie and told him I wanted a memorial for my father, and Mr. Wyllie and I planned the Joseph M. Bruccoli Great War collection at the University of Virginia." After Wyllie died, and after Bruccoli had moved to Columbia, South Carolina, to assume his new position, he attempted to buy back the collection and present it to the University of South Carolina. "The president of the University of Virginia said out of the question, and of course being what I am, I decided, all right, I am going to build a greater, more valuable World War I collection named for my father here at the University of South Carolina. My father is the only person I've ever heard of who has two major collections in the same field named for him." While there is some replication, Bruccoli said the collections are different. "This one is already better than the Virginia collection, and if I can manage not to die for ten years, I think I'll have a fair claim to saying it's the best World War I collection in America."

Yet another consequence of Bruccoli's zeal is a near-complete run of Armed Forces Editions (AFE) published between 1943 and 1947; of the 1,322 titles released in the unprecedented program implemented by the publishing industry during World War II to bring a bit of America to the troops overseas, Bruccoli has rounded up 1,309. "There were two Fitzgerald books, *Gatsby* and *The Diamond as Big as the Ritz and Other Stories*, issued in the series; when I started looking for them, I saw merit in looking for them all. We are, at the moment, thirteen shy of a complete collection." Because these books were meant as entertainment—and 132 million copies altogether were distributed—they were "read to pieces" in many cases. "Easily half the Armed Forces Edition books were sports books, mystery books, westerns—the westerns and sports books are the hardest to find." One of the key elements contributing to the "rediscovery" of Fitzgerald, in Bruccoli's view, was the popularity of the Armed Forces Editions. "Another factor was the publication in 1945 of *The Great Gatsby* in paperback. It was one of the first Bantam paperbacks issued; Bantam began in 1945 with ten titles, this was one of the first ten. At twenty-five cents, it made Fitzgerald affordable."

What Bruccoli declared flatly to be his favorite spot in the Fitzgerald Room is a section of floor-to-ceiling shelves measuring about twelve linear feet in length. "Every one of those books you see there is inscribed *by* Fitzgerald, or *to* Fitzgerald," he said. "Every one of those books Fitzgerald held, and may have read. There are more books inscribed by Fitzgerald on those shelves than anyplace else in the world." These books—known to bibliophiles as "association" copies—have unquestioned antiquarian value, but what makes them of uncommon relevance to Bruccoli is the way they function as scholarly tools. Bruccoli said he has the same high regard for books Fitzgerald inscribed with personal messages to others as he does for original manuscripts. "I learn from them," he said, citing the multiple copies of *Tender Is the Night* he has with handwritten inscriptions by the author. "The failure of *Tender Is the Night* never stopped hurting him. So when he inscribed copies of the book, he would give people instructions on how to read it." To elucidate the point, Bruccoli selected a copy of the novel inscribed to a screenwriter Fitzgerald had known during his Hollywood days, and told me to read the handwritten notation, which I did out loud, into my tape recorder:

> For Ned Griffith, who liked *Gatsby*, with a recommendation he dip into this at page 151, and if he is interested in those chapters, goes back and reads the story, with admiration, from Scott Fitzgerald, Hollywood, 1939.

"You will find that same basic inscription, using other words, but the same content, the same message, repeated at least a dozen times," Bruccoli said. "Fitzgerald was so concerned that people were confused by the flashback structure he had employed that he would go around telling people how they should read the book. I have written three books about *Tender Is the Night*, and those inscriptions have been of enormous help to me because they told me what Fitzgerald's intentions were, and I am a devout intentionalist, surrounded by colleagues who say the author doesn't know what he's doing, and even if he does, it doesn't matter. Whereas I insist if the author doesn't know what he's doing, why read the thing. Of course the author knows what he's doing. Genius always knows what it's doing. Fitzgerald's inscriptions, which help us—not just me, *us*—to understand Fitzgerald's intentions for the works he inscribed are invaluable keys to how to read *Tender Is the Night*, how to read *This Side of Paradise*, how to read *The Great Gatsby*. What he is saying here, with *Tender*, is that it was *his* fault. He's saying, I did it wrong. That's what he's saying—but it isn't true."

Published nine years after *The Great Gatsby* in 1934, *Tender Is the Night*, set in France during the 1920s, examines the deterioration of Dick Diver, a brilliant American psychiatrist, during the course of his marriage to a wealthy mental patient. Regarded as Fitzgerald's most ambitious novel, the book posted disappointing sales, and the critics had mixed feelings as to its literary merits, an ambivalence that "broke his heart," Bruccoli said. Found among Fitzgerald's possessions at his death was a copy of *Tender Is the Night*, disbound, with the chapters reordered, and a note indicating that it was the preferred version of the book. Bruccoli took down another volume from a shelf and handed it to me. "In 1951, Malcolm Cowley edited and published this so-called author's final version of *Tender*, seventeen years after the initial publication. Instead of everybody, all the readers, all the reviewers, saying, 'Boy, now, at long last, we have the book the way it should be,' it made almost no impression at all, because whatever flaws there are in the 1934 edition, that's the way the author wrote it."

Other inscribed books in the Bruccoli collection reveal layered textures of Fitzgerald's character. "Most other authors write 'Best wishes' or 'Good luck.' Fitzgerald almost always managed to say something witty, something warm, and as we just saw, he often managed to say something about the book." He then selected from the shelves a copy of *Taps at Reveille* (1935), the last book of short stories published in Fitzgerald's lifetime, and opened it to what is known as the half-title page, the page that appears immediately before the title page and the one favored by authors who like a lot of blank space to write their inscriptions. I read this one aloud into my tape recorder as well:

For Annah Williamson
—other people were young once, just like you. They broke their hearts over things that now seem trivial. But they were their own hearts, and they had the right to meddle with them in their own way.
F. Scott Fitzgerald
Asheville 1936
Courtesy of D.W.

Dorothy Williamson—the D. W. of the inscription, and the individual who presumably had asked Fitzgerald to inscribe the book for Annah, a relative—had been Fitzgerald's private duty nurse in 1936–37 in Asheville, North Carolina, during an interval in his life known as the "Crack-Up" period, so named for an essay Fitzgerald wrote of the experience. Fitzgerald's spirits had reached their lowest point; sick, often drunk, always in debt, and his professional life in a shambles, he stayed in hotels in the area to be near his wife, Zelda, who had entered Highland Hospital for treatment of her deepening mental illness. "This inscription is for someone he didn't even know," Bruccoli said. "We also have here a full-page inscription to an English lady he knew on the Riviera, reminding her of the good times they had there."

On the infrequent occasions they appear on the open market, first-edition copies of James Joyce's *Ulysses* can command six-figure sums, even more when there are interesting instances of prior ownership. The Bruccoli copy—rebound, unfortunately, but still a first-edition copy published in Paris in 1922 by the American expatriate bookseller Sylvia Beach—includes the following inscription, written on a piece of Joyce's stationery, and pasted on the endsheet by Fitzgerald:

Dear Mr. Fitzgerald: Here with is the book you gave me signed and I am adding a portrait of the artist as a once young man with the thanks of your much obliged but most pusillanimous guest. Sincerely yours James Joyce 11.7.[1]928

Beyond the obvious charm of the message, Bruccoli said there is much more to the interchange than what is contained in Joyce's notation, one he was able to determine only after pulling together other pieces of the puzzle. "This copy has Fitzgerald's annotations; in the section which is written as a series of parodies of British authors by James Joyce,

Fitzgerald attempted to identify the subject of each parody." This is particularly interesting, Bruccoli continued, "since Fitzgerald, unfortunately, didn't as a rule scribble in his books. But the best part is this," and he located a copy of *Portrait of the Artist as a Young Man*, the novel Joyce completed in 1915 before undertaking *Ulysses* and *Finnegans Wake*. "Joyce is saying over there that I'm going to thank you for asking me to inscribe *Ulysses*, and I'm going to throw in *Portrait of an Artist*. Well, here's the copy he threw in." And the copy of the book Joyce "threw in" is inscribed: "To Scott Fitzgerald, James Joyce, Paris, 11-28-[1]928." Not bad, I agreed, not bad at all, and especially impressive, I felt, was that Bruccoli had acquired the two books separately. Now, he wondered, did I want to see another tour de force from the collection? Before I had time to answer in the affirmative, Bruccoli was showing me a copy of Ernest Hemingway's novel *For Whom the Bell Tolls*, containing the inscription: "To Scott—with affection and esteem, Ernest." And while the copy seemed to be in remarkably fine condition, Bruccoli said he believed it to be the one Fitzgerald read. "Unfortunately, as I said, Fitzgerald was not a scribbler. He didn't make notes in the margins, which is a great pity, because it would teach us. It would tell us what Fitzgerald looked for in a book." We saw many more books that day, each one a great prize, each one as good as the last. "You never lose your enthusiasm for this, do you?" I asked, finally. "I'll give you an answer," he said. "I can't understand the people who *aren't* always excited about what they do."

In 1982, after close to a quarter century of sometimes rough-and-tumble deliberation, a nonprofit organization known as the Library of America began publishing affordable editions of the nation's literary landmarks, a good number of them out of print and in danger of being forgotten by a new generation of readers. For Daniel Aaron, one of the founding spirits of the enterprise and its first president, the undertaking brought to reality an idea first proposed many years earlier by his good friend Edmund Wilson, author, critic, and editor of such renown that he has been described as the "last of the great journalists who wrote for the educated man-in-the-street," arguably the preeminent American man of letters of the twentieth century. When he died in 1972 at the age of seventy-nine, the *New York Times* wrote that if there is an American civilization, "Mr. Wilson has helped us to find it, and is an important part of it." Over a prolifically versatile career that spanned five eventful decades, Wilson wrote for *Vanity Fair*, was an editor at the *New Republic*, served as chief book critic for the *New Yorker*, and contributed frequently to the *New York Review of Books*. He also wrote more than twenty books, including *Axel's Castle*, *The Shock of Recognition*, *Patriotic Gore*, *The Scrolls From the Dead Sea*, *To the Finland Station*, several volumes of poetry, a number of plays, and *Memoirs of Hecate County*, a well-received set of interlocked stories that established his credentials as a writer of fiction. In a warm introduction he wrote for a 1977 collection of Wilson's letters, Aaron described his late colleague as the "moral and intellectual conscience of his generation," and included a discussion of Wilson's mercurial politics in his own important study of the 1930s, *Writers on the Left: Episodes in American Literary Communism* (1961).

Their friendship began in 1942, when Aaron supported Wilson's nomination for a lectureship at Smith College in Northampton, Massachusetts, where he was teaching, and it continued for the next thirty years, driven partly by an interest both men had for an approach to learning that takes into account the full range of cultural life, not just literature, though literature is an essential component in the overall concept. In his writing, Wilson did not hesitate to cross traditional boundaries, treating history as literature in *To the Finland Station*, for instance, and literature as history in *Patriotic Gore*, his study of the Civil War. For his part,

Aaron is credited with being one of the earliest practitioners on the college level of American Studies, an interdisciplinary program that is now a staple at every major academic institution in the United States.

Wilson's idea for publishing neglected literary works had been fairly pragmatic, conceived out of sheer personal need as much as anything else, Aaron told me one summer morning in 2004 when we got together at Harvard University, where he has been an emeritus professor of English literature since retiring from teaching in 1983. He still spends full days in his office, usually arriving by bicycle by seven forty-five in the morning to work on his own memoirs, which have been a work in progress since 2000, the year he observed his eighty-eighth birthday. Aaron said that the concept for what would become the Library of America occurred to Wilson around 1958 when he was working on *Patriotic Gore*, a book then a dozen years in the making, that was tracing the literary traditions that emerged in the United States from the time of the Civil War, as reflected in the lives and writings of thirty representative Americans. Regarded by many observers as his most accomplished work, it prompted no less an authority than the late Alfred Kazin to declare Wilson "our American Plutarch." At eight hundred pages, it also was his longest work, and one of the most difficult to research, since its intent was to analyze minor writers of the period along with the more prominent, people like the novelist George Washington Cable, the poet Sidney Lanier, the South Carolina diarist Mary Boykin Chestnut, the Virginia author of short stories, novels, essays, and poetry Thomas Nelson Page, and the St. Louis native Kate Chopin, whose novel *The Awakening* was declared by Wilson to be a "beautifully written" expression of female emancipation, an influential opinion from an eminent critic that helped rescue it from obscurity. "The problem was that Wilson couldn't find the books of the writers that he wanted to review," Aaron told me. "They were all out of print, and nobody had copies of them. We used to talk about this at his house in Talcottville in western New York, up near Utica, where he kept all of his Americana. The place he had on Cape Cod, in Wellfleet, was usually where he kept the French, Italian, Latin, and Greek books, things like that, but the old stone house in Talcottville was all American, and we used to talk a lot about this situation there. I had a kind of antiquarian feeling about certain writers, and we were always in a sense testing each other out, you know, 'I suppose you read this,' or 'You haven't read that, but I have,' that sort of thing."

Wilson's idea was to establish an American venture modeled on a publishing project begun in Paris in the 1920s by the poet André Gide and the publisher Jacques Schiffrin known as the *Editions de la Pléiade*, or Pléiade Editions, a uniform series of impeccably produced copies of the great French writers that were based on the most authoritative texts obtainable. They were printed on fine paper, bound in leather, and published by the eminent Paris firm of Gallimard. The name of the imprint itself was selected to honor a group of French Renaissance poets calling themselves Pléiade, writers who chose not to compose their works in Latin, which was the custom of the time, but in French. The best-known member of the group, Pierre de Ronsard (1524–1585), is regarded in France today with the same esteem that is extended in Italy to Dante Alighieri, a visionary whose singular achievement as a national poet was to break with tradition and write in the vernacular of his native land. Over the years, all the great French writers—Molière, Voltaire, Baudelaire, Gustave Flaubert, Albert Camus, George Sand—would be published in elegantly produced Pléiade editions that set the standard, one that truly could be regarded as the printed record of French literary patrimony.

Not only was Wilson interested in reviving minor American writers, but there were others in the upper tier who were neglected and forgotten, and they concerned him just as much. Most of Herman Melville, for instance, particularly his early romances of the South Seas, *Typee*, *Omoo*, *Mardi*, *Redburn*, and *White-Jacket*, would be among the first volumes to be released in the 1980s, with texts edited by the noted Melville scholar

G. Thomas Tanselle. Even some of the novels of William Faulkner, the author often cited as the preeminent American novelist of the twentieth century, had fallen out of print; his novels would appear in four Library of America volumes in the 1990s, with editions prepared from the original manuscripts by Joseph Blotner and Noel Polk.

"Wilson knew we could never do the same sort of thing as the French, but it gave us a model," Aaron said. One aspect of the Pléiade editions Wilson especially liked was that all volumes were issued in the same shape and size, and all were inexpensively priced. "Wilson tried like the dickens to get it financed, and he wanted me to come in and work with him on it. He wanted little introductions written for them, and we would edit some of these ourselves. Well, the long and the short of it is that he couldn't get the money, and it fell through."

Not least among the obstacles Wilson faced was a rift that had developed with the Modern Language Association (MLA), an alliance of university instructors whose members produce their own scholarly editions of standard American texts, complete with pages of "textual apparatus," as such bibliographical annotations are known—"Wilson called that stuff barbed wire," Aaron said—that often crowd the pages and are difficult to follow, with the added complication of taking years to complete. "The MLA opposed us ferociously, and if we were going to get the federal funding we needed, they were the ones who had to be wooed. Let it be said, too, that Wilson antagonized them. He could probably have ingratiated himself had he been less brusque, but he was very rough with people he disagreed with, and the mainstream publishers were not really in favor of this either. They wanted scholarly editions with long introductions, and indeed they published some of these. They were big, clumsy books—doorstoppers. Wilson thought the MLA was being petty, but they didn't think that way at all. They felt they were guaranteeing quality, and who were we to come in and divert all this time and money that could be used for their own pet projects? The thing is, it was years before any of their volumes appeared in print. They had all these endless committees they dealt with, and then finally would come forth one of these bulky, terribly expensive volumes that nobody would buy, much less read."

Wilson's proposal was not without its lobby of supporters, enjoying the enthusiastic backing of such eminent colleagues as Allan Tate, Robert Lowell, Arthur Schlesinger Jr., Lionel Trilling, and W. H. Auden, but it was turned down first by the Bollingen Foundation at Princeton University as being out of scope to its interests, and then outright by the National Endowment for the Humanities (NEH), which gave its blessing to the MLA. In what could be surmised was a gesture of pique, Wilson in 1968 wrote a lengthy essay of what he called the "factory" approach to literary scholarship that was published in two issues of the *New York Review of Books*, and then released as a separate pamphlet; its brazen title—*The Fruits of the MLA*—left little doubt as to whether or not the powerful critic with a fiery temper had harbored any ill feelings. At the very beginning of the essay, Wilson offered a summary of his doomed attempt to get an American Pléiade project off the ground by reprinting the full text of a long letter he had sent to Jason Epstein, then the editor of Random House, who had expressed some interest in taking on the project in partnership with the Bollingen Foundation. "If we can squander billions of dollars on space rockets, nuclear weapons and subsidies to backward countries," he wrote, "why should not the United States government do something to make American literature available?"

Moving on to the MLA and its projects, Wilson offered an example of the kind of "doorstopper" that Aaron had described in his interview with me, in this instance a Samuel Langhorne Clemens project involving the participation of thirty-five scholars at a major university he chose not to identify: "It seems that eighteen of these Mark Twain wonders are reading *Tom Sawyer*, word by word, backwards, in order to ascertain, without being diverted from this drudgery by attention to the story or the style, how many times 'Aunt Polly' is printed as 'aunt Pully,' and how many times 'ssst!' is printed as 'sssst!' " Wilson cited a number of other projects, each of which carried the boldfaced imprimatur of being "AN APPROVED TEXT" sanctioned by the MLA, to which he wrote, "I propose to disapprove." Among the horror stories he chose to highlight was a forty-five-volume series of books projected on the writings of William Dean Howells, with one that devoted generous attention to *The Wedding Journal.* "In the first place, what is the point of reprinting this first novel of Howells at all? It is one of his least interesting books. What, especially, is the point of reprinting it with thirty-five pages of textual commentary which record the variations of nine of the existing texts?" Further on, Wilson asked: "What on earth is the interest of all this?" And then he offered: "What is important is the finished work by which the author wishes to stand."

With all this fire and bombast and ill will being expressed, the idea for a Library of America did not go anywhere so long as Edmund Wilson was still alive. Finally, in 1979, a nonprofit corporation was established, with seed money provided after all by the National Endowment for the Humanities, with support also forthcoming from the Ford Foundation. Two years later the first titles were announced, featuring authors that nobody could dismiss as second-string—Herman Melville, Edgar Allan Poe, James Fenimore Cooper, Ralph Waldo Emerson, Walt Whitman, Emily Dickinson—though there was some outside sniping all the same, one of the more biting criticisms coming from Francis Steegmuller, the National Book Award–winning translator of the letters of Gustave Flaubert, who took umbrage with a piece he had read in the *New York Times* announcing the series, at that time still named Literary Classics of the United States, a designation he deemed to be an "unnecessarily pretentious title."

Without wishing to agitate my literary compatriots, I would suggest that there can scarcely be, as yet, "an American counterpart" to a body of literature that has accumulated over many centuries and which, through quality, abundance and diversity, virtually proposes itself as a basic library. It may even be doubted whether literary works in the English language lend themselves at all to the Pléiade concept, with its peculiarly French tinge of institutional glory. In France the Pléiade has come to denote a measure of formal "acceptance" for the writers included, with consequent reflection on those excluded. In Britain, by contrast, the excellent editions of "standard authors" issued by Oxford and other publishing houses have never constituted such a restrictive accolade.

Regardless of whether Steegmuller's letter struck a sensitive chord or not, the name was changed by the time the first books appeared in 1982. Over the course of its first quarter century of existence, the Library of America had issued one hundred and twenty-five volumes, beginning safely with authors who wrote principally in the eighteenth and nineteenth centuries—Thomas Paine, James Fenimore Cooper, Washington Irving, Henry David Thoreau, Henry Wadsworth Longfellow, Louisa May Alcott, William Dean Howells, and Sarah Orne Jewett—then moving with measure and deliberation toward the twentieth century, and then indeed well into it, with the James Brothers, Henry and William (most assuredly *not* Frank and Jesse) leading the way, all the while making sure that deserving women were represented—Kate Chopin, Willa Cather, Louisa May Alcott, Edith Wharton, Eudora Welty, Gertrude Stein, Flannery O'Connor—and that people of color—Frederick Douglass, Zora Neale Hurston, James Baldwin, Richard Wright, W. E. B. DuBois, and a volume of slave narratives—were not ignored either. During the early years of the project, the word "canon" was used periodically to describe the choices, but that designation was quickly abandoned, though the unquestioned mandate of the program was to compile a body of important writing that was part of a heritage distinctively American in character.

Aaron said that over time, the perception of what constitutes a canon has changed significantly. "I think it has become now memorable Americana, maybe? Books that reflect a time and an idea? A period? One criterion certainly is that they all have to be well written, and they have to have had some kind of literary influence, those are factors that usually go into it." And he agreed that calling the project Literary Classics of the United States was misleading, too. "We are publishing so many books now that are not technically in the mainstream. I mean, we are doing detective stories and baseball literature, sea stories, and while even though they aren't part of the formal series, they are still being published by the Library of America, so classic is a very dubious word for me too, because it lets you do it with a certain kind of quotation mark. What exactly is *classic* American literature anyway? I suppose the mere act of selecting a work for the Library of America automatically gives it the presumption of being canonical. To tell you the truth, I don't like the word 'canon.'" So what, I asked him, *is* the canon? "A very good question, that," he said. "What *is* the canon, indeed?"

Aaron was born in Chicago in 1912 and moved to Los Angeles with his family when he was a child, growing up in the shadow of the Hollywood film colony, where he caught occasional glimpses of Tom Mix and other celebrities of the silver screen. "Both of my parents were readers, and their library was an important fixture in my life," he said. "When we came to Los Angeles, I was six years old, but my father was an invalid and my mother became an invalid, and they both died when I was ten. My mother was in a sanitarium in California; my father had multiple sclerosis and he held on for a year after she died. They were both dead by 1922. Then I went back to Chicago to live with my uncle, and that was it. My whole world was in reading. I'm beginning now to think about all of these things I've never thought about before. About being an orphan, for example, what it means, and how that compares to people who grew up with mothers and fathers."

What was telling about his early exposure to books, Aaron said, was the totally random nature of what he read. "I would read exploration books, books on New Guinea, books on Tibet. It didn't matter. When I graduated from high school, my uncle gave me a volume of Matthew Arnold's poetry. I was interested in all kinds of things, because I didn't get much out of my public high school; I have little memory of it, except that I didn't like it. It was reading that mattered. Reading was my education." After briefly considering a career in medicine, Aaron chose to study literature at the University of Michigan at Ann Arbor, where a course he took with the noted educator Howard Mumford Jones changed his life. Aaron described Jones in an essay for *Harvard Magazine* as "one of the last of the polymath educators and secular evangelists whose learning was said to be 'encyclopedic,' " a Midwesterner who wrote poetry and fiction, but whose scholarly publications in literature and cultural history made his national reputation. "He would spike his lectures with allusions to forgotten or obscure figures—a geologist, say, or the author of some pathbreaking work on calcareous manures, or a neglected political theorist or economist, or a minor regional novelist whom, he intimated, the serious scholar neglected at his peril. He was drawn to sweeping subjects, and given to writing books with the words 'civilization' and 'culture' in their titles. If neither intellectually nor stylistically 'brilliant,' they were solidly put together, packed with information, and lucidly composed."

Aaron was hooked by this exciting new approach, and when Jones left Ann Arbor to teach at Harvard, Aaron went along with him. There, he was one of the first students to sign up for a new graduate program in the history of American civilization being taught by Jones, F. O. Matthiessen, and Perry Miller, educators not much older than himself who would become powerhouses on the academic scene, introducing fresh ideas that influenced his own outlook on the world. Years later Aaron would recall how senior professors he had studied under when he first arrived at Harvard had been "desiccating" before his eyes, "and in shifting from the still strongly philologically oriented English department to the study of American literature and history, I felt that at last I was about to deal with long-skirted issues and to get a new perspective on my country and my times." The prospect of "exploring American culture on a broad scale," he admitted, was "seductive," and since there were no assigned advisers to report to, "we were expected to work up the materials ourselves." Aaron told me that he went into teaching because it seemed an agreeable way to make a living from reading. He taught at Smith College from 1939 to 1971, spending a good deal of time abroad writing dozens of essays and articles, altogether a full career for many academics, but after that he set up shop at Harvard, and taught for another dozen years.

"There's always been a social dimension with me, and that is probably a weakness, since you do have your enthusiasms, and I'm not so sure that's the best way to be a scholar." Whether or not these "enthusiasms," as he put it, helped or hindered his approach to scholarship, Aaron threw himself into the concept of American Studies, bringing everything he learned to bear in the writing of several books, most notably *Writers on the Left* and *The Unwritten War*. In the introduction to *American Notes*, a collection of his essays published in 1994, Aaron described himself as an "observer and reporter, something of a social historian and literary critic and academic scholar and journalist," and although he conceded having lived through "strenuous decades" in the United States and abroad, "and known or seen or barely missed meeting prominent persons, I have been mostly a spectator looking in from the outside, comfortable in my marginality and unsystematically incorporating what I have seen, heard, and read." In a section he called "Feeding on Books," he described his childhood years reading everything he could lay his hands on, a "heterogeneous mix" that included the *Jungle Book* of Rudyard Kipling, the *Oz* books of Frank L. Baum, the historical novels of G. A. Henty, baseball fiction, and "animal stories of all kinds" before passing through a period absorbed in what his elders referred to as "trash," plowing through these books one after the other. "I am grateful to these accomplished hacks," he wrote, "for supplying me with grit for my literary crop and helping me to appreciate their betters when the time came to concentrate on more arresting and abiding books." All of this, he realized, contributed to his life's work. And while the Library of America may be a monument to Edmund Wilson, "for me it also stands for what was best about the early American Studies movement."

Throughout his life, Aaron has kept a series of commonplace books that have recorded his reading, several of which he had in his office when I arrived for our interview. "I have kept these journals all these years, and for this book I am writing, I use them a lot." Occasionally, he said, they startle him, not with the views they express, but for the person he was when he wrote them. "The truth is that sometimes I'm ashamed of them, but then I say, 'No, everything that you did is you, because you felt this way at the time.' So you can't go against yourself when you say, 'Now, this is ridiculousness and posturing,' because that's just part of who you are."

When he started keeping these journals in the 1920s, Aaron said he felt he was keeping them for his eyes only, but as time has gone on, and as he has worked on writing his memoirs, he has found them to be useful windows through which he can view his own growth as a thinker and human being. "I suppose I had the feeling at the time that eventually someone might discover these things, but gradually, I'm glad to say, it became less a diary than a commonplace book. It records my reading, my quotations. All kinds of things that I have come across, and some of them I find terribly entertaining and amusing."

Having spent part of nine decades as an omnivorous reader of works that have both documented and illuminated American life and culture, Aaron said he has thoughts on whether or not books in and of themselves have the power to make things happen. "I do not think that literature ever changes the world, though I certainly believe that it can give the world a gentle shove," he said. "It's even harder now because there is so much noise going on, if you know what I mean, and there are so many influential things coming in from so many different directions. You would have to have the right occasion, and even something like *The Grapes of Wrath* came at a certain time, you know? But many books that are typically called the *Uncle Tom's Cabin* of this or *The Grapes of Wrath* of that, books that change people's minds, that kind of thing—it's too simplistic. Many of the books that were once regarded in this manner are now forgotten."

Asked for an example, he offered *Progress and Property* by a man named Henry George, and was astonished when I admitted that I had never heard of it. "See," he said. "Go check it out. That book sold something like two million copies in its time, and today nobody remembers anything about it." I checked Henry George out later, and learned that he had been a Philadelphia journalist who settled in California and came to own the *San Francisco Evening Post*. In 1879 he put forth his spirited argument that called for closing the gulf between rich and poor by imposing a single tax on property. "There are dozens of books like this, dozens, intensely read in their day," Aaron had told me, "but they are unknown today." Aaron has tinkered with many titles for his memoir, but nothing is etched in stone, he assured me. When *Harvard Magazine* published an excerpt of his work in progress in 2001, Aaron was calling it *Circlings: A Personal History of the United States, 1912–2000*. When we spoke in 2004, he was leaning toward *The Americanist* as the main title, something, he felt, that is more to the point of his life as educator, writer, and editor. "I take it down at night and reassemble it the next morning," he said, chuckling, hoping that he would have it ready for publication within a year or so, but not making any promises.

Though he has read many thousands of books in his lifetime, Aaron is not sentimental at all about books as artifacts; they are all pretty much the same to him, except for his commonplace books, which he dips into frequently for comfort and insight. The large, folio-sized volume he had on the day we spoke in his Harvard office was opened to a section with excerpts from the aphorisms of Georg Christoph Lichtenberg (1742–1799), whose own disorganized notebooks were called Waste Books. "Here's a man who made a big impression on me, and I have read everything I could find about him. Aphorisms are terribly important to me, you see. You really must read Lichtenberg's aphorisms. They are masterful, and quite wonderful." Aaron seemed oblivious as I snapped a few photographs while he leafed through the record of a lifetime of his own reading. "This to me is fascinating," he said. "I love it, and I read it with great interest. Why? Because this is *my* book."

After a point, he came across something he thought worth sharing, little snippets he had picked up from his reading over the years that he found mildly amusing. "I came up with some names for hurricanes here. Why not have terrible names for hurricanes instead of the pretty ones?" And he read some examples: Attila for A, Beelzebub for B, Caesar for C, and so on through Vulcan and Xerxes. "I haven't got a Z yet," he said, "but I'm working on it."

Aaron said that one of the advantages of having lived a long, productive life is that he has learned to luxuriate in choosing the books he wants to reread. "I don't read systematically these days. I have a pile. I read a lot of things simultaneously, and I like to move back and forth from one to the other. As I get older, I find now, more and more, that I'm not reading contemporary writers anymore, I just don't follow them. Every so often I do, if it's something very much in the news, like Philip Roth's new novel, for instance, that might interest me. But I've been spending this last year just rereading Proust—and I am doing it very slowly. There are so many things that occur to me as I read this, and Proust is one of them. He is really grand, I think he's just the greatest writer, he's like diving into an ocean. One writer I read that way, over a period of time some years ago, was Robert Musil. After I finish with Proust, we'll see. I'm trying to think of who I will do after that."

10.

BORN TO GRAPPLE

The flesh is sad, alas, and I have read all the books.
—STÉPHANE MALLARMÉ, "Sea Breeze" (1887)

The only thinker of consequence I have ever met who could credibly claim that there is not a single book he had ever wanted to read that remained unread, the old grumble of there being "so many books, so little time" of no relevance to him, is Harold Bloom, the critic, author, and educator whose book *The Western Canon* set off a flurry of discussion when it was released in 1994, praised by those who respect his work as a courageous statement against political correctness, scorned by others for its supposed insensitivity to diversity. "I gave you that line from Mallarmé the last time we met," he reminded me when we spoke in the summer of 2004, referring to a conversation of ours six years earlier and a quotation he had shared that I used in my book *Patience & Fortitude*, and which I have chosen as the epigraph of this chapter.

Conceded by admirers and detractors alike as being one of the most assiduous readers in the world, Bloom's great personal hero is Samuel Johnson (1709–1784), acclaimed by generations of acolytes to have been the greatest reader of them all. "Dr. Johnson is the number one for me, to be sure," he said unhesitatingly when I asked him to identify his role models, and then singled out the essayist William Hazlitt (1778–1830) as his number two. "Johnson, it is fair to say, had read *everything*, not just what we call national literature, but anything that an educated mind could read that was available up to the time of his death. He defined a kind of paragon of learning in a literary critic that is today impossible. For Hazlitt, that is equally true, though in his case once you get beyond what you might call high literature and philosophy, which he read copiously, as Johnson did—and of course all questions of art history were of great interest to Hazlitt also—the range and scope are a little less wide than with Johnson. There are other learned people in the English and American traditions I admire, but they are really literary critics, and they are not of the eminence, critically speaking, or in terms of general literary accomplishment, of Samuel Johnson and William Hazlitt. So I suppose yes, I would have to say they remain forever impossible ideals for me to emulate. John Ruskin would be on that list, I think, if we were to press the issue."

Bloom said that what he finds most remarkable about Johnson is the "extraordinary tenacity and ferocity" the famously cantankerous man of letters had as a reader. "There is a wonderful painting of him by Joshua Reynolds in which you can actually see him engaging a book for what interests him while at the same time discarding what he doesn't want from it. I cannot say that I read in quite that way anymore, though I used to be like that. Indeed, I had developed some freakish built-in mechanical aids when I was young that served me through my early manhood and on through most of middle age and early old age, and now here I am in my seventies. My once absolutely insane reading rate has slowed down, unless I deliberately rev it up, and my once—even to me—incredible ability to hold on to a work word for word where it had impressed me enough, even if it were prose, isn't quite what it was anymore. Though still, if I find a really good poem that I've never seen before, it will memorize itself."

The image Bloom described of Samuel Johnson was validated first-hand by James Boswell in his great biography of the doctor, and by other contemporaries of his who left accounts of their impressions. Whenever Johnson picked up a book, Boswell recalled, he "seemed to read it ravenously, as if he devoured it, which was to all appearance his method of studying." One erudite acquaintance who experienced Johnson's aggressive approach to the task had a similar opinion. "He knows how to read better than any one," the poet Mary Knowles exclaimed after watching in awe as Johnson worked through a volume of history that was lying about. "He gets at the substance of a book directly; he tears out the heart of it."

The economist Adam Smith told Boswell that Johnson "knew more books than any man alive." One can only imagine the satisfaction Johnson enjoyed in later life when he was granted free access to the incomparable private collection assembled by King George III, one of the truly outstanding royal bibliophiles through history, whose books quite literally form the core of the British Library in London, a six-story tower of rarities shelved behind glass at the center of the building at St. Pancras that opened in 1998. Boswell recounted the details of a celebrated encounter Johnson had with the king in 1767 during one of his periodic visits to the palace library. King George remarked how he had heard that Johnson made a recent trip to Oxford, and asked if he liked going there. Johnson said that he did somewhat, but added how he always enjoyed returning to London, prompting George—"with a view to urge him to rely on his own stores as an original writer," according to Boswell—to reply, "I do not think you borrow much from any body." Johnson countered by saying that he thought he had "done his part as a writer" anyway, evoking from the king: "I should have thought so too . . . if you had not written so well."

The son of a bookseller with ready access to the written treasures of the world, Johnson read poetry, drama, history, religious tracts, and philosophical treatises in English, French, Latin, and Greek from the time he was a "child in petticoats." He demonstrated his versatility best, perhaps, in the production of his *Dictionary of the English Language*, a virtuoso work of some 40,000 illustrative definitions published in two volumes in 1755, which included 114,000 quotations drawn from the works of "the best writers" in the English language in every field of learning during the previous two centuries, all of whom he had read, digested, and knew thoroughly, many from memory. One biographer, Walter Jackson Bate, has estimated, in fact, that Johnson selected something on the order of 240,000 quotations for the dictionary, and that the final work was pared down for space considerations by the consortium of booksellers who had commissioned it. Lauded in its time as a national monument, Johnson's magnum opus remained the standard lexicon of the English language for more than a century, the only time it could be said that a great dictionary was produced by a single individual, in fewer than ten years to boot. It was superseded only by the *Oxford English Dictionary*, assembled by hundreds of lexicographers under the direction of James A. H. Murray, which began to appear in 1884. Lord Macaulay called Johnson's compendium "the first dictionary which could be read with pleasure," emphasizing that it was an artistic performance in its own right. "The definitions show so much acuteness of thought and command of language, and the passages quoted from poets, divines and philosophers are so skillfully selected, that a leisure hour may always be very agreeably spent in turning over the pages." Bate, one of the most respected literary biographers of the twentieth century, ranked the work "as one of the greatest single achievements of scholarship, and probably the greatest ever performed by one individual who labored under anything like the disadvantages in a comparable length of time."

A good deal of the research was done among the well-thumbed volumes in Johnson's private library, described by Sir John Hawkins in his 1787 life of the doctor as "a copious but a miserably ragged" variety of books. Johnson borrowed and annotated other books freely, and, as Hawkins wrote, returned them "so defaced as to be scarce worth owning, and yet, some of his friends were glad to receive and entertain them as curiosities." Visiting Johnson on April 3, 1776, Boswell told how he "found him very busy putting his books in order, and as they were generally very old ones, clouds of dust were flying around him. He had on a pair of gloves, such as hedgers use." Boswell thereupon described the doctor as a "robust genius, born to grapple with whole libraries." Johnson's general approach, according to Boswell, was to forage "a great deal in a desultory manner, without any scheme of study, as chance threw books in his way, and inclination directed him through them," and he recalled one "curious instance of his casual reading" that Johnson had shared, of a period during his youth that had been marked by a keen curiosity:

> Having imagined that his brother had hid some apples behind a large folio upon an upper shelf in his father's shop, he climbed up to search for them. There were no apples; but the large folio proved to be Petrarch, whom he had seen mentioned in some preface, as one of the restorers of learning. His curiosity having been thus excited, he sat down with avidity, and read a great part of the book. What he read during these two years, he told me, was not works of mere amusement, "not voyages and travels, but all literature, Sir, all ancient writers, all manly: though but little Greek, only some of Anacreon and Hesiod; but in this irregular manner (added he) I had looked into a great many books, which were not commonly known at the Universities, where they seldom read any books but what are put into their hands by their tutors; so that when I came to Oxford, Dr. Adams, now master of Pembroke College, told me I was the best qualified for the University that he had ever known come there."

Two months after Johnson's death in 1784, his private library of 2,922 volumes went on the auction block at Christie's in 650 lots. A woefully inadequate catalog of the sale survived, one that "can claim the distinction of being the worst book catalogue ever produced," according to the bibliographer who edited a copy for publication two centuries later, but it does at least afford an appreciation of the doctor's eclectic tastes. An annotated copy of the catalog that survived describes the library as being "in general in most woeful condition," a not surprising detail given Johnson's predilection to consume his books with great gusto. There were few rarities, only one title from the fifteenth century known as an incunabulum, a 1491 Boethius, further evidence that these were books to be used, not admired as objects. Fundamental to Johnson's approach was that literature exists to be enjoyed, that there is genuine pleasure to be derived from *reading*, a concept that is at the heart of everything Harold Bloom preaches in his books, in his lectures, in his public appearances, and in his interviews. As obvious a statement as that may sound—it is almost embarrassing to state something that should be so apparent to everyone—it is central to the complaint Bloom has for the teaching of literature today on the college and university levels.

"The parameters of the university today are the parameters of what might be called the elite constructionist society," Bloom has said, a view that is shared by the critic Robert Alter in *The Pleasures of Reading in an Ideological Age*, an elegant paean to a precious activity that has been placed on the academic margins, he asserted, by a "bold enterprise of systematic analysis that situates literary studies among the *sciences humaines*." The result is that literature has come to be studied "against the backdrop of philosophy, psychology, anthropology, and linguistics," while "the most urgent issues of politics, history, personal and gender identity" are "boldly exposed" through the examination of literary texts. The "central failure," in Alter's view, "is that so many among a whole generation of professional students of literature have turned away from reading. One can read article after article, hear lecture after lecture, in which no literary work is ever quoted, and no real reading experience is registered." Perhaps most discouraging, in Alter's view, is that college faculties are "increasingly populated with scholars who don't particularly care for literature."

In the summer of 2004, the National Endowment for the Arts released the results of a survey it had conducted over a twenty-year period of seventeen thousand adults, disclosing that less than half of the adult population now reads literature for the first time in "modern history," and these trends "reflect a larger decline in other sorts of reading." Called *Reading at Risk*, and available online (see endnote), the study took into account competition from other media, most obviously the Internet, but the central message was clear—fewer people than ever are now reading novels, short stories, plays, and poetry, with the drop steepest among adults aged eighteen to thirty-four, down 28 percent from 1982 to 2002. Whether any of this is related to *how* literature is being taught today—or, indeed, specifically *what* literature is being taught—was not addressed directly in the study, and is a matter that can be argued on both sides of the issue. But it seems safe to suggest that if fewer people develop what Robert Alter called the "pleasure of reading" early in life, then the likelihood is that fewer still will engage in what the NEA report explicitly called *literary reading*.

What has been described variously as a "culture war," a "war of ideologies," and a "battle of the books" has raged for centuries. Indeed, the phrase "battle of the books" itself derives from a famous essay by the satirist Jonathan Swift, who in 1697 described a pitched battle between the "ancients and the moderns" in literature, with his sympathies firmly on the side of the ancients. At the core of this dispute—which has been waged heatedly and shows no signs of cooling down—are books that a long tradition has held truly *matter* in the world, and whether or not they should be regarded as "canonical," a word that itself sparks considerable controversy.

A lightning rod of controversy for his oft-stated criticism—he, in fact, uses the word "contempt" for the heat he generates in the world of academe—Bloom has found himself in the odd position of being exceedingly well known nationally, but the subject of intense fire from people who under normal circumstances might otherwise be regarded as his colleagues. At Yale University, where he has taught since 1952, Bloom—who observed his seventy-fifth birthday in 2005—takes pride in being a professor in what has been called a "department of one," meaning that he is his own boss and free to teach whatever he deems relevant. Maverick or otherwise, he remains one of the most popular lecturers on the New Haven, Connecticut, campus. When I interviewed Bloom for the first time in 1994, he made it very clear to me that he would continue teaching until carried out the door "feet first in a body bag," a commitment he repeated in similarly colorful language each time we spoke over the next ten years, and which he shows no sign of abandoning, serious medical problems—including major surgery—notwithstanding. "I loathe what has happened to the teaching of literature in the universities, and I want to be there to do it the way I think it should be done, right down to my dying moment. Two, I'm a solitary individual, a lot of my old friends are dead, I find it hard to make new friends, I can't stand being alone all the time, I can't just drive my wife crazy. I think I would get very depressed, and I would go mad and die if I didn't teach. Most of all I will never retire because I have a kind of religious bent of what the future of literature is, and it seems to me that after my generation there will still be some good people teaching, but we're not really going to be replaced."

Bloom said he left the Yale English department in 1976 "when I got the Yale Corporation to appoint me professor of absolutely nothing, you know, Sterling Professor of Humanities Without Colleagues. When I did that, I also wrote a letter of resignation to the Modern Language Association, and another one to the English Institute, in which I blasted both. I said, 'You're not studying literature anymore, you're just agitating. This has become purely political. You are fighting culture wars, and you are destroying aesthetic, humane, scholarly, cognitive, and intellectual value.' The MLA used to stand for aesthetic values and aesthetic interests, but they don't believe in that anymore. They now make *aesthetic* a curse word."

Founded in 1883, the Modern Language Association passed its first century with a minimum of controversy, its members contenting themselves over that time with publishing papers they wrote on various projects that elucidated their specialties, agreeing on standards for scholarly publishing ventures, and getting together every December for a meeting of what theretofore had been a clubby group of professional colleagues. There were occasional spats, as the tussle with Edmund Wilson discussed in the previous chapter documents, but the tone shifted sharply in the 1980s, as traditionalists began to skirmish with new factions—postmodernists, multiculturalists, feminists, Marxists, gay groups—that had become increasingly powerful, all with agendas, all demanding not only to be heard but that they become major forces on faculties, and that courses more responsive to race, gender, and sexuality be incorporated into the curriculum. If there were any doubts at all about conflicting philosophies, they came to the surface in 1988 in an address delivered at the MLA annual meeting by Barbara Herrnstein Smith, a professor of English at Duke University at that time completing a one-year term as president of the organization. Responding directly to a year in which numerous articles had appeared in the popular press reporting what purported to be a "siege on the canon," Smith took note of "a generational shift within the academy" that had tailored courses being taught to reflect "demographic changes" apparent in the country itself. As to the canon itself, she expressed the salient issue: "who shall determine what texts shall be studied and taught, in what spirit, and to what—and of course to *whose*—ends."

To the "demographic and status" shifts in American society that she enumerated—increasing numbers of Asian and Hispanic peoples, increased percentages of black children and immigrant families, more women in the workplace and in the schools, "previously excluded or invisible groups," including "people who are openly gay"—Smith added the point that "a large number of us now practice some form of post–New Critical criticism and engage more or less explicitly with questions of theory and methodology," and less, it would appear, on aesthetics, a word she never used in her address. "Given the increasingly diverse character of contemporary college students," she summarized, "it is no wonder that many of us have revised our conceptions of the primary aims of literary education, revised our courses in order to meet those aims more effectively, and find ludicrous the notion of a uniform, durable set of self-evidently 'best' texts for all to teach and study." On the matter of Great Books—and she used the phrase—Smith offered this, and supplied the emphasis:

> As a result of research activities of the kinds I mentioned a moment ago and others—that is, historical and archival investigations, textual and conceptual analyses, explorations of methods and theories in adjacent disciplines, and so on—we have begun to develop more sophisticated models of canon formation or, as it might be said now, *models of the dynamics of the cultural transmission of privileged texts.* If I use such terms, and do not speak of, say, *the facts we have uncovered about the appreciation and endurance of great works of literature*, it is because, after the past half century of developments in the field, these latter, once familiar, once transparent-seeming terms cannot be used so easily.

In 1994, the Association of Literary Critics and Scholars (ALCS) was established as an alternative to the MLA, declaring simply in a mission statement that "there ought to exist in America an organization devoted to literary studies." The ALCS began to have meetings of its own, with literary papers delivered by its members. In December 2004, as the 120th annual meeting of the MLA was about to convene in Philadelphia, the *New York Times* published an article that poked fun at some of the conference papers that were about to be presented, offering a bit of history that went back to 1989, the year after open warfare was declared. "Basking in this unaccustomed level of public notice, Modern Language Association scholars brought increasingly attention-grabbing papers to the convention through the 1990's, 'queering' the 'canon,' some said, and championing the 'postcolonial,' proposing wild theories about everything from comic books to hip-hop to television and movies," John Strausbaugh wrote, leading him to conclude: "What any of it has to do with teaching literature to America's college students remains as vexing a question to some today as it was a decade ago."

While the banter may sometimes bewilder outsiders with the bitter level of vitriol only academic infighting can engender, it is deadly serious, and can get very personal. One reviewer of Bloom's 1990 book, *The Book of J*—Barbara Probst Solomon in the *Washington Post*—anointed him in the lead paragraph of her piece as "our reigning literary terrorist critic," a clear indication that she was not about to take warmly to the thesis put forth in that book, that a woman was the author of central strands of the Pentateuch, or, for that matter, at least by implication, his continuing fusillade against a power structure that had redefined the essence of education in the United States by declaring irrelevant what has traditionally been regarded as essential elements of our shared culture. And the annoyance with Bloom has manifested itself in other ways, most notably by ignoring, wherever possible, his contributions outside the field of conflict, as it were. A fairly recent example comes by way of Bloom's writings about the Bible. "The scholar who best indicates the joy that should invariably emanate from any serious encounter with the scriptures and the great historical puzzles they enhull, is not, however, one of the guild of full-time biblical scholars," Donald Harman Akenson wrote in *Surpassing Wonder: The Invention of the Bible and the Talmuds*, an erudite exploration of the making of these great texts: "It is the literary critic Harold Bloom." What impressed Akenson most profoundly—and what should resonate with anyone who picks up at random any book written by Bloom—is the astonishing energy he brings to the task at hand, and the full measure of passion that he invests in it.

An expression just beginning to gain currency when *The Western Canon* was published in 1994 was DWEM, short for the Dead White European Males, whose writings were perceived by some to be dominating the core curriculum at institutions of higher learning throughout the United States, Shakespeare, Chaucer, Dante, Cervantes, Dickens, Goethe, Montaigne, Voltaire, Tolstoy, and Proust being some of the more prominent, while squeezing out works of purportedly equal merit that reflected the accomplishments of minorities and women. Taking on what he chose to call the School of Resentment, Bloom reaffirmed his conviction that great books should be read because they are great, with aesthetic originality the only criterion for admission, and not because they support any kind of agenda being propounded at any given moment. "I don't pretend to be a canon maker," Bloom told me in our first interview, an apparent contradiction to some of his detractors, given that he had just devoted 578 pages of *The Western Canon* to discussing what he regarded as the twenty-six cornerstone writings of the tradition, though he qualified his statement. "I simply say that this is the best that I can make on the basis of what I've read twice." But his most provocative point—one he continued to maintain when we picked up the topic in our later discussions—was that literature should be exalted above petty politics and special interests, and that what he was mourning most of all was that there was very little joy left in the reading of superior literary work in college classrooms.

Central to Bloom's displeasure is his belief that literature has taken on a political context, with various factions demanding a share of the curriculum in colleges as a way of projecting their guiding principles and beliefs, and not for reasons of literary excellence or merit. "There are of course some very honorable exceptions, there are real teachers still at many universities, but by and large the universities and the colleges of the English-speaking world are in a deep sense willing victims of that whole phenomenon. This all began in the 1960s, and it is still called by the archaic and inaccurate term the 'counterculture,' and it is not a good thing, but there is nothing to be done about it. The parameters of the university today are the parameters of what might be called the elite constructionist society, and I make very clear that I am saying this as a liberal Democrat who regards the Republican party as the enemy of the human race. So it's not political on my part, quite the contrary." It is for this reason above all others, he asserted, that he intends to go on teaching and writing to the "very end."

To read, according to Bloom, is to first become a "common reader" in the spirit of Samuel Johnson, who coined the expression, and Virginia Woolf (1882–1941), who appropriated it as the title of two volumes of her literary essays. In the opening sentence of her first collection, published in 1925, Woolf cited a passage from Johnson's biographical portrait of Thomas Gray in *The Lives of the Poets*, an observation, she suggested, "which might well be written up in all those rooms, too humble to be called libraries, yet full of books, where the pursuit of reading is carried on by private people." Johnson had expressed abundant pleasure in being able to report that Thomas Gray's great poem of consolation, *Elegy Written in a Country Churchyard*, enjoyed widespread admiration among the general population, not just the rarefied few. "I rejoice to concur with the common reader," Johnson had written, "for by the common sense of readers, uncorrupted by literary prejudices, after all the refinements of subtilty and the dogmatism of learning, must be finally decided all claim to poetical honours." Picking up on that sentiment, Woolf offered the following: "The common reader, as Dr. Johnson implies, differs from the critic and the scholar. He is worse educated, and nature has not gifted him so generously. He reads for his own pleasure rather than to impart knowledge or correct the opinions of others. Above all, he is guided by an instinct to create for himself, out of whatever odds and ends he can come by, some kind of whole—a portrait of a man, a sketch of an age, a theory of the art of writing. He never ceases, as he reads, to run up some rickety and ramshackle fabric which shall give him the temporary satisfaction of looking sufficiently like the real object to allow of affection, laughter, and argument."

Two of my interviews with Bloom were conducted in his New Haven house, with him seated in a cushy leather chair that dominated the center of the living room, surrounded by piles of books, all within arm's reach. Well-stocked shelves surrounded him, with other titles kept in a flat he and his wife, Jeanne, maintained in New York City. Bloom told me that he follows a strict regimen of preparation for reading that combines principles learned from Johnson, Sir Francis Bacon, and Ralph Waldo Emerson, the latter a "third sage of reading" and "fierce enemy of history and of all historicisms, who remarked that the best books 'impress us with the conviction, that one nature wrote and the same reads.' " One endless injunction expounded by Dr. Johnson that he has embraced as his own is to "clear the mind of cant." In his book *How to Read and Why*, Bloom defines "cant" as "speech overflowing with pious platitudes, the peculiar vocabulary of a sect or coven," or more to the point in his worldview, the "academic cant" he has been decrying for the better part of four decades. "I turn to reading as a solitary praxis, rather than as an educational enterprise," he maintained, and stressed just one unalterable injunction: "first find Shakespeare, and let him find you."

One reason Bloom has been able to read everything that interests him, of course, is that he has been reading continually from the age of five, and because he can sustain a pace upward of a thousand pages an hour, more than fifteen pages a minute. "There is no one in the world who has read as much and remembered as much as Harold," a colleague of Bloom's told a writer for *New York* magazine in 1990. "It's scary to watch him read." I asked Bloom if that mind-boggling speed applies to works that he relishes and savors word for word, and he said no, not at all. "I don't speed-read Shakespeare, but I know it all by heart anyway, so it doesn't matter. I've taught all thirty-eight of the plays again and again, and since 1985 or so I've done nothing but teach Shakespeare. So I'm very deep in all of them."

Having read so many books, Bloom is often asked what he flippantly calls the "desert island" question, to choose the one book above all others that he would take with him on a forced exile. "I require at the very least three choices, and that is because a complete Shakespeare is so easy to choose as my number one. Then I want a Bible. It would be hard to choose between the Hebrew Bible and the King James, so I would want a text of both, make that choice 2A and 2B. Then things get tricky, very tricky indeed." Bloom paused here, wrestling between selecting a copy of *Don Quixote* or *The Divine Comedy*. "I really do feel that Shakespeare's only possible rival, though he doesn't quite match Shakespeare in Western literature since the ancient world, is Dante. He scares the life out of me, he fascinates me, and I intend to go on reading him until I die. I intend to go on *learning* from him until I die. But the truth is that I don't love Dante the way I love Cervantes, and it would be very hard to do without a copy of him. So he would be my third choice. Then, if permitted, I would take the Dante, and after that, it would be very hard to say."

When it comes to choosing what he picks up to read at any given moment, Bloom said he never has reason to despair. "I try every day, no matter how tired I am, to go and sort of muse among my own shelves, and just pick up things that I've read and haven't seen for years. I think I *have* read all the books. So now I reread all the books. I have done nothing but read. And I go on reading, and I reread things all the time. I meet with Shakespeare daily. I recite poems to myself all the time as I walk around."

"Why should anyone but a poet care about the problems of American poetry?" the poet Dana Gioia asked in a widely quoted essay published in the *Atlantic Monthly* in 1991. "What possible relevance does this archaic art form have to contemporary society?" Apparent skepticism notwithstanding, Gioia, who was named chairman of the National Endowment for the Arts in 2002, was not joining the chorus of naysayers who have been claiming for decades that poetry has become an exercise of interest to a limited audience; his questions were predicated on a sense of gloom that has been expressed over a manner of artistic expression that has been with the human race for thousands of years. And he was by no means alone in his concern. "Who killed poetry?" the poet Joseph Epstein asked in a 1988 essay. The concern for both of these writers was not that poetry was in any danger of disappearing, far from it, but that fewer and fewer people are making it a part of their lives.

For Helen Vendler, one of the most influential poetry critics in the world, poetry is not something that appeals to every sensibility, but that does not, in her view, diminish the power it has to impact people's lives. "Poetry will never *not* be relevant," she told me in a calm, even voice that suggested she has dealt with this question more often than she might like. "Poetry is one of the evolutionary skills that a certain number of us is born with. Just the way that the composing of music is everywhere, and will never stop, so too the composing of poetry is everywhere. But it is not something that most people can *do*, or can do *well*, any more than composing string quartets, which most people cannot do, or certainly not do well. But there will always be a minor group of people, or a minority of people, maybe what Ruskin calls the 'saving remnant,' who will be able to do this, and also to enjoy it, because just as there are different levels of talent in composition, so too are there different levels of appreciation, from children all the way up to adults."

Beyond the certainty she has of poetry's continued composition and relevance is the question of its enduring power to influence the way we live, and on that score, Vendler said she regards it as one of "many streams" that impact cultural change, and which can never be minutely quantified. "I am not someone who believes that you can point your finger at one person, or one event, and say this made that happen," she said. "The evolution of thought is shaped by all forms of representation of human life, so that whether it is photography or poetry, people see their own lives reflected back at them from many of these media of representation, and eventually, somehow, cultures evolve. Nobody quite knows how. But then they all make mistakes, like probably cutting off the king's head in England in 1649, the fanaticism and religious enthusiasm that allowed that to happen, and then they sort of learned that wasn't such a good thing to do, and so they don't do that anymore. There were eleven thousand highly opinionated pamphlets written during the period when Oliver Cromwell was running England, when everybody had his or her say about the way government should or should not be run, and who can say if those pamphlets were responsible for anything happening? Obviously, that's a massive outpouring of pointed opinion, and they all had some effect, but we can't actually track them."

Committing poems to memory has become something of a quaint conceit in this day and age, an exercise once required in elementary schools by authoritarian teachers not immune to inflicting a dose of corporal punishment every now and then to recalcitrant students, but rarely mandated today, if at all. As a girl growing up in Boston, the then Helen Hennessy was drawn to what for her was a magical form of human expression, and the works that meant the most to her were ones that she routinely "learned by heart." Brought up in a staunchly Roman Catholic household in which she was required to attend Mass every morning, Vendler's initial goal was to attend Radcliffe College, a dream that was quickly dismissed by her parents, who considered instruction at a secular school a mortal sin. She enrolled instead at Emmanuel College in the suburbs of Boston, abandoning thoughts of studying French literature, the idea being fruitless, given the listing of such essential authors as Voltaire, Baudelaire, Molière, and Montaigne on the church's Index of Prohibited Books.

After getting her bachelor's degree in 1954, Vendler turned her full attention to literature, spending a year at the University of Louvain in Belgium as a Fulbright scholar studying French and Italian, followed by further study in the United States, receiving her Ph.D. from Harvard in 1960 in English and American literature. Before joining the Harvard faculty in 1981, she taught at a number of prestigious institutions, including Boston University, Smith College, and Cornell University, lectured at Swarthmore and Haverford colleges, and in 1978 became poetry critic for the *New Yorker*. She has written hundreds of essays and reviews for many publications, a number of which have been collected in *Part of Nature, Part of Us* (1980), *The Music of What Happens* (1988), and *Soul Says* (1990). She has written a dozen important books, including monographs on William Butler Yeats, George Herbert, Wallace Stevens, and Seamus Heaney, and edited an edition of the odes of John Keats; her *Art of Shakespeare's Sonnets* was published in 1997, *Coming of Age as a Poet: Milton, Keats, Eliot, Plath* in 2003. In 1990, Vendler was named University Professor at Harvard, the first woman in the long history of North America's first institution of higher learning to be so honored.

As this truncated résumé suggests, Vendler's reputation is second to none, her influence formidable. "Ms. Vendler is so feared that many refuse to speak publicly about her," Dinitia Smith wrote in a *New York Times* feature that ran under the colorful headline "A Woman of Power in the Ivory Tower," reporting a number of instances where unflattering reviews from the A. Kingsley Porter University Professor prompted one Pulitzer Prize–winning poet, Philip Levine, to deride her as "an elitist the likes of which we've never had before." In her literary criticism, Vendler told me, she tries to stay away from studying any outside forces that may or may not have influenced the creative process, in particular details from an artist's life that others might find pertinent to their understanding, choosing instead to focus her attention on the work itself, "these beautiful whole things," as she is wont to describe exquisitely sculpted poems. "If we were required to know the biography of the poet to appreciate poetry, that would really be too bad, wouldn't it, because we know next to nothing about Shakespeare, to give you just one example," she said. But would it help, I asked, to know the books that Shakespeare read and at the very least sifted through to charge his imagination? She shook her head, an emphatic *no*.

"There are writers that you cannot read unless you know the Bible, I will grant you that," she said. "For instance, so many nineteenth-century poems come straight out of Exodus, because that was a popular text. You can't read Dante without knowing the Bible, and St. Thomas Aquinas, at the very least, and sure, when you see 'On First Looking into Chapman's Homer,' you certainly can see that Keats has been reading the *Odyssey*, and it would be a mistake not to take that into account, or when Keats writes a poem, 'On Sitting Down to Read *King Lear* Once Again,' you have to take that into account. So there are indispensable books, but frankly, you don't really get that much. I was reading the prototype for *Romeo and Juliet*, two very nice little Italian stories, and Shakespeare did change it, of course. So if you want to know what he added, then you want to read them. But it is in no way essential to your enjoyment of *Romeo and Juliet* that you should read the stories that he cribbed it from." There are even cases, Vendler continued, where poets will respond to their own work. "There's a lot that's explicit. Milton wrote 'Il Penseroso' as a response to his own 'L'Allegro.' Now I know that to many people the biography comes first, and the life interests them. I encountered poems in my youth through anthologies, and the anthologies in those days had no biographical information to speak of, so they were all poems that had no life history attached to them. If I liked the poems enough, then, sure, I would go out and get the life history, I would go find some pictures, but that was all subsequent to my attachment to the words."

What Vendler does do—and her skill in this regard is legendary among her peers—is to penetrate with excruciating care the work of art itself. Seamus Heaney has called her "the finest close line reader in the world," using a standard phrase that Vendler said she personally does not like, "though it does have currency," she acknowledged. "I don't like the phrase because people don't understand it. They say, 'Well, I can read, too, and I can understand everything that Seamus Heaney says in his poems.' But poems have maybe fifteen levels, with the simplest being the phonetic level; then you go up to the grammatical level, you go up to the syntactic level, you go up to the arrangement of images level, you go up to the propositional content and statements level, the asseverations, you go to the emotional level where questions of exclamation are different from declarative sentences, whatever. The *context*, as I see it, is the other poems in the same volume, and then the *other* poems written by the same poet. It's a series of concentric circles."

A determined critic who follows this approach ultimately will have read all of a poet's other work, she continued, "and eventually, when you read a single poem, all of these things are reverberating, and you see how they mesh, how the phonetic is meshing with the grammatical, how the images are meshing with the syntax, how the propositions that are being

asserted are being undermined by certain tones of voice in the poem, perhaps, that you register are in contrast to the asseverations. If you feel that
certain *words* have great weight or that certain *images* have great weight,
that is because you have read other poems by the poet. The words shim-
mer and resonate, and even the syntax shimmers and resonates because
you know it's another poem. So you see more in a poem because you are
bringing so many levels of awareness to bear, whereas most people just
bring a single level of awareness, which is, 'What does the poem say?'
And they treat it as though it were an essay with a topic sentence."

Vendler said that she spent a good deal of time in her youth committing poems to memory, no fewer than twenty Shakespeare sonnets by the
time she was fifteen. This came in response to a question I asked about an
oft-quoted observation of hers that a good poem can be a companion
through life, and how the magic had worked for her over the previous
half century. "I learned most of Gerard Manley Hopkins, I learned various things of Wordsworth, lots of Dylan Thomas. This is all when I was
a teenager, when I was in high school, once I woke up to the fact that
poetry was about adult life. I also loved the Psalms because they were
dangerous poems. I was so wild inside myself as an adolescent, and I
didn't have anything mirroring that back to me except the Psalms, so
that's how I learned about emotional life, through poetry, and if you
don't memorize it, you don't have it to take around with you. So as I was
straphanging back and forth to school on streetcars, I needed something
to do with my head, and I would say these poems over to myself. I find
you possess them very differently when you know them by heart."

My first meeting with Vendler was occasioned in 1997 by publication
of the critical evaluation she had just done of Shakespeare's 154 sonnets,
an incisive work that she told me at the time she had put off writing for
decades because she had felt inadequate to the task, quite an extraordinary admission for a woman acknowledged to be among the most articulate, the most influential, the most knowledgeable critics of poetry in the

English-speaking world, especially with an artist she had memorized as a teenager. "I had to be worthy of the challenge," she said. "The first poet I seriously acquired was Shakespeare, but not his plays, not *Venus and Adonis* and so forth, just the lyrics, just the sonnets. So there was Shakespeare when I was fifteen, then there was Keats, and then there was Dylan Thomas, and then there was Hopkins, also when I was fifteen, and then there was Yeats. But with Shakespeare, I had to be worthy of the challenge."

Part of the attraction poetry has always held for Vendler is the economy of transmission, the idea that it is a "beautiful little thing," with the emphasis on *little*. "I do like nonfiction prose very much, especially if it is explaining something to me, but I don't like popularizations of science. I hate the big fact-dumps, though I do like a well-written biography if it's short. What I want is the direct transfusion of emotion, from one person to another, and that, it seemed to me in my youth, only happened with music and poetry. Novels were too diffuse and worldly and often comic or ironic; I wanted the straight narcotic of emotion intravenously transfused. Music did it very much for me, and so did poetry."

For a poet, being "discovered" by Helen Vendler can mean the difference between floundering in obscurity or being embraced as an artist of significance, a reality not lost entirely on Vendler, though she has very definite views on the long-term merit of critical approbation. "I do think brokering is necessary, otherwise we would all be out of business," she joked when I asked her if writers require the intervention of a "champion," a mediator, such as herself, not only to explain the importance of a work but to herald its arrival. "It does help to read something about a mysterious book that opens it up for you more, especially when you are young, and I think as Frank Kermode said in his essay 'What Is a Classic?,' books that many generations can relish. Maybe it is only many generations of writers who have relished Montaigne—maybe it's only many generations of writers who have liked *Don Quixote*—but then the prestige accrues to the books, they do not fade, they are still delightful hundreds of years after they are written, and most books are *not* delightful hundreds of years after they are written. On the contrary, they are boring and dated."

While critics certainly have the ability to recognize literary genius—and in some instances, such as James Joyce and *Ulysses*, for example, which is known to so many readers not from having read the challenging novel at all but through the inspired analysis of mediators such as the scholar Richard Ellmann—Vendler said that she firmly believes that classics are established by other forces. "In the final analysis, it is not critics who create literary canons, it is other writers who create them," she said. "A writer can have published thirty-seven volumes, but if that writer doesn't interest other writers, they will all molder in the library and nobody will ever want to read them again. Other writers—they're the ones who define and continue the canon, because you have to be doing something that your peers admire." The best poems of every century, she said, are "kind of pulled out of the air" by their creators, works of art that are "invisible to everybody except the person who pulls them down." It seems almost inevitable, she continued, that somebody eventually would write timeless works like *Paradise Lost* or *The Divine Comedy*. "It was all just waiting there. Hell, Purgatory, Heaven, all the doctrines, all the scholasticism. Virgil was the poet who took you down to hell. It was just there, and so was the vernacular when everybody else was writing in Latin. But it takes some kind of courage to reach up into the air and pluck down one of those clouds and make it real, and other writers admire that very much. There are little canon makers—a good review, a critic, a teacher who puts the book in the syllabus—but that won't last if writers don't admire it. It has to be writers. It's the same with composers. It's composers who admire other composers. It's artists who admire other artists."

As influential as her criticism is, Vendler said she likes to think of her primary audience as the poet she is writing about. "What I would hope is that if Keats read what I had written about the ode 'To Autumn,' he would say, 'Yes, that is the way I wanted it to be thought of.' And 'Yes, you have unfolded what I had implied,' or something like that. It would not strike the poet, I hope, that there was a discrepancy between my description of the work and the poet's own conception of it. I wouldn't be happy if a poet read what I had written and said, 'What a peculiar thing to say about this work of mine.' "

There were two occasions to note on the morning I arrived in the office of the British critic Christopher Ricks at Boston University. The date was June 16, 2004, the hundredth anniversary of the day Leopold Bloom set out on a Homeric adventure about the streets of Dublin in James Joyce's 1922 novel *Ulysses*, "the most celebrated single day in literature," the *Irish Independent* proclaimed in an excusable moment of national pride, as millions of admirers around the world prepared for a day of revelry. "Happy Bloomsday," I said, and Ricks returned the greeting. "Do you find it curious," I asked, "that what is by far the most celebrated day in the world for a work of literature"—and, indeed, there would be reports from around the globe of various festivals and events marking the occasion to support the claim of the Irish newspaper—"is being celebrated by people who, for the most part, have never read the book?" Ricks said he found the circumstance "comical, but apt," and recalled for me a comment of the British poet and critic William Empson (1906–1984). "Empson once said, endearingly, that he only had to think of *Ulysses* when he was walking down the street, to find himself laughing, happily."

The other event of significance was to offer my congratulations on a book Ricks had just written on the lyrics of the singer Bob Dylan, which had reached an impressively high ranking on Amazon.com that morning, placing it among the company's best-selling books of the moment, quite an achievement for what amounted to a work of literary criticism, albeit one of an iconic figure in contemporary American culture. "I suspect a good deal of that has to do with the subject, Mr. Dylan himself," Ricks said. A champion of Dylan's music since the 1960s, Ricks—like Helen Vendler, widely regarded to be one of the best "close readers" of poetry in the world today—considers the American singer a genius of perception, with lyrics that demand the kind of attention normally afforded some of the deepest thinkers in the land. I had arranged the meeting with Ricks primarily to talk about his new book—I regard the contemplation of song lyrics to be a compelling concept to consider—but we covered a wide range of topics, all of them related to the art and craft of reading.

One of the difficulties in discussing Dylan's work is that it was written to be performed, not to be read on a printed page, a reality that raises the kind of issues confronted when dealing with dramatic literature that playwrights intend to be acted on the stage. "There is a fundamental difference between the two, the page and the stage," Ricks said, "and not just because of performance, for song is a different performing art from drama. I talk in the book a little bit about different systems of punctuation, which sounds like a very small thing but is not. T. S. Eliot was right to say that the difference between poetry and prose is that they are different systems of punctuation. They're not different media, they're not different genres, they have the same medium: language."

The book Ricks wrote about Dylan is very much an examination of what he calls a "mixed media art," music combined with words combined with voice. "I think a literary critic is allowed to attend to the words, provided one does not forget that words are only *part* of the art. The same is true with Shakespeare. It is now questioned by scholars as to whether there was a clear-cut distinction between the stage and the page, something we have always taken for granted with him. There is a school of thought out there now that says one of the reasons we have Shakespeare's plays in such different forms is that there was a move toward preserving them in print, a move that gave us 'unactorably' long versions that were meant to be read, and other versions intended for performance. We are used to saying that Shakespeare wasn't interested in whether his plays would be preserved since he never lived to see them published, but that's not entirely certain anymore."

Ricks's appreciation for Dylan's performances, which he has attended frequently over a period that spans five decades, set in motion a kind of deep reading that some purists might judge to be decidedly unconventional, especially with regard to the comparisons he makes of the songwriter's work and great poetry, placing the musician's songs in company with some of the most accomplished writers of verse of his generation. Writing—and speaking—as a critic who enjoys enormous international respect for the depth of his insights on every manner of literature, Ricks is ever mindful of the potshots he has exposed himself to by picking the oeuvre of a popular singer and songwriter as a literary project. "I'm contrite about having been snobbish," he said when I asked him about the initial reticence he had felt forty years earlier when he first encountered Dylan's work, as against now when he proclaims it brilliant. "I believe it was stupid of me in 1965 to suppose that to take Bob Dylan seriously would be slumming." Ricks was teaching at the time at the University of California, Berkeley, a place were contrary views were very much a part of the cultural landscape, so Ricks could enjoy what he was hearing without necessarily having to openly embrace it, but by 1968 he accepted that he had encountered genius. "I think the moment that you know when something is really good is when there is what I might call two-way gratitude. You're grateful to the song that illuminates something about, say, a person that you're in love with, and then you're very grateful to the person you're in love with, because the love really illuminates the song. So there is this lovely occurrence of what I think of not as a vicious circle, but a beautifully virtuous circle. It is what happens when I read a Robert

Graves poem; Graves's poems have that very beautiful accessibility. You read a Graves love poem and you think, 'Very strange that he so knew this about me, since I've never met him.' "

In his conversation about Dylan, and in his book, Ricks's reading is everywhere apparent, and the connections he makes from one to the other are seamless, and a delight to experience. Dylan's thirst for personal privacy, for instance, is well known, but it is understood here in a manner that acknowledges the vicissitudes of fame. This is how Ricks discussed it with me: "Henry James foresaw everything that would happen to somebody like Dylan. His description of the great actress in *The Tragic Muse* is a description of the price that a person may have to pay for being a celebrity; Miriam Rooth hopes that she will be able to travel around the world and continue to act without becoming a travesty of herself. That is the whole world of celebrity. I take it that the celebrity is like the cuttlefish that announces where it is in order to not be caught. Dylan's decision has been the opposite of Beckett's. Beckett didn't give any interviews, and he wonderfully said to somebody, 'No, not even for you, and in any case I have no *views* to *inter*.' The interview is like living death. Dylan has done the opposite thing, which is terrific self-exposure, like Norman Mailer, but at the same time remaining extraordinarily unknown."

I suggested that what Dylan was doing, perhaps, was exposing himself, but revealing next to nothing. "Exactly," Ricks answered. "You expose yourself in order not to reveal yourself. I think he's talked very well in interviews about the dangers of self-consciousness. That is, in a way about—how shall I put this?—about the dangers of self-knowledge. We tend to say 'know thyself,' this is an aspiration. But it's difficult to know things without becoming *knowing* about them. That is, just as we want people to be self-conscious but not *self-conscious*, we want people to know themselves, but not to suppose that they're knowable. One of the things I hate in Rousseau is that he thinks he knows himself. He begins as though he really knows himself. I don't think he did know himself, and one of the things he didn't know was how unknowable you are, even to yourself. I mean Proust is wonderful, isn't he, on this? Is this the person you really want to deceive all the time: you? So that I think there's a certain kind of self-knowledge and self-understanding that Dylan would think comes between you and felicity, this being something that happens by a kind of chance. Dr. Johnson loves that term, 'felicity.' A good effect of poetry is felicity. It's something which falls out happily, which you couldn't will into existence, and which wasn't even the consequence of knowing something. Knowing that you would receive grace—I mean, I'm an atheist—but *knowing* that you would receive grace would have to be incompatible with receiving it. The point about grace is that you can't know—you better be prepared if it arrives to recognize it for what it is. Keats writes beautifully about this, that it's as if his best things have been written by somebody else. He can't believe that he wrote them. He says, 'I cannot conceive how I came upon it.' And of course we must remember Blake—'Though they are not mine, I call them mine.' The point is that you don't really know what goes into the making of them."

A graduate of Oxford University and a former professor at Cambridge University, Ricks accepted an invitation to set up shop in Boston partly because he has a love of structure. "I am terrifically in favor of syllabi, incidentally, and one of the reasons I wasn't happy in Cambridge was that there was no syllabus, essentially. Because there is no common body of books that your students have all read, you have to study something that does not depend on any particular books, such as narratology. That is, all novels are in some touch with narratology. For a while there was a war as to what books to study, and then if you can't agree on what books to study, what you agree on is a form of study which doesn't depend on what the particular books are."

On the formation of literary canons, Ricks took particular issue with the word "canon" itself. "What that word 'canonical' immediately does is locate importance in the university. These days the university is the most powerful patron that literature has. But it's not good for the university to be told, or come to believe, that being the most important patron is the most important thing—that is canonical. Nobody ever wondering whether to read a book says, 'Is this in the canon?' No decent human being ever thinks like that. The canon is really a syllabus. When they say, 'Is it in the canon?,' what they really mean is, 'Is it taught? Does the MLA authorize the teaching of it?' The trouble with the word 'canon' is that it sells short the past. It's funny. The word 'syllabus' was an honorable word once because it was frankly pedagogical. The word 'canon' is a dishonorable word because it comes over from the sacred texts. Perhaps I think about canons the way I do about liberty. Liberty is a very good idea, I'm in favor of it. But what crimes are committed in its name? Here, I think, Helen Vendler is right in saying that what matters most is what artists make of previous art. That's how most art stays alive. Canons tend to crush that. I think it cuts you off from the readerly instincts of the people who in the end keep books alive."

Asked to give his version of what, exactly, it means to be a "close reader" of poetry, Ricks said the exercise takes on the form of interpretation. "I sometimes tell my students that it's much easier to *attend* lectures than to attend *to* them. Poetry needs a certain kind of attention, and this, if it's not careful, will sacrifice some very, very important things. So I take it that close reading is predicated on realization. Unless certain ideas and convictions and wisdom are realized in the very words, then all you are talking about is an abstraction or a sketch. So I take it that the close reader's job is to help people notice things they otherwise wouldn't have noticed, and not only noticing things, but noticing relations *between* things that they have noticed."

As a critic of modern poetry, Ricks's influence has been enormous, with recognition from him often seen as a validation of purpose, in no small measure an affirmation, if not outright discovery, of talent. Early essays he wrote about the poets Seamus Heaney and Philip Larkin, for example, have been credited with heralding the arrival of what have become fruitful careers. "I think a lot of that is overstated, the work is the work," Ricks said modestly when I asked him to discuss his role in the process. "I am very pleased to have reviewed Seamus Heaney's first book very favorably, and to have reviewed his second book very favorably, and in general to have continued to believe in his work. I am very pleased to have written what was probably the first essay that was written on Geoffrey Hill, which was in the *London Magazine* a long, long time ago. I am pleased to have written about Samuel Beckett when I was an undergraduate at Oxford in the mid-'50s. That's not so early from Beckett's point of view, but it was pretty much so from the world's point."

Ricks said one experience he found enormously satisfying was the chance discovery of a Victorian Irish poet named James Henry, "whom I started reading only because I was tickled by his not being Henry James, so I took down this book in the Cambridge University Library, where I was browsing. I later learned that James Henry had published, at his own expense in Dresden, in the 1860s, this volume of poetry, which was then presented by him to Cambridge University Library. Well, when I came across the volume it was never opened, the pages were uncut, and this to me was quite poignant. So I thought of this Victorian doctor sending his book of poems from Dresden, and here it was, more than a hundred years later, lying unopened. He was never reviewed by anybody. He got into the *Dictionary of National Biography* as a Virgilian scholar, so it's not that James Henry is totally unknown, but his poetry was in no anthology. Well now, since I included his work in my edition of the *New Oxford Book of Victorian Verse*, he is in quite a few. And he's a lovely poet too, he writes these wonderful openings. There's one that begins, 'By what mistake were pigeons made so happy.' He has an extraordinary view of the world. He's an anti-Christian poet. He's very devout in his human pieties, he thinks that paganism is wrong, but isn't as bad as Christianity at any rate. Well, for me, there is some real pleasure in having recognized something in him, though to suggest that I am the midwife to his work overdoes my part. It's mostly luck, that's what it is. It's the idea of felicity again. Something happens which is a happy happenstance. If I'd been living in Oxford as I did for ten years, instead of in Cambridge as I did for ten years when working on this anthology, I never would have read James Henry, because there is no stack access in the Bodleian Library for scholars, and I'd have never run across it."

Yet another felicitous discovery had taken place in about 1953. "I happened to be in Paris on holiday at a time when Beckett had just published *Watt*. It was brand new, hot off the press. I happened to pick up a numbered copy in the rue de Seine for 29 shillings. I read the first page and I thought, 'This is really weird and funny, and I may be the only person in the world who will have read it.' I mean this was a clear fluke. I could easily enough have been somewhere else that day, but there I was, and that was my introduction to Beckett."

The Dead White European Male controversy that continues to simmer provoked mild amusement for Ricks when I asked him to weigh in on it, and occasioned yet another reasoned observation that drew on insights from his reading. "I think Shaw was right, that next to personal conduct, the most powerfully influential thing is art. It falls short of personal conduct in some respects as an influencer, and in other respects it goes ahead of personal conduct, partly because you can be influenced by those persons who are no longer around. I mean the terrible thing about the phrase Dead White European Males was the opprobrium attached to the word 'dead.' Males? It's never been clear to me why being cloven instead of clustered necessarily makes you terrible. But Dead? The wonderful thing is to be in conversation with people who are dead, and it has many of the advantages of conversation, while being free of the many disadvantages of conversation. It's got a wonderful disinterestedness to it."

The idea of conversing with the dead, needless to say, prompted me to ask whether Ricks indulges in such an exercise. "I think so," he said after some thought, and answered by expressing satisfaction in a review of his Dylan book that had just appeared in the *New York Times*, which had taken note of his tendency to "put the poems" of disparate artists together in tandem for scrutiny, be they John Keats, T. S. Eliot, Alfred, Lord Tennyson, Philip Larkin, or D. H. Lawrence. "That reviewer felt that I am interested in the ways in which artists speak to one another. It might be a Donne poem talking to a Dylan song, for instance, and that observation pleases me because I *did* set them up so that they are in conversation, which is different from saying that the one *alludes* to the other. That is, there is a kind of conversation going on across the generations. Somebody says, 'Come, Madam, come, all rest my powers defy,/ Until I labour, I in labour lie.' Well, there is a relation between that, and 'Lay, Lady, Lay.' 'Come, Madam, come' returns. It doesn't matter to me whether Dylan knows Donne—though he has recently said that he does—I'm interested to read *his* talking to dead artists in his songs. I'm sort of pleased about it, actually."

II.

THE HEALING ART

*If I needs must mention something else that I owe to Goethe, it is
this—that a deep concern for justice goes with him everywhere. When,
at the turn of the century, theories began to prevail that whatever had to
be done should be done without regard to the right, without regard to
the fate of all those affected by the change, and since I myself did not
know how these theories which influenced us all were to be met, it was a
real experience for me to find everywhere in Goethe a longing to avoid
the sacrifice of the right in doing what had to be done.*

—DR. ALBERT SCHWEITZER, *Goethe Prize Address* (1928)

A word that crops up again and again in the writing and conversation of Dr. Robert Coles is "character," a sentiment the
Harvard University psychiatrist and Pulitzer Prize–winning
author of sixty books told me springs directly from the inspirational stories and novels passed on to him by his parents when he was a boy growing up in Boston in the 1930s and '40s. "That's my mother talking right
there," Coles said when I asked him to discuss the relevance of the word
to his life and work, and how it continued to animate every reach of his
daily thought. Indeed, it was the question I chose above all others to
begin our conversation one bright summer morning in 2004 when we met

in the kitchen of his Concord, Massachusetts, home, a quaint, comfortable house that looks out on old apple trees, and stands a short distance from the historic dwellings of Ralph Waldo Emerson, Henry David Thoreau, Nathaniel Hawthorne, and Louisa May Alcott, about as writerly a community that anyone with a passion for American literature could want to visit, as many thousands do every year. "That entire fascination I have for character flows from my mother's deep interest in spiritual matters and from the lessons that she gave my brother Bill and myself about behavior, and the idea that *good* is so important. In fact, she often told the two of us, quoting from Emerson, that character is *higher* than intellect. For years I quoted that line in my lectures, that character is higher than intellect; to tell a group of Harvard students that character is higher than intellect, I think, is a grandiose statement to make." Coles told me that his working definition of the word comes from his father: "He said character is how you behave when no one is looking. What he meant is that it's a rock-bottom way of behaving that you either know or ought to know."

Another concept Coles learned from his parents centered on the power narrative has to shape character. "My mother preached that everyone needs stories they can live their lives by," a conviction he said he has professed as his own ever since, using the sentiment as the focus for one of his most compelling books, *The Call of Stories*, and placing it at the heart of the philosophy he embraces as physician, educator, social commentator, activist, and author. "She was making a connection between the reader and the moral implications of a story. Are you going to read from an abstract distance not connected to your life, or are you going to read in such a way that what you read informs the way you live? That is what she was saying, that is what she was doing. I can still recall my mother and father contemplating Jude Fawley, being Thomas Hardy's *Jude the Obscure*, and I remember my mother saying to me, 'This was a young man who had all kinds of abilities, but who was being brushed aside because he was from the poor.' That was prophetic, don't you think, given the work that I would later do?"

Learning values from parents is endemic to the human experience, of course, though Coles carried what he acquired to uncommon heights, evolving from a young man whose driving ambition was to teach high school English to becoming a physician who worked in the Civil Rights movement and championed children's welfare, an author who wrote numerous penetrating books while pioneering a program of university instruction that uses storytelling as a device to develop better, more sensitive physicians. "My father came from England, he was from Yorkshire, and my mother, she was a schoolteacher who came from Iowa, and they both used to read to one another every night, that's how I got involved in all of this, if you want the psychoanalytic part. I got into all this by remembering my parents reading out loud to one another, a practice that was their lifelong passion. My father would read to her from Dickens, especially, whom he loved, and Hardy, of course. My mother loved Willa Cather, Mark Twain, and Booth Tarkington; she was passionate about the great Russian writers and she reread Tolstoy throughout her life. So every night, without fail, he would read aloud to her, and then she would read aloud to him. My father once explained to me that what they were doing was 'drinking from the great reservoirs of wisdom.' He told me they felt 'rescued' by these books, and that they read them with enormous gratitude. I remember my father introducing me to George Eliot, and *Middlemarch*. Now that's a *tough* book. I used to think *War and Peace* was too long, too, and *The Brothers Karamazov* too long. But my parents knew how to excerpt, and when they got to a paragraph or a sentence that meant something—this even now gets me all choked up—they'd read it again, slowly, and then again, so they would together savor the message."

Captured early by the siren call of story, Coles entered Harvard College in 1946 with every intention of pursuing a life among books, a road followed by his younger brother William, who went on to teach literature at the University of Michigan. At Harvard, he studied under Perry Miller (1905–1963), a renowned author of American history and educator whose most influential work, *The New England Mind: The Seventeenth Century* (1939), analyzed the nature of Puritan piety and thought. His other works included *Orthodoxy in Massachusetts* (1933), *The New England Mind: From Colony to Province* (1953), and *Errand into the Wilderness* (1956). With Miller as his guide, Coles began reading the poems, essays, and short stories of William Carlos Williams (1883–1963), a practicing physician in New Jersey who drew on his daily experiences with everyday people to create a distinctive body of writing. "Perry Miller allowed me to study William Carlos Williams at a time when something like that was a controversial act in the English Department. Very few living writers were studied at Harvard in the late 1940s and '50s, believe it or not, T. S. Eliot maybe, but that's about it. Yet Perry Miller still encouraged me. This was quite a singular act on his part." In his junior year, Coles wrote a lengthy essay on *Paterson*, Williams's extended poem of life in America during the Depression, published in separate volumes between 1946 and 1958. When the paper was finished, Miller suggested that Coles send a copy to Williams in New Jersey. "I was reluctant to do this, but Miller said, 'Did it ever occur to you that Dr. Williams just might be interested in what a Harvard undergraduate thinks about his work?' So I sent it to him, and before long I got a letter back from Rutherford, New Jersey: 'Dear Mr. Coles, thank you for writing about me; not bad for a Harvard student.' " More consequential was Williams's suggestion that Coles "drop in" for a visit if he ever found himself in the neighborhood, an offer that proved irresistible.

Up until then, medical school was the furthest thought from his mind. "I wrote a fan letter, that's really all that it was, but it changed everything for me," Coles said. "We developed a friendship that lasted until he died. When I visited him he invited me to tag along on his medical rounds to the tenements. I was so impressed, so enamored of his way of dealing with life that when he suggested I think about medical school, I frantically squeezed in some premed courses my senior year at Harvard, and miracle of miracles, I was admitted to the Columbia College of Physicians and Surgeons. 'There's a lot to keep you busy in medicine,' he had told me, 'and you get to forget yourself a good deal of the time.' I did this only because Dr. Williams thought it was a good idea. I had decided to become a doctor as a response to his life. I also liked the idea that I would be in New York, where I could cross the Hudson River from time to time and say hello, and even if he died—he'd had a heart attack and was not a well man—I would be near where he lived. *Paterson* had that tremendous an impact on my life, and that sense of place was very important to me."

Once admitted to medical school, Coles found the rigorous program not entirely to his liking, but he continued to find succor in reading. "I used to bring books with me into the anatomy lab because I couldn't take a lot of the science without some modification of my own. I'd bring a book of poems to histology or physiology, and I figured if I can just take a minute off and look at a poem, that'll help me get through these labs. I remember one or two teachers in medical school who wanted to share stories that some of their patients had shared about themselves, and that resonated with me. And then of course right across the Hudson was Dr. Williams, dying, but Paterson was there, Rutherford was there, all of New Jersey that he had showed me was there. And I had *Paterson* close to me, and I would read a line, another line, and somehow it was nourishment, it was like vitamin pills helping me feel a bit stronger."

It was during this time also that Coles discovered the work of Dorothy Day (1897–1980), the dynamic founder of the Catholic Worker Movement. "I had been so involved in my own problems and with what I was going to do with my life—I was in despair, really, since I was not all that enamored with medical school—and it was my mother, an Episcopalian with a long-standing interest in the Catholic Worker

Movement, who said to me, 'Why do you think only of yourself? Why don't you do something where you can touch the lives of people who are really hurting?' That was when I made my way to the Lower East Side and sought out Dorothy Day." So he devoted whatever spare time he could muster to working at St. Joseph's House in her soup kitchens; ultimately he would write a biography of the woman, the greatest tribute he feels he can offer people who have impacted his life, a practice he repeated several times, with William Carlos Williams, with the novelist-physician Walker Percy (1916–1990), and with the noted child psychoanalyst Erik H. Erikson (1902–1994), one of the world's leading figures in human development, who described such concepts as "ego identity" and "life cycle" in his work.

With the encouragement of Dr. Williams, Coles tried his hand at pediatrics. After receiving his M.D., he took a residency in Boston, but found the going difficult. "My first work was with children who had polio and who had to face limitations of movement and the possibility of death. I also worked with children who had leukemia at a time when we did not have a cure for the disease as we do now." It was in the midst of this work that his career "veered from pediatrics to psychiatry, because I was so moved by the moral testimony of these children under such duress, facing life's hazards if not the loss of their own lives. They became morally reflective in a way that was very surprising to me, and gave me a great deal of moral pause myself."

Drafted into the air force in 1958, Coles was assigned to a hospital in Biloxi, Mississippi, at which point serendipity intervened once again. During a visit to New Orleans for a psychiatric conference in 1960, he was delayed in a traffic jam caused by a cluster of angry people taunting a six-year-old black girl who was being escorted by federal marshals into a newly integrated public school. Coles would later recall that the child—her name was Ruby Bridges—paused to pray for her tormentors, a demonstration of extraordinary moral courage that moved him so profoundly that he arranged later to meet with the child, setting in motion a lifelong effort to produce The Children of Crisis series of five books that would earn him a Pulitzer Prize in 1973.

As he followed Ruby and other students who were entering Southern schools in the 1960s, Coles found a focus for his life's work, opting to study how children handled the stresses of integration, and employing a method of inquiry based on listening to what children had to say that he christened "documentary child psychiatry." His underlying concern became the psyche of America itself as the country experienced profound social change, undergoing what his mentor Erik Erikson would call an "identity crisis." With his wife, Jane Hallowell Coles, who died in 1993, Coles spent three decades traveling throughout the world, to Northern Ireland, Poland, Nicaragua, South Africa, Brazil, Canada, everywhere they went asking children to share their views on religion and politics, to discuss their fears and anxieties, to speculate on the future. Children responded by telling their stories, and he paid close attention to everything they said. Three volumes dealing with political, moral, and spiritual concerns, collectively called The Inner Lives of Children, would emerge from these sessions, and lead him to write about these experiences in *The Call of Service: A Witness to Idealism.*

While living in the South, Coles discovered the work of the Southern Gothic writer Flannery O'Connor (1925–1964), whose life he also would profile in a biography, and whose writings he would later include in his teaching. His attraction to yet another Southern writer, Walker Percy, was due partly to the fact that both he and Percy had turned to writing deeply moral and philosophical works after receiving their medical degrees. For Percy, the medium of expression was fiction, beginning in 1961 with *The Moviegoer*, a work of enormous power that won a National Book Award in a richly competitive year, finishing ahead of Joseph Heller's *Catch-22*, John Updike's *Rabbit, Run*, and John Steinbeck's *Winter of Our Discontent*. The two men became close friends, prompting

Coles to write a biography that was excerpted in two issues of the *New Yorker*. Percy, in turn, dedicated what would be his last novel, *The Thanatos Syndrome*, to Coles.

Orphaned as a teenager and raised by his father's cousin, the Mississippi writer William Alexander Percy, Walker Percy had been stricken with tuberculosis not long after graduating from medical school, and it was this illness that set in motion an important life in letters, and stimulated a deep interest in the Danish philosopher Søren Kierkegaard (1813–1855), whose pseudonymous writings developed many themes that would later be associated with existentialism. During a lengthy convalescence, Percy spent a great deal of time contemplating the human condition, experiencing an intellectual epiphany that led to the writing of an eminent body of work, and his conversion to Roman Catholicism. "He read and he read and he read," Coles said, "and this was when he went through his spiritual—I won't call it a *crisis*—but his spiritual *life*, let's say. That's when he became truly awake and alive and connected to the reflections in the Bible and the whole tradition. He told me how he had read St. Augustine and Pascal, how he had devoured Thomas Mann's *Magic Mountain* and Dostoyevsky's *The Idiot* and *The Brothers Karamazov*, and of course above all else there was Kierkegaard. Walker used to tell me that before Freud, there was Kierkegaard, that it was Kierkegaard who understood the unconscious and how it works better than anyone else, that he understood how the negatives can become the incendiary fire in a person's life, how accurately he articulated the concept of dread and anxiety in *Fear and Trembling*. So he was a master psychologist in other words, and Walker kept telling me, '*your* buddy Freud'—I'd say, 'Walker, *my* buddy Freud?'—'*Your* buddy Freud would have a lot to learn from Kierkegaard.'"

The key element in Percy's progression from medicine to writing, Coles emphasized, emerged from his reading. "You have to remember that Walker's sense of tragedy was personal. His father was a suicide and his mother had died in an automobile accident when he was young. Through novels he found kindred spirits, writers who could conjure up this world, help him to understand his own world, and also make him feel less lonely, because when you read, you are in the company of another person. The other person's words and thoughts become part of yours, and connect with you, and reading is a kind of human connection. It's an embrace of another person's thoughts, ideas, suggestions, premises, worries, concerns—the whole list of nouns is what I think reading enables, and prompts in a person. We are the creature of language, and through language we affirm ourselves, we find out about the world, including ourselves, through words, and we share with one another through language."

Fittingly, the epigraph to *The Moviegoer* is a line from Kierkegaard, a passage from *The Sickness Unto Death*, regarded as a key text in the evolution of existentialism: "The specific character of despair is precisely this: it is unaware of being despair." In Percy's novel, despair is central to the experiences of his narrator, thirty-year-old Binx Bolling, a prospering New Orleans stockbroker and Korean War veteran who is "floating tolerantly on the surface of life," but yearns for a spiritual catharsis. Because Walker Percy is on my short list of great American writers, one of my prize possessions is a first-edition copy of *The Moviegoer*, along with a letter Percy wrote to the former owner of the book, both of which I acquired from an antiquarian bookseller in 1984. Written by hand in 1979 on a "Walker Percy, M.D." letterhead—with the M.D. crossed out—Percy had offered some words of comfort, from the context of the letter, obviously in response to some communication he had received from the man:

The place you find yourself—which is despair—may not only not be the worst thing that ever happened to you—but may be the best. This sounds presumptuous and may only succeed in angering you but I'll take the chance. All I know is that the bleakest times of my life have also *invariably* been the times when I have most nearly come to myself, felt all of a piece, whole enough and free enough after awhile to know what you want to do. You know what my old friend Kierkegaard said: Consciousness of despair is the beginning of hope. The only real despair is the despair which is not conscious of itself.

When I went to interview Coles in Concord, I brought the letter with me, and presented him with a copy. "That's Walker, always trying to help someone, always caring about others," he said in quiet admiration. *The Moviegoer* is a staple in the enormously popular undergraduate course Coles has taught at Harvard since 1963, which is listed in the curriculum catalog as General Education 105: The Literature of Social Reflection, but known among students as Guilt 105 for its emphasis on writing that seeks to connect moral ideas with daily life, linking stories and experience in meaningful ways. "I had that book with me when I was in New Orleans," Coles said, "and I read it over and over and over again."

Another author Coles requires his students to read is Elie Wiesel, survivor of Auschwitz, author of numerous books relating to the Holocaust, and winner of a Nobel Peace Prize. "I've taught Elie Wiesel for years, and the book of his I assign is *Night*. Because we read *Night*, and because we also read the writings of Dorothy Day, the students nickname that whole part of the course Night and Day. So what we have is Guilt 105, within which we have Night and Day." Coles has also taught courses at Harvard in the medical, business, law, divinity, architecture, and education schools, in every instance using literature to make connections with various academic disciplines. In 1995, he was named the James Agee Professor of Social Ethics at Harvard, a position that meant he was free, essentially, to teach anywhere he wanted in the university, to "wander about," as he put it. The chair is named for the author James Agee

(1909–1955), whose novel *A Death in the Family* won a Pulitzer Prize in 1959, and whose masterpiece of social commentary, *Let Us Now Praise Famous Men*, is the piece of writing Coles tells students taking Guilt 105 to read first. Written as a magazine feature for *Fortune* magazine in 1936, *Let Us Now Praise Famous Men* achieved legendary status for passionately describing life in the deep South during difficult times, and for the quiet rage Agee expressed at the misery he witnessed, and also for the stark black-and-white images of Alabama tenant farmers taken by the photographer Walker Evans. A decidedly unconventional work of literary journalism, the submission was so poignant that Henry Luce, who had assigned the essay, then refused publication, finding it, perhaps, a bit too cutting-edge for the staid readers of his conservative publication; five years would pass before the Agee-Evans collaboration saw the light of day, issued finally by Houghton Mifflin in a hardcover edition that recorded modest sales when issued, and quickly went out of print. Over time, however, the work acquired a certain resonance, a cachet of significance that made it a classic of social commentary, and a forerunner of what would become known as the New Journalism.

"*Let Us Now Praise Famous Men* began as a book with no audience," Coles said. "I always begin my course with that book because it drives the students a little crazy. They don't know what to do with Agee, with the writing, with a lot of those jibes at the intellectual world, that whole chapter he has on education. I just can't do it without James Agee. He is like a spiritual father, he provides the whole flow to the course." The Walker Evans photographs, Coles stressed, are of comparable importance to the total impact as Agee's text. His belief, in fact, that these two forms of print, the textual and the visual, work as a form of synergy, inspired formation of *DoubleTake*, a literary quarterly he established in 1995. "It's pictures and words, words and pictures, since we are creatures of both. When we dream at night, it is images that cross our minds. When we wake up, we use words to convey what those pictures, as they were seen by us, enacted by us in our dreams, mean, and we tell a story, which is the report about what we dreamed. So we are the creature who is constantly picturing things to ourselves at night and during the daytime, when we have what are called *daydreams*. Then we use language to narrate, to tell of, to talk about, those pictures. And in fact Erik Erikson, who was an artist before he became a psychoanalyst and a writer, once said to me he always asked his patients, 'What did you *see* last night?' "

Coles said, in fact, that he uses this approach with his own patients, and that he avoids using the word "dream" in his discussions. "I will say, 'What did you *see* that you're trying to tell me about?' They'll say they had a dream, and I'll say, 'Will you tell me what you *saw*?' I don't say, 'in the dream,' I'll say, "Will you tell me what you *saw*?" And they know immediately to pick up on it. What I'm trying to do is accentuate the visualization side of the dream experience so that it doesn't get lost in a lot of talk, not that talk doesn't do justice to a dream by conveying through words what was seen, but dreaming is a visual experience. Dreaming is seeing things. It's acting, it's talking, but above all, it is *seeing*. Dreaming is a movie with sound. It's not a still photo, it's a moving picture. And it is narrative. Dreams are stories told to us by ourselves, then remembered, and if we are fortunate, and if we work at it—as Freud told us, you have to work at it because you have to 'keep it in mind,' so to speak—then you become your own student."

With a person of such supreme intellect as Leonardo da Vinci (1452–1519), questions of what someone may or may not have read become almost pointlessly irrelevant when measured against what the individual was able to accomplish through initiative and perception, be it as artist, architect, engineer, philosopher, mathematician, zoologist, botanist, anatomist, inventor, or scientist. "To write a book about Leonardo without once using the word 'genius' would be a feat worthy of the French author Georges Perec, who contrived to write a book without using the letter *e*," the British author Charles Nicholl admitted in a recent biography. When dealing with Leonardo, a good place to begin is with the polymath's resolve to constantly learn something new, and to do it through observation, a quality that prompted Kenneth Clark to proclaim him the "most relentlessly curious" person in history.

"Leonardo called himself an unlettered man," Dr. Sherwin B. Nuland, author of several highly regarded books about medicine and its history, said in an interview, and urged me to check out a famous description the Italian offered of himself when confronted with suggestions that he lacked formal instruction. The phrase Leonardo wrote in his notebook, *omo sanʒa lettere*, is clear enough—that he was a "man without letters." What is mildly amusing about this brash confession is that Leonardo did not despair his inability to "quote the learned experts" of the day, in fact he scorned it. "I will quote something far greater and more worthy, experience," he declared, summarily dismissing his critics as "trumpeters and reciters of the works of others," mere charlatans who "inflate themselves" with secondhand information.

Leonardo was too poor to attend university, and while not fluent in Latin or Greek, he is known to have read a few books in Italian translation, and recorded in his notebooks the purchase of an occasional volume or two, including a mathematical treatise of 1494, *Summa de arithmetica, geometria e proportione* (Everything about Arithmetic, Geometry, and Proportions), compiled by the Franciscan monk Fra Luca Pacioli, with whom he collaborated on a later project. Leonardo's fiercely independent nature is appreciated best, perhaps, by the uniquely personal writing style he developed that was disdainful of convention, the setting down of letters on a page from right to left, an accommodation he made with the circumstance of his being left-handed.

"The rules don't apply to people like Leonardo," Dr. Nuland said. "I don't know what combines to make it happen, but the more I learn about him, the more I am convinced that his mind was beyond the brightest intellect of almost any time. He never learned the paradigm—he never learned the way fifteenth-century people saw evidence—and he refused to explain things on a supernatural basis. He didn't know what the supposed scientists were thinking, so he invented his own way of looking at things." In medicine, Leonardo executed anatomical drawings that introduced a new visual language for the description of body parts, and his zeal for direct investigation amounted to a total revaluation of tenets that had been formulated in ancient Greece by Galen, Hippocrates, and Aristotle, and after the passage of fifteen centuries were still the basis of medical education in Leonardo's time.

Leonardo's disdain for "learned experts" aside, there are nevertheless medical texts that can be looked upon as benchmarks, which was the thrust of Nuland's 1988 book, *Doctors*, a work that traced the development of modern medicine through profiles of its most revolutionary advancements. "This book was written in a library, a sanctum containing the lore and the collected reminiscences of the art of healing," Nuland stated in his introduction. A professor at Yale Medical School for forty years with a busy surgical practice, Nuland wrote how he had often found refuge in the school's Medical Historical Library, a "safehouse from daily disquiets and a nurturing spring for renewal and strengthening of purpose." Located just a few minutes from the operating rooms where he spent much of his days, the library was a place where vast holdings of medical literature were readily available to him, and where visitors are still greeted by a plaque bearing a simple admonition: "Here, silent, speak the great of other years." The subtitle of *Doctors* is *The Biography of Medicine*, with the emphasis on accomplishments as expressed in books by those who achieved them. It is not likely that many readers whose interests fall outside the field of medical history will recognize all of the works cited in Nuland's fourteen chapters, let alone swear to have read any of them, but their impact on people's lives is beyond dispute. Nuland began, though, with one luminary whose contributions are universally admired, Hippocrates of Cos, a Greek physician who practiced during the latter half of the fifth century BC and is credited with formulating the earliest system of empirical medicine based on clinical experience; the Hippocratic Oath he composed continues to express the moral standards of the healing arts.

A major exhibition at the Grolier Club in New York in 1995 of One Hundred Famous Books in Medicine—a spiritual descendant of earlier Grolier gatherings showcasing the one hundred most influential books in America and the one hundred books famous in science—featured the writings ascribed to Hippocrates, and displayed three volumes from the fifteenth and sixteenth centuries containing the oldest surviving texts as the first exhibit. How influential was Hippocrates over time? "Aristotle quoted from *The Nature of Man*," Hope Mayo wrote in the Grolier catalog, referring to one of Hippocrates's writings. "Diocles of Carystus and Herophilus of Chalcedon each alluded to several treatises; Apollonius of Citium builds the discussion in his treatise *On Joints* around the Hippocratic book of the same title; and Erotian in the first century AD devoted a dictionary to difficult Hippocratic words; it is in the preface to this work that the first list of Hippocratic titles (about forty) is found. Galen dealt at great length with many of the writings and raised 'Hippocrates' to a quasi-divine status as first discoverer of the medical art." That reputation carried through the Middle Ages, Mayo continued, with Hippocrates appearing in both Arabic and Latin translations. The Greek *editio princeps*—the first *printed* edition—was published in 1526 by the famed Venetian printing house of Aldus Manutius, and a complete translation of the corpus was completed in Ravenna toward the end of the sixteenth century.

Another medical innovator ranking high in both the Grolier and Nuland hierarchies is the French military surgeon Ambroise Paré (1517–1590), a physician who wrote voluminously, with the added virtue

of having written well, according to Nuland. His first published work—
issued in two editions in 1545 and 1551—bears a long title that neatly
summarizes its content: *The Method of Treating Wounds Made by
Arquebuses and Other Firearms, Darts and Such; Also on Combustion Made
Especially by Cannon Powder*. Among the innovations Paré introduced for
gunshot wounds, which up to that time were regarded as poisonous
injuries, was to substitute egg yolk and turpentine for boiling oil, and to
apply arterial ligature instead of cauterization, strategies that were soon
adopted around the world. "Because he wrote in the conversational
French of his fellow surgeons, his works were soon translated into plain
English, German, Dutch, and other languages which were available to
colleagues throughout Europe," Nuland wrote; copies of his books that
survive are usually well worn and tattered from continued thumbing and
consultation.

Among other medical pioneers profiled by Nuland is the Italian
pathologist Giovanni Battista Morgagni (1682–1771), whose monumental work comparing clinical symptoms with postmortem findings, *De
Sedibus et Causis Morborum per Anatomen Indagatis* (The Seats and Causes
of Disease Investigated Through Anatomy), was issued in two volumes
the year he died at the age of seventy-nine, and drew on the vast store of
records compiled during his long career. "There is hardly a phase of
pathological anatomy observable with the naked eye that Morgagni did
not cover," Hope Mayo wrote in her description of the book for the
Grolier Club. Another Nuland notable is William Harvey (1578–1657),
physician to King Charles I of England and doctor of physic at Oxford,
whose *Anatomical Study of the Motion of the Heart and of the Blood in
Animals* (1628) explained how blood is pumped throughout the body and
recirculated, establishing a model for all subsequent research on the heart
and blood vessels. Harvey's second book, *Essays on the Generation of
Animals* (1651), formed the basis for modern embryology.

De Humani Corporis Fabrica Libri Septem (On the Fabric of the

Human Body), by Andreas Vesalius (1514–1564), caused a sensation when it appeared in 1543, not only for the accuracy of its comprehensive text, but also—and perhaps most significantly—for the remarkably detailed woodcuts which remain, according to Hope Mayo, "the most famous series of anatomical illustrations ever published." Nuland said he ranks it in importance to Darwin's *Origin of Species*.

A spiritual descendant of Leonardo and a contemporary of Ambroise Paré, Vesalius was a firm believer in direct observation who argued that Galen had relied too heavily on the dissection of primates, and that the only way to understand human anatomy was to study human beings. Born in Brussels, Vesalius studied medicine in Louvain, Paris, and Venice. Anatomy, he wrote in the preface to his landmark work, known familiarly as the *Fabrica*, must "be recalled from the dead, so that if it did not achieve with us a greater perfection than at any other place or time among the old teachers of anatomy, it might at least reach such a point that one could with confidence assert that our modern science of anatomy was equal to that of old, and that in this age anatomy was unique both in the level to which it had sunk and in the completeness of its subsequent restoration." Not only was Vesalius way ahead of his time in his scientific approach, his perceptive use of illustrations changed forever the design and content of textbooks. Vesalius did not identify the artists he used for the woodcuts, though he commissioned the remarkably detailed depictions of muscles, bones, vessels, nervous system, the viscera, and supervised their production. "If you ask me whether the illustrations in this case are essential to the text—whether the book can stand alone without the drawings—I answer by asking whether the text is really essential to the illustrations," Nuland said. "If truth be known, the illustrations are the core of that book. You could say that Vesalius broke the paradigm that Leonardo never learned, a paradigm that had to be broken shortly after Leonardo by Vesalius."

As a dedicated reader of medical history, Nuland offered the opinion that the one skill physicians must nurture above all others is a willingness to *listen* closely. "The taking and recording of history is a lost art," he said. "It is interesting to me that the emphasis on narrative is relatively new, maybe in the last ten years, and it comes up just at a time when medicine has become so technological that these kids—and by kids I mean students, residents, people in training now to be doctors—feel that they can find out everything they need to know by ordering the right tests. In my day, clinical physicians considered themselves masters of history taking and of the physical exam. Today kids are masters of the menu. They see a patient, the patient has a complaint, an algorithm goes through, this, this, this, this, and depending on what that shows, you order this, this, this, and you are going to get a completely objectified diagnosis. The art of history has lost its value to these people, and they don't realize how important it is. So there's that aspect, which is the taking of the history, allowing the patient to speak, guiding the patient along so that a real description emerges."

It is at that point, Nuland continued, where an element just as vital comes to the fore. "What is important now is that you record what you have just heard as a narrative. It isn't enough to jot phrases down in short bursts simply because you have ten lines on a chart to fill out. I used to say, and I still do, that it's a little bit like producing a play. When you have finished taking a history and recording it, the person reading that history ought to be able to visualize everything about that patient, including the origins of the symptoms, including the image of the patient first doubling up with pain, or the image of the patient just sort of becoming aware that something's not right. You know, Dickens's only advice to writers was to make them *see* it. And that's why I think narrative is so important. By the time that you've recorded that history, you should be able to make them see it. Pain. It's very important to know, did the pain start slowly, rapidly, suddenly, or with immediacy. It is just that sort of narrative that leads you through the diagnosis. We demand in medicine to know what's happening so that we can visualize it in our mind's eye."

Medical schools throughout the United States are now adopting literature courses that nurture this kind of sensitivity. In the spring of 2005, the University of Pennsylvania Press issued a DVD-ROM developed by three University of Oklahoma College of Medicine educators who approach the topic from several directions. Designed as an interactive guide to what is called the "medical humanities curricula," *Medicine and Humanistic Understanding: The Significance of Literature in Medical Practices* is the brainchild of Jerry Vannatta, a physician and professor of internal medicine, Ronald Schleifer, a research professor of English literature and adjunct professor of medicine, and Sheila Crow, an assistant professor of pediatrics and program director for curriculum development at the University of Oklahoma College of Medicine. The DVD includes presentations from a number of prominent physician-writers, Oliver Sacks, Richard Selzer, John Stone, and Rita Charon among them, and includes numerous works of literature. In a section on sensitivity training, for instance, students read and discuss Tolstoy's *The Death of Ivan Ilych.*

The video portion of the program opens with a telling statement of purpose: "The links between storytelling, literature, and medicine can present to physicians—but also to patients—ways in which practices of healing, or alleviating suffering, and of simple caring for those who suffer can be made better and more efficient. They can help us define and in practical ways help to achieve competence in 'narrative knowledge' that contributes, often as much as 'biomedical knowledge,' to the everyday goals of medical practices." Narrative knowledge, they continue, "arises out of encounters with stories and storytelling," and that "through practice, analysis, and discussion in relation to literary narratives, we can become better at recognizing stories, comprehending their implicit parts, rearranging them in new contexts, responding to them, and acting upon the knowledge we have gained. Narrative knowledge and practice, so defined, can help medical practitioners become better physicians and the rest of us to become better patients."

At Yale New Haven Medical Center, where he held the position of clinical professor of surgery in a career that spanned four decades, Dr. Nuland treated more than ten thousand patients. Helping people to get well was the mission, but inevitably there was loss, and over the course of time he developed an acute sense of the eternal process he was observing on a daily basis. It was from that experience that he wrote *How We Die*, an eloquent, erudite, sensitive, deeply informed discourse on the many ways that illness takes away life. "Poets, essayists, chroniclers, wags, and wise men write often about death but rarely have seen it," he explained of his purpose. "Physicians and nurses, who see it often, rarely write about it. Most people see it once or twice in a lifetime, in situations where they are too entangled in its emotional significance to retain dependable memories." A national bestseller in 1994, the book won the National Book Award and the National Book Critics Circle Award for nonfiction. Central to that effort—and central to his guiding outlook on his profession—is that "medicine is never going to be a science, it's an art that uses science, and one of the reasons that I think of it as an art is not just because Hippocrates and the Greeks referred to it that way, because ultimately it is the expression of your scientific knowledge, the wisdom that you acquired by living on this earth, and by your reading and by your previous experience to the illness—I deliberately say illness, and not disease—to the *illness* of one individual, which by its nature has to be distinctive to that individual, so that nobody in history has ever had that particular illness. They may have the same disease, but not the same illness, because illness is the way disease influences the person who has it."

In remarks given on the occasion of receiving his National Book Award in 1994, and later in a memoir he called *Lost in America*, Nuland told how he grew up in New York in the 1930s the son of Jewish immigrants who spoke only Yiddish, and how his teachers in public school changed his life. "We were seven people living in four little rooms in an apartment in the Bronx, and out there was this whole, amazing world. I used to take these long walks with my parents, and I would ask, how do you get into this world. I quickly realized that the key to America is the language, and I owe everything to my teachers. They told us—and there were Greek kids, Italian kids, lots of others in the same boat as me—that we had to read the books they assigned. We had to memorize poetry. We had to get a library card. It's ours, they said, and it's going to be yours. I owe them everything I ever became because they opened this up to us, and I became an omnivorous reader."

And the most important book he read in English, he said, was the King James Bible. "I had been reading the Hebrew Bible because I was brought up in an Orthodox household and had spent a lot of time in synagogues. Then I went to Yale and decided to take a course in the Bible. I didn't know the New Testament at all, so I took a year's course. The first semester was what they called the Old Testament, and the second semester was the New Testament, and of course it was the King James version. The Bible was treated as literature in that course, and it opened my eyes in ways that I had never imagined. It was the cadences, the sounds. The Hebrew Bible only has something like five thousand different words, that's all there are. But the King James Bible, the way they translated it, you can hear it ringing. And if you read it out loud, it's all poetry. You get that rhythm in your head, and it never leaves you, and when I started writing, I realized after a while that the reason I enjoyed reading my own writing was not the language so much as it was the sound of it. Those sounds came to me from the King James version of the Bible."

As physicians who have turned to writing, Robert Coles and Sherwin Nuland joined an interesting fraternity of creative people with medical backgrounds who also wrote literary works for publication, and the tradition is as old as the printing press itself. The French satirist François

Rabelais (c. 1490–1553) is best known for the outrageous popular comedies he wrote of the gigantic buffoons Gargantua and Pantagruel, but after a rocky experience as a freethinking Franciscan monk with humanistic leanings—he was placed at one point in solitary confinement for his persistent reading of secular texts in Greek, Hebrew, and Arabic that were regarded as heretical—he studied medicine at Montpellier, lectured on anatomy at Lyons, and served as head physician at the hospital of Pont-du-Rhône. Other prestigious postings included several tours to Rome as personal physician to the French envoy, though his decision in 1537 to conduct a public dissection of a hanged criminal caused a minor uproar. An inventive man, Rabelais constructed devices for the treatment of hernia and fractured bones, and published his own translations of Hippocrates' *Aphorisms* and Galen's *Ars parva*. But it was his ribald, outrageous irreverence that occasioned coinage of the adjective *Rabelaisian* to evoke a lusty sense of humor and that managed to get all of his works placed on the Vatican's Index of Forbidden Books, quite an accomplishment for a former man of the cloth. In the "author's epistolary dedicatory" address to the fourth book of *Gargantua and Pantagruel*, Rabelais asserted that he was motivated to write his satiric tales partly to amuse his patients, having learned "that many languishing, sick, and disconsolate persons, perusing them, have deceived their grief, passed their time merrily, and been inspired with new joy and comfort." Rabelais died in Paris, his final words, if accurately reported by Pierre Antoine Motteux, his first biographer, entirely in character: "I am going to seek a great perhaps; draw the curtain, the farce is played out."

In seventeenth-century Britain, the writings of Sir Thomas Browne (1605–1682) include *Religio Medici* (A Doctor's Religion), a philosophical meditation in which the Norwich physician, philosopher, and essayist asserted the right to rely on his own reason in cases where guidance was not forthcoming from Scripture. Never overtly intended for public distribution—Samuel Johnson expressed mixed feelings on the author's intent—

the first two editions of the treatise nevertheless were published without the author's permission, then followed by twenty editions during his lifetime that were authorized. It remained in print continuously through the eighteenth century, and was translated into Latin, Dutch, French, German, and Italian. In his biographical essay of Browne, Dr. Johnson wrote that the *Religio Medici* was no sooner published "than it excited the attention of the public, by the novelty of paradoxes, the dignity of sentiment, the quick succession of images, the multitude of abstruse allusions, the subtlety of disquisition, and the strength of language."

It was these very qualities that made Browne's meditation a particular favorite of Dr. William Osler (1849–1919), the first professor of medicine at McGill University in Montreal, Canada, and author of *The Principles and Practice of Medicine* (1892), a standard textbook for more than thirty years. A consummate bibliophile, Osler's gift to McGill of his eight thousand rare medical books became the core of a specialized library that now contains forty-three thousand books. In a recent biography of Osler, Michael Bliss wrote how the man some regard as the "most famous physician of the nineteenth century" found in the *Religio Medici* "a stylistically beautiful, intellectually complex, profoundly tolerant, and, for him, richly satisfying argument." As a follower of both revealed religion and the mysteries of nature, Browne had written what for Osler was an inspirational work that anticipated arguments for the reconciliation of Christianity and human reason. "Aphoristic and elusive, the *Religio* requires and repays reading. During his life Osler came to use it virtually as a surrogate Bible. Eventually he knew the *Religio* and Browne's other writings almost as well as his parents knew their Old and New Testaments."

Browne, like Osler more than two hundred years after him, was a serious bibliophile and collector of books, so devoted to the volumes he had gathered with taste and discrimination throughout his life that at his death, on his seventy-seventh birthday in 1682, it was learned that he had made the following declaration in his will: "On my coffin when in the grave I desire may be deposited in its leather case or coffin my Elsevier's Horace," a book, he wrote, that had been "worn out with and by me." What remained of his library—and it was regarded as among the strongest of the day—made its way ultimately to the auction tables, being sold off in 1711, though the contents were recorded in a catalog. Among those attending the London sale were Jonathan Swift and buyers bidding on behalf of Sir Hans Sloane, one of the original benefactors of the British Museum library, now the British Library, where a number of the books repose.

Though not known at all for any medical triumphs, the poet John Keats (1795–1821) did attend Guy's and St. Thomas's hospitals in London as a student in 1815, taking weekly lectures in anatomy, surgery, dissection, medicine, and chemistry, with every apparent intention of entering the profession. He was licensed to practice as an apothecary and surgeon the following year, and worked briefly as a wound dresser and junior house surgeon, but quickly turned his full attention to the writing of his timeless poetry; his first book, *Poems*, was published in 1817.

The Russian playwright and short-story writer Anton Chekhov (1860–1904), who graduated from the School of Medicine at the University of Moscow in 1884, once confided to his older brother Alexander that medicine was his "legal wife," his writing something else entirely: "I have a mistress, literature. But I never mention her, for those who live outside the law shall perish outside the law." As his fame as a writer grew—Chekhov enjoyed considerable celebrity during his lifetime—the dual identity was scrupulously maintained. "I write and doctor," he wrote elsewhere, describing not only his daily routine but his principal interests.

Other notable writers and poets who either trained in medicine or practiced it without formal instruction include: John Locke (1632–1704), Tobias Smollett (1721–1771), Oliver Goldsmith (1730–1774), George

Crabbe (1754–1832), Friedrich von Schiller (1759–1805), Oliver Wendell Holmes Sr. (1809–1894), Arthur Conan Doyle (1859–1930), Mikhail Bulgakov (1891–1940), W. Somerset Maugham (1874–1965), Sir Geoffrey Keynes (1887–1982), and in our time, the Americans Oliver Sacks, Lewis Thomas, John Stone, Michael Crichton, Perri Klass, and Ethan Canin.

Dr. Albert Schweitzer (1875–1965)—humanitarian, philosopher, theologian, lecturer, missionary, organist, winner of the Nobel Peace Prize in 1952, and, by his own description, a "jungle doctor" in tropical Africa—was also a prolific author, whose oeuvre included *J. S. Bach*, a biography of the great composer in two volumes, *The Quest of the Historical Jesus*, an impeccably reasoned inquiry upon which his reputation as theological scholar was established, and a dozen other books, *On the Edge of the Primeval Forest*, *The Decay and Restoration of Civilization*, *Civilization and Ethics*, and *Christianity and the Religions of the World* among them. The debt Schweitzer felt to the writings of Johann Wolfgang von Goethe (1749–1832) was lifelong, and energized his entire philosophy of life. "The great Goethe and Indian humanist saint Gandhi have made the deepest impress on my life and philosophy," he said a week before he died in 1965, expressing a conviction that he had stated on many occasions in his correspondence, in his journals, in his lectures, and in his writing.

Schweitzer's kinship with Mahatma Gandhi is evident to the most casual of students, both men renowned as paragons of peace and principle, each having manifested by word and by practice a deep reverence for life. Schweitzer's profound feeling for Goethe—the author of *Faust* and the sentimental novel *The Sorrows of Young Werther*, the towering figure of Western literature who created lyrical poetry so transcendent it was set to music by Mozart and Bach—was no less sublime or powerful, and one he frequently acknowledged. "I cannot tell exactly the extent and the intensity of Goethe's influence upon me," Schweitzer wrote in a letter to Charles H. Joy, who translated into English and edited for publication four lectures he had given on the writer over a period of twenty years.

On the occasion of his receiving the Goethe Prize in Frankfurt, Germany, in 1928, Schweitzer told how he had come "into touch" with the great writer through a reading of the poem *Harzreise im Winter* ("Winter Journey in the Harz Mountains"), which tells how Goethe set out in 1777 to visit a young acquaintance who had called out to him for help. "And it impressed me wonderfully that this man whom we regard as an Olympian should have set out in the midst of the rains and mists of November to visit a preacher's son who was plunged in deep spiritual distress," Schweitzer said. "I learned to love Goethe, and when it happened that I had to undertake some work in my own life for the sake of some man or other that needed help, I said to myself, 'This is your *Harzreise.*'"

Four years after delivering those comments, Schweitzer was again invited to speak in Frankfurt, this time to mark the occasion of the one hundredth anniversary of Goethe's death. The date was March 22, 1932; the world was in a state of growing apprehension and turmoil, and within nine months Adolf Hitler would become chancellor of Germany. Without citing anyone by name, Schweitzer was clear about the anguish he felt swirling around him in his native country, leading him to wonder whether "we should not let this day pass in silence," deciding nonetheless to "do honor to Goethe today," but with "peculiarly mixed feelings" that he had no intention of disguising:

Proudly we remind ourselves of those imperishable and invaluable elements which we find in him and in his works. At the same time we cannot but ask if he has not become a stranger to us, since the age in which his life and labor fell know as yet nothing of the needs and problems of our time. Does not the clear light that streams from him shine on to the coming days, which once more will reach the heights where he dwelt, without penetrating the dark valley where we live?

Toward the end of his remarks, Schweitzer wondered if "what is now taking place in this terrible epoch of ours" was not "a gigantic repetition of the drama of Faust upon the stage of the world? The cottage of Philemon and Baucis burns with a thousand tongues of flame! In deeds of violence and murders a thousandfold, a brutalized humanity plays its cruel game! Mephistopheles leers at us with a thousand grimaces! In a thousand different ways mankind has been persuaded to give up its natural relations with reality, and to seek its welfare in the magic formula of some kind of economic and social witchcraft, by which the possibility of freeing itself from economic and social misery is only still further removed!" In his summation, Schweitzer suggested that Goethe "is summoned as no poet or thinker to speak to us in this hour. He looks into our time as one most out of place in it, for he has absolutely nothing in common with the spirit in which it lives. But he comes with the most timely counsel, for he has something to say to our time which it is essential that it should hear." Concluding, he quoted directly from Goethe's epic poem *Hermann and Dorothea*, written during the time of the French Revolution:

> *For the bonds of the world are all loosed,*
> *What ties them together*
> *But the need, need alone, the highest,*
> *That now confronts us.*

Thirty years later, in the aftermath of a horrific war that had intervened and scorched so much of the planet, the American author Rachel Carson was so moved by the selfless example and conviction of Dr. Albert Schweitzer and his abiding tenet, "reverence for life," that she dedicated *Silent Spring* to this gentle man, and began her landmark book that presaged a different kind of Armageddon, one brought on by industrial pesticides and pollution, with a quotation directly from him: "Man has lost the capacity to foresee and forestall. He will end by destroying the earth."

REACHING OUT

"But, my dearest Catherine, what have you been doing with yourself all this morning? Have you gone on with Udolpho?"

"Yes, I have been reading it ever since I woke; and I am got to the black veil."

"Are you indeed? How delightful! Oh, I would not tell you what is behind the black veil for the world! Are you not wild to know?"

"Oh! Yes, quite; what can it be? But do not tell me, I would not be told upon any account. I know it must be a skeleton; I am sure it is Laurentina's skeleton. Oh, I am delighted with the book! I should like to spend my whole life reading it, I assure you; if it had not been to meet you, I would not have come away from it for all the world."

"Dear creature, how much I am obliged to you! And when you have finished Udolpho, we will read The Italian together; I have made out a list of ten or twelve more of the same kind for you."

"Have you indeed? How glad I am! What are they all?"

—JANE AUSTEN, *Northanger Abbey* (1798)

As he approached his fifty-ninth birthday in 1964, Jean-Paul Sartre (1905–1980) published a searching memoir he called *The Words* (*Les Mots*), a compact recollection of the first ten years of his life that was centered entirely on an awakening awareness of books. Though by no means the French existentialist philosopher's best-known literary accomplishment—indeed, the headlines Sartre would make that very year came when he declined to accept a Nobel Prize for literature and refused the generous stipend that came along with it—the work offers a revealing window into the making of a formidable intellect and on the myriad ways that reading had shaped a brilliant mind. "I began my life as I shall no doubt end it," he declared, "amidst books."

An only child whose father died when he was one, Sartre and his widowed mother, Anne-Marie Sartre, moved into the apartment of her parents on the sixth floor of a building overlooking the housetops of Paris. His grandfather, Charles Schweitzer—an uncle of Dr. Albert Schweitzer—was a professor of German at the Sorbonne, the author of numerous published works, and a translator of such supreme self-confidence that he "regarded world literature as his raw material." It was this imposing man who took it upon himself to tutor Jean-Paul, whom he called Poulou. Anne-Marie, meanwhile, pampered her son with loving attention, dressing him in frilly clothing, letting his hair grow long, and reading aloud to him constantly from various volumes in her father's eclectic library. "In my grandfather's study there were books everywhere," Sartre would recall half a century later. "It was forbidden to dust them, except once a year, before the beginning of the October term. Though I did not yet know how to read, I already revered those standing stones: upright or leaning over, close together, like bricks on the bookshelves or spaced out nobly in lanes of menhirs." From the time of his first exposure to these wondrous objects, the boy knew that his life would never be the same, and he schemed of ways to have some of his own. "I had found my religion: nothing seemed to me more important than a book. I regarded the library as a temple," and because he had no siblings or playmates to distract him, books were his "first friends." Sartre realized years later that having grown up in a world without other children, he had been "a miniature adult" exposed to thoughts and ideas intended for older people, and while his strict grandfather brooked no frivolity, he had encouraged the child to "breathe the rarefied air of belles-lettres; the Universe would rise in tiers at my feet and all things would humbly beg for a name; to name the thing was both to create and take it. Without this fundamental illusion I would never have written."

During those glorious interludes when his mother read to him, Sartre noticed a dramatic change in her voice. "I didn't recognize her speech. Where had she got that assurance?" Before long he believed that what he had been listening to was not his mother at all—it was the *book* that was speaking to him. "Frightening sentences emerged from it: they were real centipedes, they swarmed with syllables and letters, stretched their diph-thongs, made the double consonants vibrate." The ritual charmed him at first, but soon he "resolved to take her role away" and claim it as his own. Removing a book one day from the shelves, he rushed off to a storeroom and buried himself in the black marks and symbols imprinted on the pages. He was four years old at the time, and the book he had chosen was Hector Malot's novel, *Sans Famille* (No Family), a work that held no special import for him other than it was what might be called today the "enabling" text. "When the last page was turned, I knew how to read," he recalled with clarity. "I was wild with joy. They were mine, those dried voices in their little herbals, those which my grandfather brought back to life with his gaze, which he heard and which I did not hear!" The days and weeks that followed came to him as in a whirlwind. Though he could not under-stand all the meanings at first, Jean-Paul began to write his own words on paper, more often than not adventure stories with himself cast as the hero, but also entries in a diary that he had begun to maintain, and in verse he wrote for the amusement of his incredulous grandfather. "It was in books that I encountered the universe: assimilated, classified, labeled, pondered, still formidable; and I confused the disorder of my bookish experiences with the random course of real events. From that came the idealism which it took me thirty years to shake off."

Another unconventional exposure to reading had a similar impact on a towering figure of the nineteenth and twentieth centuries, the American inventor Thomas Alva Edison (1847–1931), an authentic Horatio Alger character whose early life and meteoric rise to prominence is without modern parallel, with his 1,093 registered patents—the incandescent lightbulb, the phonograph, the motion picture projector, the first electrical generating system, the automatic telegraph, the stock ticker, dozens of devices and concepts that have altered life for billions of people the world over—remaining by far the record for one individual. Born in Milan, Ohio, Edison moved with his family to Port Huron, Michigan, when he was four years old, where his public school education amounted to three short months, an unsatisfactory experience that ended when a teacher declared him to be "addled," and sent him home to his mother. That falling-out may well have been the most fortunate event in Edison's early life, because it was then that Nancy Edison, a onetime Sunday-school teacher, took over and began nurturing her son's sharp curiosity and keen mind with a steady diet of challenging ideas and things to capture his attention.

"My mother taught me how to read good books quickly and correctly, and as this opened up a great world of literature, I have always been very thankful for this early training," Edison told a group of schoolchildren many years later in a talk about his path to success. And Edison's biographers totally agree with that assessment. "Nancy's role in educating her son was the primary parental influence on his intellectual development," Paul Israel, director of the Thomas A. Edison Papers Project at Rutgers University, stressed in a meticulous biography of the inventor, and discussed in an interview with me. A good many of the books Nancy Edison passed on to her son, Israel said, included titles that were already in the family library, put there by Samuel Edison, his father, a local businessman. It was in this manner that young Tom Edison had his first exposure to William Shakespeare and Charles Dickens, and read all of Edward Gibbon's *Decline and Fall of the Roman Empire* and David Hume's *History of England*. An early reading of Thomas Paine's *Age of Reason* had a remarkable influence on the youngster, prompting Edison to remark years later how he could still recall "the flash of enlightenment that shone" from the pages, an affinity for the work so genuine that Edison agreed to write a laudatory preface to an edition of the book issued in 1925 by the Thomas Paine National Historical Association. But the greatest literary influence on him by far was Shakespeare, whose incisive insights into the timelessness of human nature Edison regarded as an important source of inspiration for his own creativity. Israel quoted no less a source than Edison himself: "Ah Shakespeare! That's where you get the ideas! My, but that man had ideas! He would have been an inventor, a wonderful inventor, if he had turned his mind to it. He seemed to see the inside of everything. Perfectly wonderful how many things he could think about. His originality in the way of expressing things has never been approached."

In addition to giving him a full grounding in the humanities, Nancy Edison channeled her son's energy in productive directions, an affirmative response to the boy's burgeoning interests in science and the natural world. When he was nine, she gave him a copy of Richard Green Parker's *A School Compendium of Natural and Experimental Philosophy* (1854), a science primer that described numerous experiments, and "the first book in science I read when a boy," Edison declared years later. When he was eleven, the youngster set up a laboratory in the basement of his family's home, spending hours on end conducting experiments while other children were playing games, spending the money he earned from odd jobs on chemicals he bought at a local pharmacy and collecting bottles, wires, and other useful supplies.

"Edison read very widely, and he never let up," Israel told me.

"Throughout his career, when he was working on various technologies, reading was as much a part of his approach as anything else. There are only two areas in his life where you could say that Edison was extravagant, in demanding the best equipment he could get for his laboratory, and in the books he acquired for his reading." Edison had three libraries, the largest one at the main laboratory in West Orange, New Jersey, which had its volumes shelved dramatically in a three-floor, balconied enclosure that swept around the interior of the building. "Edison saw two things as the source of knowledge," Israel said. "One was nature, which he felt was the font of all new technology, but to understand nature he felt he needed books. They were the most important source of knowledge he had. He was a very pragmatic man, and his pragmatism led him to other reading. He was living a life of practical invention, and if he was going to anticipate people's wants and needs, he had to know cultural, economic, political, and social thinking."

In the project Israel directs at Rutgers, some five million pages of documents are being selected, edited, and prepared for use in a series of books being published by the Johns Hopkins University Press, expected to comprise fifteen volumes. Established in 1978, the Thomas A. Edison Papers Project has been granted access to holdings in every major repository of Edison material. In addition to technical papers and drawings, there are company archives, workshop diaries, notebooks, letters, and Edison's own books, many of them annotated, which until recently have undergone only superficial scrutiny, although two of Israel's colleagues in the Rutgers project, Theresa M. Collins and Lisa Gitelman, have done a preliminary evaluation of the library. In 1998, they prepared a paper, "Reading as Invention: Thomas Edison and His Books," for presentation at a conference organized by the Society for the History of Authorship, Reading and Publishing (SHARP), which they kindly shared with me. Two of Edison's earliest known possessions, they noted in the essay, are books, a copy of Isaac Pitman's *Manual of Phonography*, or phonetic shorthand, and a Latin grammar, both of which he had acquired during his early years as an itinerant telegrapher, and both of which he carried with him from city to city until settling in West Orange. The first book gave Edison the name for his phonograph, though there is no evidence that he ever mastered Latin. "Edison's marginalia suggests that the inventor's reading formed a kind of dialogue," they determined, "though usually a nuanced combination of several dialogues. He read in dialogue with himself, read in dialogue with an author, and read in dialogue with nature." To illustrate this, they referred to a 1920 copy of Albert Einstein's general theory of relativity, in which Edison wrote in the margin of page four: "To this point it is easy to see that Einstein like every other mathematical mind has not the slightest capacity to impart to the lay mind even an inkling of the subject he tries to explore."

It was Edison who coined the phrase that genius is "one percent inspiration and ninety-nine percent perspiration," with reading, Gitelman and Collins suggested, comprising a good portion of the latter. "If he combed the globe, he also foraged along his own shelves and through printers' trade catalogues to find the right geological conditions for certain ores, to find the right chemical compound for specific purposes, to find prices and supplies for equipment, a good published source on this or that." In an 1859 edition of Henry Noad's *Manual of Electricity*, Edison frequently wrote the words "make," "get," and "try" in the margins. From all of this investigation—with much more study of the books still yet to be done—they offered this provisional conclusion:

> Edison did not read in dialogue with an unidentified party, but rather read in dialogue with an unidentifiable party. The result was contradiction. He had a strong, even cranky sense of self, yet in reading he continued to invent himself, suggesting an ego that was loud, not rigid. His perspective was emphatic, not forever inflexible. He turned to his bookshelves with a desire for useful knowledge, part of

his ideology of the practical, and yet in reading he felt free to doubt and correct, as well as to speculate and to delay for further consideration. He read with confidence, that the world was knowable and authors plain spoken, yet he misread, lost interest, got frustrated, let his ego interfere. He looked to books for authoritative information, yet authored himself in their margins.

The triumphant achievement of Helen Keller (1880–1968) to become both a reader and a writer of distinction remains one of the most inspirational success stories of all time, a victory of will and intelligence over extreme disability. Unable to see or hear from the time she was nineteen months old, Keller conquered her drastic handicaps with the determined help of the woman she always called Teacher, Anne Sullivan Macy (1866–1936), who had been persuaded by the Keller family to come south to Tuscumbia, Alabama, from Massachusetts, and work with their child. Helen's mother had read in Charles Dickens's book *American Notes* of the success the Perkins Institution for the Blind in Boston had achieved with another similarly afflicted child, Laura Bridgman. As Keller recalled in her 1903 memoir, *The Story of My Life*, written in both Braille and on a manual typewriter during her junior year at Radcliffe College, the great breakthrough came on April 5, 1887, at the Keller home:

> We walked down the path to the well-house, attracted by the fragrance of the honeysuckle with which it was covered. Someone was drawing water and my teacher placed my hand under the spout. As the cool stream gushed over one hand she spelled into the other the word water, first slowly, then rapidly. I stood still, my whole attention fixed upon the motions of her fingers. Suddenly I felt a misty consciousness as of something forgotten, a thrill of

returning thought, and somehow the mystery of language was revealed to me.

It was only a matter of weeks before the next major advancement came, one that Keller recounted with precision and clarity. "I read my first connected story in May 1887, when I was seven years old, and from that day to this I have devoured everything in the shape of a printed page that has come within the reach of my hungry fingertips." When she went north with Sullivan to Boston for more intensive training, Helen was allowed to "wander from bookcase to bookcase, and take down whatever book my fingers lighted upon" in the Perkins Institution library. At first she just read "parts of many books" that came her way, without finishing any of them in any comprehensive manner, until the day she discovered Frances Hodgson Burnett's *Little Lord Fauntleroy*, "which was the first book of any consequence I read understandingly." By the time she entered Radcliffe, she was reading every manner of text through touch, but that first book forever remained her "sweet and gentle companion." Keller turned to other books of increasing complexity, and everything she encountered was a revelation, every author a bearer of beautiful gifts. "They laid their treasures at my feet, and I accepted them as we accept the sunshine and the love of our friends," she wrote. "Circumscribed as my life was in so many ways, I had to look between the covers of books for news of the world that lay outside my own."

For all the people who refused to believe that a woman unable to see or hear from childhood could read through the miracle of touch—and there were thousands of disbelievers—there were just as many who regarded the eloquence and erudition of a former slave, Frederick Douglass (1818–1895), as a transparent hoax, especially at a time when it was a criminal act in parts of the United States to teach people of color how to read. The release in 1845 of *Narrative of the Life of Frederick Douglass, an American Slave*, published seven years after the great orator's escape from a Maryland plantation to freedom—and sixteen years *before* the outbreak of the Civil War—offered convincing proof to the contrary, and once again it was a thirst to read at an early age that led the way. Tutored by Sophia Ward, the wife of his master, at the age of nine, Douglass was immediately captured by the sound of the woman's voice. "The frequent hearing of my mistress reading the bible—for she often read aloud when her husband was absent—soon awakened my curiosity in respect to this *mystery* of reading, and roused in me the desire to learn," he wrote.

> I frankly asked her to teach me to read; and, without hesitation, the dear woman began the task, and very soon, by her assistance, I was master of the alphabet, and could spell words of three or four letters. My mistress seemed almost as proud of my progress, as if I had been her own child; and supposing that her husband would be as well pleased, she made no secret of what she was doing for me. Indeed, she exultingly told him of the aptness of her pupil, of her intention to persevere in teaching me, and of the duty which she felt it to teach me, at least to read *the bible*. Here arose the first cloud over my Baltimore prospects, the precursor of drenching rains and chilling blasts.

Aghast at the news, "Master Hugh" Auld forbade his wife to continue with the lessons, arguing that literacy would render the youngster "forever unfit for the duties of a slave," that if "you learn him now to read, he'll want to know how to write; and, this accomplished, he'll be running away with himself." The lessons abruptly ended, but there was no stopping Douglass from realizing what he perceived to be his destiny. He vowed that "the very determination" Auld had "expressed to keep me in ignorance, only rendered me the more resolute in seeking intelligence. In learning to read, therefore, I am not sure that I do not owe quite as much to the opposition of my master, as to the kindly assistance of my amiable mistress. I acknowledge the benefit rendered me by the one, and by the other; believing, that but for my mistress, I might have grown up in ignorance."

Since its release in 1945, *Baby and Child Care* by Dr. Benjamin M. Spock (1903–1998)—by general consent the first modern parenting book—has been translated into thirty-nine languages and sold more than fifty million copies worldwide, giving it a range of influence that is superseded in the United States by few other books published since 1900, probably none except the Bible. And it is a book that people own and keep in their houses, usually in affordable paperback editions, not a volume they might otherwise borrow from a public library. Indeed, the title does not even appear on the Online Computer Library Center (OCLC) list of the top one thousand books owned by the 50,540 libraries in eighty-four countries that report their holdings to its database, and the titles that top that list are instructive. In July 2005, the title that weighed in at number one was *not* the Bible—which, with 271,534 copies among member libraries was number two—but twenty-eight volumes of statistical records grouped under one heading called *the census*, with 403,252 holdings reported. The Bible, of course, is by far the more impressive statistic of the two, since it is a single volume that is kept in millions of American homes as well—undoubtedly a majority of them—while it is safe to assume that the number of people owning personal copies of the federal census is so low it is probably impossible to measure statistically.

The Spock book, on the other hand, is not, as these figures suggest, something a mother would normally go to the library to consult, especially with an infant at home requiring her undivided attention. It is instead a volume that by and large is bought for quick and ready reference, some might even say guidance, with the consultation typically coming at a time of pressing need, a humbling reality not lost on Dr. Robert Needlman, a Cleveland pediatrician who updated and revised the eighth edition, which was released in 2004. Several generations of parents, he noted in his preface—and the emphasis is his—have "raised their children *by the book*," which is the ultimate compliment any piece of writing can get, to be regarded, in essence, by several generations of admirers as the "last word" on something, regardless of what that something may be.

Another twentieth-century "self-help" publication that could be argued shares this distinction includes *Alcoholics Anonymous*, a confessional written in 1939 by a man who identified himself as "Bill W." (William Griffith Wilson), and has been known to its adherents ever since as the "Big Book" for the twelve-step program it offers to treat substance dependence. Such a list might also include the low-carbohydrate diet book introduced in 1972 by the late Dr. Robert C. Atkins as *Dr. Atkins' Diet Revolution*; certainly the work compiled by a research team under the direction of Dr. Alfred C. Kinsey and issued in separate studies in 1948 and 1953 under the titles *Sexual Behavior in the Human Male* and *Sexual Behavior in the Human Female*, which for the first time documented in a scientific manner American sexual practices and is collectively known as the Kinsey Report, would have to be considered as well. But Dr. Spock's nurturing advice, and the influence his laid-back philosophy brought to bear on the politics of his time—"Trust Yourself *and* Your Children" was the title of his first chapter—connected with people in all walks of life, and continues to have a significant impact after half a century. The headline that ran over his obituary in the *Los Angeles Times* pretty much said it all: "Baby Doctor for the Millions Dies."

Spock was a hands-on kind of author who insisted that he prepare his own index, a tedious task usually assigned by publishers to others. "I knew I would have a better notion of what words mothers would look for," he explained years later, and he was right, with more than fifteen hundred handy entries keyed to the parenting anxieties of the moment, be it hiccups, insect bites, diarrhea, masturbation, poison ivy, or weaning from the breast. The book has been revised over the years to include medical advances and to cover new problems like the influence of television, and to reflect cultural attitudes that are constantly changing.

The eighth edition, released in 2004, and the first since Spock's death six years earlier, included a new chapter written by Dr. Needlman on "reading aloud," drawing on material developed by a literacy program he had founded in 1989 in Boston with another pediatrician, Dr. Barry Zuckerman, called Reach Out and Read, that makes the systematic promotion of literacy an essential part of a child's medical care. As the story has been passed down by their colleagues—indeed, it has taken on the patina of legend—Needlman and Zuckerman had independently determined that a supervised program of preschool reading could contribute to the making of healthier, better adjusted, brighter children, and that together they established the concept of using regular medical checkups as a means of making it happen. For Zuckerman, director of pediatrics at Boston City Hospital, an inner-city facility now known as the Boston Medical Center, the moment of inspiration came when he realized that children's books he was bringing into the office from his home for casual use in the waiting room were disappearing at a rapid rate, prompting him to think about ways to establish a formal program that would make guidance on reading aloud to parents—and the ceremonial gift of a book to the young patient—a part of regular medical checkups. Needlman, a resident in pediatrics, noticed a similar phenomenon, and mentioned it to Zuckerman, his supervisor, who showed him the plan he had already drawn up but had set aside for lack of outside interest.

Together, they renewed the effort, secured some funding, and established Reach Out and Read, targeting their efforts primarily at preschool children growing up in or near poverty, since statistics show that they are

the ones less likely to have parents reading to them during their most crucial years of development. "What Robert brought to this program was
his passion for children and his commitment to make a difference in their
lives," Zuckerman said in an interview. "Serendipitously, we were both
on the same page, and now millions of kids have books in their homes
who might not have had them otherwise." Few people would dispute that
literacy is important in a modern society, but the idea hit upon by
Needlman and Zuckerman—that reading is critical to the health and
well-being of children, as essential to their growth as food, clothing, and
shelter, and that it should be regarded as a "clinical intervention" that is
part of their primary pediatric care—struck a nerve among pediatricians
nationwide, and received the enthusiastic support of two first ladies,
Hillary Rodham Clinton during the presidency of her husband, Bill
Clinton, and later while serving in the U.S. Senate, and Laura Bush, who
made it a key project in the Ready to Read, Ready to Learn Educational
Initiative she has promoted during the administration of her husband,
George W. Bush.

As Reach Out and Read entered its sixteenth year in 2005, sanctioned
programs were in place at 2,337 sites in all fifty states, the District of
Columbia, Puerto Rico, and Guam, operating in hospitals, clinics, health
centers, and private pediatric practices, involving the active participation
of fifteen thousand medical providers. Every program that is sanctioned
has a contractual agreement with the National Center, which is located in
Boston and affiliated with the Department of Pediatrics at the Boston
Medical Center and the Boston University School of Medicine. In 2004,
some three million books were presented to two million children, along
with advice and guidance for the parents on how to participate in the
process. The programs serve mostly children growing up in poverty, or at
"socioeconomic risk," to use the bureaucratic term. With continued support from private sources, including a number of children's book publishers, most notably Scholastic Press, Inc., which has donated hundreds of

thousands of books since the program began, and the U.S. Department of Education, which in 2004 committed $10 million toward the purchase of others, it is anticipated that those numbers will be doubled by the end of the decade.

For Perri Klass, a Boston pediatrician, author, professor of pediatrics at Boston University School of Medicine, and the medical director and president of Reach Out and Read, the gift of a book is just one element of an effective model, which is why timing plays such an important role in the process. "We deliberately wait until a child is six months old, because we feel strongly that the baby is more likely to respond positively to the book at that age," she said. "A younger baby is very interested in voices, in people; it is very important to *talk* to your baby, sing to your baby, but the book itself is not going to be that interesting immediately. They just can't focus that far away yet, their eyes are still developing, and they are really much less likely to reach and grasp and enjoy an object before they are that age."

This is also around the time that babies are beginning to sit up by themselves and develop distinctive social personalities, Klass said, and withdrew a volume from a canvas bag she always has with her, identifying it as "one of our six-month-old books," and explaining that one of the reasons it fell into that category was its extra-textual features. "These are built for people with small hands, and they're very chewable, but also— and I always point this out to the doctors we train for the program—they are engineered for people *without* pincer grasps, because babies don't have pincer grasp until they are about nine months old. When they grab, they use the whole hand, so if you open this book, the pages all separate—which you can't do at all with a paper book. Now, if you hold this book out to a six-month-old, the baby will smile, the baby will reach for the book, the baby will vocalize. Even if the parent thinks that this is a strange or silly idea, the parent is going to see a reaction. Then, of course, the baby will grab the book and chew it. But starting at six months, it's very deliberate." At that age, each child who comes into a clinic that is participating in the Reach Out and Read program will get a new book, and that practice will continue at every medical examination until the child is five years old, "and then we stop, because at that point we hope the child is in school and there's at least someone else in the child's life who is talking about books and reading. The idea is to target that window when for many children there isn't anybody else pushing books and reading aloud."

So over a period of fifty-four months, if everything goes according to schedule, each child who comes in for a regular medical checkup twice a year not only will be given ten books, but the pediatrician will offer advice, give instructions, and assess progress by performing a series of diagnostic tests. "I give a lot of talks," Dr. Klass said, "and one of the interesting things I get from talking to day care providers, Head Start teachers, and first-grade teachers is the unanimity with which they all say that on the first day of school, you can look around the room and tell which children have never handled books. There are always some children in the room, at whatever age, three, four, five, who don't know how to hold a book, they don't know what it's for, why it's appealing, they don't know how to listen to a story, they don't understand the narrative arc of a story. I had never thought about this before I started this work, but how is it that you know when you're listening to a voice whether somebody is talking or reading? What is it about my voice right now that signals to you that I'm talking, not reading? Or when you're listening to a lecture, how do you know whether the lecturer is speaking from notes or reading? Children who are read to understand that difference at a very early age, and you can tell they understand it, because there's something they do that we call book babble."

Klass asked if I wanted a demonstration of what she meant by this term, which sounds almost like an oxymoron. "Book babble is this wordless language, but it's syllabic and it has the cadences of reading aloud. It *sounds* like reading aloud, that's why it's so cool when you hear it. I can't really do it well, but it's like *adda-dadda-dadda-radda-adda*, kind of like that. We're all familiar with babies who start to babble in conversational cadences, question-and-answer babble—well, just as you can have a conversation with babble, babies who get read to also develop a babble that sounds like reading aloud, and that comes very early. Way before they get to school, they can do what you're doing when you listen to my voice and just know whether I'm talking or reading—they understand that there's something about that particular rise and fall, that rhythm, that means reading aloud. I know I can hear the difference. I don't know *what* I'm hearing—but I can hear the difference."

If it were just a difference in sound, then book babble would be little more than an amusing curiosity, but what is happening, Klass said, is that the child is acquiring a skill that humans alone are capable of mastering, and it is a wonder to behold. "In addition to the actual work of decoding spoken language, the brain is somehow taking in and responding to the question, 'What does this word mean?' As a child, you have to learn to decode all kinds of things. What is the emotional content? Is this information? Is this a prohibition that I'm hearing? Why am I hearing this? By the time you get to school, you want to know, 'Oh good, that's somebody reading a story,' and then, 'I'm going to pull up close so I can see the pictures, and I'm going to listen, and I want to know what happens next, and this is going to be fun.' Children who have not been read to, this is all news to them, and I think it's a much harder job for teachers, getting them from there to the work of learning to read, because it's a real struggle. One of the things I have come to understand working with this program is just what an impressive thing it is—what a hard job it is—that we learn to read."

A graduate of Radcliffe College in 1979 and Harvard Medical School in 1986—with time for graduate work in zoology at the University of California, Berkeley, and the birth of a son in between—Klass is passionately articulate about what she does and the interests that motivate her, personally, emotionally, and intellectually. Aside from her work as a physician, Klass has written nine books in several genres, including *Other Women's Children*, a novel; *Love and Modern Medicine*, a collection of short fiction; and two collections of essays, *Baby Doctor: A Pediatrician's Training* and *A Not Entirely Benign Procedure: Four Years as a Medical Student*. Five of her short stories have won the O. Henry Award, and her articles have appeared in numerous national publications. It was a lengthy feature she wrote about pediatrics for the *New York Times Magazine* in 1992, in fact, that introduced Klass to Dr. Needlman, who was about to leave Boston for a position with Case Western Reserve Medical Center in Cleveland, prompting her to ask, "What's going to happen to that nice little book program you run?" The answer he gave, she told me, pretty much changed her life: "He said, 'I'm looking for someone who can take it over, because otherwise it probably will just wither away.' I believe his exact words were, 'I'm afraid they won't pay you anything, but it will only take about an hour or so a week.' " Klass accepted the challenge, and signed on. Encouraged by Barry Zuckerman to expand the program, she submitted applications for grant support and prepared a manual to help train other pediatricians. "Barry had this vision that we could help other programs do this sort of thing, that this idea of promoting reading aloud and giving out books at pediatric physicals was something that had the potential to become as standard as giving shots. I don't think either of us had any idea how it would catch on, but as it grew it kind of took over bigger and bigger chunks of my life. I suspect that I have now probably become a fanatic."

In one essay she wrote about Reach Out and Read, Klass offered this about what has become the central focus of her professional life: "When I think about children growing up in homes without books, I have the same visceral reaction as I have when I think of children in homes without milk or food or heat: It cannot be, it must not be. It stunts them and deprives them before they've had a fair chance."

In her conversation with me, I asked Klass to elaborate on that thought. "I don't know if you've looked at two-year-olds recently," she said. "It is hard to look at two-year-olds because they are essentially uncooperative, and whatever it is that you want them to do, they won't do, and they'll do the other thing. But if you look at a reasonably bright, normal two-year-old who has been read to, that child's level of engagement with books is very profound, and very complicated, and very intense. They use books as transitional objects. Many of them have one book that they carry everywhere, and that they take to bed with them. They want to hear the same books over and over and over, and they know exactly what belongs on every page, and they memorize them, and if you change a single word, the two-year-old will correct you. They have this incredibly intense, powerful relationship with books, and this can be with hundreds of books. We're talking about children who have just started talking, we're not talking about very sophisticated or very grown-up children. So when you think about a two-year-old missing that, not having any chance to make those connections, to relate to books in that way, in that very powerful early way, something is just missing. Some tremendous opportunity has been lost, something that could help make that child's brain grow."

Again and again in our conversation, Klass stressed that the presentation of a book at a medical checkup should not be confused with what in another context might be the ceremonial gift of a lollipop to a cooperative child. "This involves so much more than giving books away," she said. "Lots of well-intentioned groups give books away to children, many of them at birth, but part of what we do is add something extra to a child's visit to the doctor. One of the reasons this program is so popular among pediatricians is because it helps them understand the child better. We have fifteen minutes in these checkups, and there is a whole list of imperatives that we try to fulfill in this time. You talk about discipline, you talk about nutrition, you talk about growth, weight, height. But you also talk about development, so what I try to do when I do a physical, I try to come into the room with a book, give the child a book, and then, as I'm saying, 'Hi, how's it going, oh my gosh, you've gotten so big,' I watch and see what the child is doing with the book, and watch and see what the parent says."

By the time children reach the age of two, they are supposed to have a working vocabulary of about two hundred words, Klass said, "and when they speak, about fifty percent of their language is supposed to be intelligible for someone other than their parents." By making reference to the book that was given to the child six months earlier, the physician can get answers to a lot of these questions. She gave me an example from just the previous week. A woman came in with her eighteen-month-old twins for their regular checkup. "I had two different board books, and I said to the mother, 'Who gets which?' And she said, 'He gets that one because he loves animals, and he gets the other one.' She started talking about how much they love their books, and this one knows this, and this one knows all the animal sounds by heart. So then I don't need to say to her, 'OK, by eighteen months, you should have some words beside mama and dada, now does he? Now when he says those words, are you the only one who can understand them?' Those are kind of standard pediatric questions, developmental questions, because between one year and two years, part of our brief is to pick up things like speech delay, and we're supposed to pick up developmental delay. Most important, we're supposed to refer any child who's not learning to talk on time, get those children hearing tests and speech therapy. When I do this right, by having the book in there, by having the parent talk about the child dealing with books, by watching the child with the book, I get a lot of those questions answered."

As a prolific writer in her own right—and as a prominent member of

PEN, the international writers' organization, a great champion of book culture—it is fair to assume that Klass would favor the printed page over the computer, a device that younger Americans are often more adept at using—and much more comfortable with—than their elders. It happens that she does prefer the book, but for altogether different reasons than might be expected. "I would take the computer in a heartbeat if I thought it could provide the same benefits as a book," she told me, and snapped her fingers for emphasis. "I have given this a lot of thought and I believe it has to be an object. I see this every day, right here, with the children who are my patients. There are an awful lot of ways in which there's nothing as satisfying as a book, starting with a six-month-old who can chew it and handle it, and kind of map through and manipulate it. And then there are books for a one-year-old, they're a little bigger and a little heavier—they're still indestructible—but they're a little more conceptual. They have baby animals, maybe, and a little more of a story. But the pages of these books don't all separate and pop up. You need a pincer grasp, you need to turn the pages. That's so important to kids, handling the book, controlling the book, manipulating the book, having it in your home, owning it."

And that is all within the first eighteen months of the program, with more to come. "One of the really exciting things that happens when you turn two," Klass continued—and at this point her enthusiasm was palpable—"is that these kids can now *turn* paper pages. They have the pincer grasp, and they can *turn* pages. A lot of this depends on how much the child has been read to. A lot of these kids have been growing up in homes with no books; a child who has been growing up in a home full of books, and has learned to be careful with books, knows how to handle them by two. By then they definitely have the control and they can turn the pages without ripping them. So the feel of the book is extremely important. For babies, part of the appeal of the book is that if you wave the book at Mom, and Mom's going to read it to you, that means that you're going to be on Mom's lap, and you get Mom's voice, and you get Mom's one-on-one attention, which is very much what babies want. A six-month-old, or a one-year-old, or even a two-year-old would probably rather have the parent one-on-one than anything. So one of the things you get is not just the tactile quality of the book, but you get on a parent's lap, and the physical contact with a parent, the parent looking at you, looking *with* you at the book, holding you, and I suspect that is where some of those positive associations come from—your first repeated exposure to the sound of someone reading aloud—to words on a page, or to the object of a book, in this most safe, most protected, most familiar, most important person in the world, most important voice in the world. And the book is one of the ways to get that person all to yourself."

For those who do not learn to read in childhood, literacy is still achievable at any age, with few examples more compelling than the experiences recalled by the social activist Malcolm X (1925–1965) in a memoir written with the author Alex Haley and published shortly after the dynamic leader of the Black Revolution was shot to death in the Audubon Ballroom in Manhattan. An admitted street hustler in his youth, the man variously known as Malcolm Little, Detroit Red, Satan, El-Hajj Malik El-Shabazz, and Malcolm X taught himself how to read during the six years he was an inmate at the Norfolk Prison Colony in Massachusetts, 1946 to 1952, convicted on fourteen counts of felony burglary. In his first-person recollections, Malcolm X recalled being motivated to change his life on the strength of a basic realization, a fact of life quickly perceived moments after the barred doors had been locked behind him. "As you can imagine, especially in a prison where there was heavy emphasis on rehabilitation, an inmate was smiled upon if he demonstrated an unusually intense interest in books. There was a sizable number of well-read inmates, especially the popular debaters. Some were said by many to be practically walking encyclopedias. They were almost celebrities. No university would ask any student to devour literature as I did when this new world opened to me; of being able to read and understand."

He began his course of self-study simply enough, with a dictionary, taking the first word he saw, "aardvark," and copying it down on a piece of paper, then continuing on from there, one word after another. "I couldn't even write in a straight line" at the time, he admitted, but after several days of this, a richer awareness of language began to kick in. "That was the way I started copying what eventually became the whole dictionary." Malcolm X estimated that he wrote a million words during his incarceration, and along with mastery of the manual skills of writing came a dedication to absorbing the words he was now able to comprehend. "Available on the prison library's shelves were books on just about every general subject," he recalled, many of them donated by a generous benefactor, most "still in crates and boxes in the back of the library— thousands of old books. Some of them looked ancient: covers faded; old-time parchment-looking bindings," and he began spending every available minute devouring their contents. "I read more in my room than in the library itself. An inmate who was known to read a lot could check out more than the permitted maximum number of books. I preferred reading in the total isolation of my own room." He would become "outraged" when the lights were ordered out each night at ten p.m., as it "always seemed to catch me right in the middle of something engrossing." But right outside his door was a corridor light that shone into his cell. "The glow was enough to read by, once my eyes adjusted to it. So when 'lights out' came, I would sit on the floor where I could continue reading in that glow" to three or four in the morning, pausing only to jump into his bunk and feign sleep when the guards came by on their regular rounds.

"Ten guards and the warden couldn't have torn me out of those books," he told Haley. "I have often reflected upon the new vistas that reading opened to me. I knew right there in prison that reading had changed forever the course of my life. As I see it today, the ability to read awakened inside me some long dormant craving to be mentally alive. I certainly wasn't seeking any degree, the way a college confers a status symbol upon its students. My homemade education gave me, with every additional book that I read, a little bit more sensitivity to the deafness, dumbness, and blindness that was afflicting the black race in America. Not long ago, an English writer telephoned me from London, asking questions. One was, 'What's your alma mater?' I told him, 'Books.' You will never catch me with a free fifteen minutes in which I'm not studying something I feel might be able to help the black man."

On the evening of December 15, 2004, I attended the most unusual graduation I am ever likely to witness, an informal ceremony held in a bare conference room on the campus of the University of Massachusetts in the town of Dartmouth, a suburb of New Bedford on the southeastern coast of the state. Before each of the four young men who had taken the college-level literature course over the previous three months would receive a certificate of completion—along with a book donated by the Library of America as a memento of their successful participation—they would have to spend two hours discussing their reading of a work of fiction with Robert P. Waxler, a professor of English at the university, who with Judge Robert Kane of the nearby New Bedford District Court in 1991 established what is euphemistically known as an "alternative sentencing program" for criminal offenders, one that substitutes reading American fiction on a supervised basis in lieu of doing hard time behind bars in a state penitentiary.

On this particular night, the topic of discussion was "Sonny's Blues," a short story written by the African-American author James Baldwin, first published in *Partisan Review* in 1957 and collected in *Going to Meet the Man* in 1965. There is a lot in "Sonny's Blues" that young men of the twenty-first century can relate to, and everyone in the room that night apparently did. It tells the story of two brothers who move about in New York City in the middle of the twentieth century, one of whom, the unnamed narrator, has tried to assimilate himself into the mainstream of society. The music of the period may be jazz and blues, and the language occasionally dated—who today is referred to as a "cat"?—but anguish, aspiration, and anxiety know no generational bounds, as everyone in the class made clear, especially with regard to Sonny, the piano-playing brother whose arrest for selling "horse" has caused a rift between the siblings. There is a decided distance, until the narrator, a schoolteacher, hears his brother's music. "I had never before thought of how awful the relationship must be between the musician and his instrument. He has to fill it, this instrument, with the breath of life, his own. He has to make it do what he wants it to do." And only then does he realize that freedom "lurked around us and I understood, at last, that he could help us to be free if we would listen, that he would never be free until we did."

For the young men completing this course—none of them over thirty, and for this group, only one of them a minority—the experiences related in the story are from another generation and from another ethnic experience, yet a prevailing opinion expressed was that this may have been the most moving work they had read in the course. "James Baldwin is very good at portraying the ghetto," the one minority student said, telling me afterward that before he got in trouble with the law he had spent a good deal of time "moving around from place to place and doing a lot of different things," with all that implied left pointedly unspoken. "I see parts of myself in there that I don't like," another student said. "This guy is rocking back and forth—I know that feeling," a third offered, and the fourth wondered aloud why the narrator has no name. "I like him, I wouldn't mind being like him," he said. "To tell you the truth, I like

Sonny," came another response. "I say that because I have the feeling he has a story he wants to tell, and I have a story. I want people to understand it, just hear it, whoever listens; that's all any of us really want, is to have people listen to our music. You know? I think that's the first time his brother actually *listened* to him."

As assignments go, this one, at thirty-five pages, was among the least demanding in terms of length, but it was the final requirement of the course, and the one that meant the difference between pass and fail. Though books vary from week to week and class to class—there are separate programs for women, usually involving more works with strong female characters, and there will be certain books more appropriate to different ethnic groups—Waxler said some have proven to be staples on the regular reading list. They include James Dickey's *Deliverance*, J. D. Salinger's *Catcher in the Rye*, John Steinbeck's *Of Mice and Men*, Elie Wiesel's *Night*, T. C. Boyle's *Greasy Lake*, Jack London's *Sea Wolf*, Richard Wright's story "The Man Who Killed a Shadow," Ken Kesey's *One Flew Over the Cuckoo's Nest*, Harry Crews's *The Knockout Artist*, Raymond Carver's story "Tell the Women We're Going," Zora Neale Hurston's *Their Eyes Were Watching God*, Tillie Olsen's "I Stand Here Ironing," and Alice Walker's "Everyday Use."

Asked to cite the one work above all others that seems to have the greatest impact on the students, Waxler, Wayne St. Pierre, a probation officer, and two lawyers attending the session that night all agreed it was Ernest Hemingway's *The Old Man and the Sea*. "That's one story that always comes alive in the discussions," Waxler said, "and it's all about the old man, Santiago. Here's a guy, going out in his boat every morning, never catches anything, and how many people going through this sort of thing every day are likely to give up? His heroism, his endurance, the pain he goes through, speaks to these people in ways they understand. Literature does this. You know that it can happen, and it does happen all the time." To one extent or other, these writings allow the instructors to generate conversations about such concepts as violence, identity, friendship, love, family, and responsibility. "We are always looking for relevance, and it has to be accessible," Waxler said. Poetry, essays, and drama have their place, but in this program, it is narrative that seems to have the greatest impact. "But number one, they have to read the book. There are no excuses, and no exceptions. Just as important, in our view, is the discussion. We know immediately whether or not they have done the reading, because nobody gets a free pass in the classroom; everyone is required to contribute."

As mute testimony to the latter point was the obvious fact that only four people were in the classroom that night. "We started out with ten," Waxler said. "Six guys, for one reason or another, washed out, and that's an unusually high attrition rate," a figure he attributed in this instance to having men who were generally younger than many in the other classes, where there is the prevailing sense of a last chance having been put on the table, with few alternatives being available. "It is not very pleasant to contemplate," St. Pierre, the probation officer, explained to me. "These are not petty crimes we're dealing with here, and being accepted into this program is not a slap on the wrist." Showing results, Waxler added, is the one factor above all others that has allowed the program, formally known as Changing Lives Through Literature (CLTL), to survive. The success rate has been such that programs based on his model have been organized in six other states, with more than three thousand "graduates" having successfully completed courses of instruction since its inception. Sensitive to suggestions some might have that this just might be another example of Massachusetts liberals trying out their permissive policies on the rest of the country, Waxler pointed out that one of the most enthusiastic CLTL affiliates is in Texas, which enforces what is far and away the strictest penal code in the United States, including the imposition of twice as many death penalties as any other state. Other programs have been set up in Arizona, Maine, New York, Rhode Island, and Kansas. "This really transcends politics," Waxler said. "Liberals and conservatives have embraced this program. They all use it because they say it works."

With Jean R. Trounstine, a colleague who teaches a similar course to women offenders, Waxler edited an anthology of writings specifically for use in the program, aptly titled *Changing Lives Through Literature* and published by the University of Notre Dame Press. In the introduction, he told how he came up with the program and proposed it to Judge Kane, who was receptive to an idea that might "break the dull round of a court system dizzy with turnstile justice," and for Waxler, provide an opportunity "to talk about good books with a group that ordinarily would not come to the campus" for such a discussion. He asked the judge to take "eight to ten criminal offenders appearing before his bench, headed to jail, and sentence them instead to a series of literature discussions that I would design and facilitate at the University of Massachusetts, Dartmouth." The first group "collectively had 148 convictions before coming into the program," yet all took it seriously. "As one of the men suggested, these discussions were as challenging to him as anything he had ever found peddling drugs on the streets. I too found myself thinking about the stories in new ways, seeing fresh perspectives, and understanding that the boundary between me and the criminal offenders was very thin indeed."

In order to qualify for CLTL, the men and women who apply must first convince officials of a genuine desire to turn over a new leaf; eligibility requires an eighth-grade reading level, and the ability to read a standard-length book. "Teaching people how to read is not the function of this program, literary intervention is something else entirely," Waxler said, since participants have to read six novels and an equal number of short stories during the three-month course. "If they cut class and don't have an excellent reason for not being here, or if they come to class unprepared, they go to jail," St. Pierre said. Numerous studies have been made and professional papers written, a typical one published in 1998 in the *Journal of Offender Rehabilitation* titled "Combining Bibliotherapy and Positive Role Modeling as an Alternative to Incarceration," whose authors, G. Roger Jarjoura of Indiana University and Susan T. Krumholz, a colleague of Waxler at the University of Massachusetts, compared the records of thirty-two men who completed the program with a "matched comparison group" of forty other probationers, finding "a reconviction rate of 18.75 percent in the study group, compared with 45 percent in the comparison group."

What is distinctive about CLTL is that the preferred offender is one who has a history of getting into trouble, not someone who has made one or two mistakes. "These are high-risk offenders," Waxler said. "The only people we won't allow into the program are those who have been charged with a sex offense or murder." As a consequence, there is a decidedly "hard-core" element involved, with students typically having more than one criminal offense on their records. To cite one documented example, the average number of prior convictions for the first two groups of men to participate in the program was 18.4 per person. "There has to be the real fear of going to jail, otherwise it doesn't work," Waxler explained, noting that those who drop out—or those who are washed out—are subject to immediate incarceration. "Participation in the program is in lieu of a jail sentence—not probation, but prison. You don't read forty pages and you go to jail? That is a very strong motivating factor."

When the evening program was over, and each participant had received his certification of completion, there was an unmistakable sense of relief. One of the men confessed that the reading had proven a chore for him. "I thought the books were going to be more related to our situations," another said, noting that none of them knew any of the others. "Basically, what we were dealing with was issues. We all read the same books, but our backgrounds made us look at them differently." One of the more obviously relieved graduates allowed that he is a "very slow reader," and that he needed help occasionally to get through the assignments. "I paid a kid to read *Deliverance* to me," he said, which Waxler found unconventional, but acceptable all the same. "It mattered enough to him that he was going to read the book, one way or the other," Waxler told me after the room had cleared, and he was closing up for the night. "I have always believed that there is a universal quality to literature, that the power of story, the power of literature, is that it truly can bring about a kind of salvation."

FULL CIRCLE: A FINAL STROKE

In the spring of 2003, the British Library took a thirteen-hundred-year-old book known as the Lindisfarne Gospels from the wings of its main gallery and made it the centerpiece of an exhibition that depicted a medieval people in the grip of monumental change. Known as an illuminated manuscript for the exquisite artwork that adorns its vellum pages, the book is remarkable for many compelling reasons, not least among them the extraordinary circumstance of its making on a tidal island off the coast of Northumbria that gave the volume its name.

Remarkably, all of the paintings and calligraphy are believed to be the work of a single artist who toiled in splendid isolation in the early years of the eighth century, a brilliant cleric who drew inspiration from a multitude of cultural influences. Typically, books produced in the scriptoria of medieval Europe were group efforts, with many specialists contributing to the task. The Book of Kells, for example, was made off the western coast of Scotland on the island of Iona about AD 800 by no fewer than eight craftsmen.

The Lindisfarne text consists of the Four Gospels of Matthew, Mark, Luke, and John, each written out from about 715 to 720 by the abbot of the monastery, Bishop Eadfrith, from the standard version of the New Testament known as the Latin Vulgate of St. Jerome. Around 950, a priest named Aldred prepared a version of the text in Old English, and inscribed each word he had translated beneath its Latin equivalent in the Gospels, making what is known as a running gloss. The book, as a result, is also the earliest known account of the Bible in the language of the

Anglo-Saxons, and while that milestone is considerable in and of itself, there is much more to this book than the words it contains. Michelle P. Brown, curator of illuminated manuscripts at the British Library and organizer of the 2003 exhibition, called Painted Labyrinth, wrote that the Lindisfarne Gospels was made at "an uneasy restless time during which one of the great shifts in world history was taking place and cultures were metamorphosing and melting into one another, giving birth to new identities."

The Romans who had occupied Britain for four centuries had left the region toward the end of the fifth century, and though some Christian outposts had been established on the islands prior to their departure, invasions by Saxons, Angles, and Vikings had driven most of them to the north and the west. The process that resulted in Britain's total conversion to Christianity began in 597 with the arrival of St. Augustine from Rome on a mission to turn "Angles into Angels." In 664, doctrinal differences that had developed between indigenous Celtic and outside Roman factions were finally resolved at the Synod of Whitby.

Little more than a generation after that rapprochement—and less than a hundred years after the arrival of St. Augustine—Eadfrith began his work on the Lindisfarne Gospels, boldly combining Celtic and Anglo-Saxon artistic elements with Roman, Coptic, and Eastern traditions to create a unified vision that was apparent throughout the book. There seems little doubt, according to Brown, that Eadfrith "consciously drew upon the ornamental repertoires of a variety of cultures" to create his masterpiece, producing what she is confident is the earliest example of multicultural art to be produced in Britain.

Eadfrith's fusion of motifs is everywhere apparent, and particularly striking at the opening sections of each gospel. His portraits of the four evangelists—each pictured with a quill and scroll—were clearly influenced by Italian and Byzantine models. Immediately following them are meticulously decorated leaves known as "carpet pages," so called because their intricate designs resemble prayer mats that probably originated in eastern Christian and Islamic lands, possibly even Coptic Egypt. After each carpet page appears an "incipit," or opening page, in which the first letters of the gospels are elaborated with interlacing and spiral patterns strongly influenced by Anglo-Saxon jewelry and enamel work.

As part of his preparation, Eadfrith drew outlines for his images on the reverse side of each page with a lead point, predating by three hundred years the invention of the pencil. This circumstance raises the question as to whether he might also have devised an early version of the light box to project images from behind so that they could be traced on the front. For his paintings and decorations, Eadfrith used a wide range of vegetable and mineral pigments imported from all over Europe to formulate subtle shadings of purple, lilac, red, pink, green, and yellow, with blue lapis lazuli coming from Afghanistan. For the page surfaces themselves, it is estimated that the skins of three hundred yearling cattle were used to fabricate the vellum sheets.

This "encyclopedic masterpiece," as Brown called it in her monograph, influenced work produced throughout the region, and was later carried across the channel by Irish and Anglo-Saxon monks who were establishing monasteries throughout Europe. The Painted Labyrinth exhibition featured jewelry, coins, sculpture, metalwork, and textiles borrowed from numerous museums. The many examples of Anglo-Saxon, Celtic, and other European artifacts produced in the northeast of England, Scotland, and Ireland—joined by Coptic Egypt, Byzantine, Judaic, Islamic, and Buddhist materials—offered graphic evidence of just how pervasive that influence was on the world of the Middle Ages.

Brown compared an examination of the Lindisfarne Gospels to a study of all great artistic monuments, be they timeless paintings such as Michelangelo's Sistine Chapel frescoes or archaeological wonders such as the Valley of the Kings. Each generation of scholars, she wrote, comes to these creations with "new questions, new perceptions, and new technologies" to interpret them. In the instance of the Lindisfarne Gospels—which is far too precious and much too fragile to allow perusal by anyone other than its immediate custodians—the making of high-resolution digital images now allows scholars the unprecedented opportunity to pore over the ancient leaves without ever having to handle or touch them.

Centered around a single artifact, Painted Labyrinth came almost forty years to a day after the British Museum had mounted its Printing and the Mind of Man exhibition in the old King's Library. The Lindisfarne Gospels were not included among the 440 books displayed then, for the obvious reason that it predated the invention of movable type by more than eight hundred years. The timing of the two shows was just a coincidence, I was told, though to me the glory of the grand continuum was everywhere apparent, one that the curator, Michelle Brown, touched on in the study she wrote expressly for the 2003 exhibition.

"Books are about people," she made clear in *The Lindisfarne Gospels: Society, Spirituality and the Scribe*. "They can embody many different aspects of human activity—intellectual, literary, spiritual, ideological, artistic, historical, political and economic. They are portals into past lives, facilitating that vital organic communion between past, present and future. Whenever one such witness survives the ravages of time and the vagaries of fortune it presents a valuable testament."

NOTES

This work draws substantially from the author's personal interviews, which are fully referenced and identified in the body of the text. Biographical information for the principal subjects is contained there as well, and can be located by referring to the index. Sources cited in the Notes by the author's last name or by a short form of the title are to be found in the bibliography.

Chapter 1: The Magic Door

1 *"No teacher"*   In Becker, v–vi. The Harvard University copy of May Lamberton Becker's *Reader's Guide Book* is in the Houghton Library of rare books and manuscripts, according to the HOLLIS online catalog, because it is from the library of the poet, biographer, bibliophile, and Harvard benefactor Amy Lowell (1874–1925), who, it can be surmised, had a high regard for Becker's opinion.

2 *"dispose of this question . . . reading"*   Becker, 13–23.

3 *"found on the top . . . the bookcases"*   Ibid., 3–12.

6 *"books are the physical . . . make lightly"*   See www.schwartzbooks.com/.

7 *"It was something . . . through and through"*   Jim Higgins, "Bookseller at War With Tolstoy and Cancer," *Milwaukee Journal Sentinel*, March 17, 2004.

8 *"I was forced"*   Waite, *Footfalls*, xv.

8 *"First, I hold it"*   Waite, *Taken on Trust*, 114–15.

9 *"I want to savour . . . a book"*   Ibid., 204.

9 *"Now about something else"*   Frank, 669.

10 *"I'm allowed to read"*   Ibid., 310.

10 *"We always long"*   Ibid., 386. On July 15, 1944, just a month before her arrest, Anne wrote about a book just smuggled into the annex from the public library "with the challenging title of *What Do You Think of the Modern Young Girl*," discussing at length a chapter about "Daddy and Mummy don't understand me"; Ibid., 712.

10 *"I can hardly wait"*   Ibid., 611.

11 *"The book woman's coming"*   Appelt and Schmitzer, passim.

11 *"That room"*   Nafisi, 8.

12 *"Poet Laureate of the Negro Race"*   Vendler, *Voices and Visions*, 353.

12 *"Then it was"*   Hughes, 4.

12 *"Melodramatic maybe"*   Ibid., 3.

13 *Nicolaus Copernicus's*   For a spirited account of one man's twenty-year effort to track down every first- and second-edition copy of *De Revolutionibus Orbium Coelestium*, see Gingerich, passim.

13 *Thoreau . . . Gandhi*   See Manfred Steger, "Mahatma Gandhi and the Anarchist Legacy of Henry David Thoreau," *Southern Humanities Review* 27, no. 3 (Summer 1993), 201–15.

13 *Robert H. Goddard*   See Jeffrey Kluger, "Rocket Scientist," in *Time*, March 29, 1999.

15 *Permitting the Destruction of an Unworthy Life*   See Basbanes, *Splendor*, 216–19.

Chapter 2: One Out of Many

18 "Why, *it might be asked*"   Carter and Muir, vi.

18 *"one of the proudest"*   Muir, 24.

20 *"unique in the history"*   Carter and Muir, 69.

20 *"Creative literature"*   Ibid., 8.

21 *"initiated a novel"*   Ibid., 229.

21 *"caught the public ear"*   Ibid., 245.

22 *"George Washington, President"*   Paine, 433.

22 *"In the four quarters"*   Quoted in Buell, 11.

22 *"Young Emerson was highly susceptible"*   Buell, 21–22.

23 *"They were concerned"*   One Hundred Influential American Books (hereinafter referred to as Grolier 100).

25 *"not for what it is"*   Ibid., 102.

26 *"The mail order catalogue"*   Ibid., 109–10. See also www.bgsu.edu/departments/acs/1890s/sears/sears4.html.

27 Eclectic First Reader   Grolier 100, 76–77.

27 *"The announcement . . . of the people"*   Ibid., 17–22.

29 *"What awaits the intrepid explorer"*   In Pastoureau, 3.

32 *"surmounting the barrier"*   Dickinson, ix.

35 *"brilliant commentary"*   In Devine, Dissel, and Parrish, 21–22.

35 *"The stuff of poetry"*   Ibid., 249.

35 *"By confining itself"*   Cowley, 239.

36 *"Sooner or later"*   Ibid., 4.
36 *"The important question"*   Ibid., 35.
37 *"All these"*   Ibid., 93.
38 *"ticketed through life . . . the twentieth"*   Adams, 723.
38 *"found its most responsive"*   Cowley, 45–57.
39 *"little immediate effect"*   Ibid., 129–42.
40 *"It will be interesting"*   Ibid., 124.
41 *"By now"*   Ibid., 241.
41 *"deeply barbarous . . . literary style"*   In *Hitler*, unpaged insert, titled "A Review of *Mein Kampf*," by Dorothy Thompson.
42 *Modern Library*   For fiction, see www.randomhouse.com/modernlibrary/ 100bestnovels.html; for nonfiction, see www.randomhouse.com/modernlibrary/ 100bestnonfiction.html.
43 *"For over fifty-five years"*   Silvey, xii.
45 *Little Red Book*   See Oliver Lei Han, "Sources and Early Printing History of Chairman Mao's *Quotations*," in *Antiquarian Book Review* (London, November 2003).

Chapter 3: Eye of the Beholder

50 *"I have regretted"*   Montaigne, 465.
51 *"shake" . . . "spear"*   Anthony Burgess, *Shakespeare*, 233–34.
53 *Shakespeare's reading*   See Thomas W. Baldwin, *Shakspere's Small Latine and Lesse Greek* (Urbana: University of Illinois Press, 1944).
54 *"green ey'd monster"*   Shakespeare, *Othello*, act 3, scene 3.
54 Vero Nihil Verius   See www.shakespeare-oxford.com/.
54 *"No mention . . . empty hours"*   Ogburn, 270–94.
56 *"a considerable stock"*   Rowse, 14.
56 *"What Shakespeare did acquire"*   Schoenbaum, 23–24.
57 *"from my twelfth year"*   John Milton, *The Second Defence of the English People* (1654), in Roy Flannagan, ed., *The Riverside Milton* (Boston: Houghton Mifflin, 1998), 1115–1116.
58 *"I enjoyed an interval"*   Ibid.
58 *"might be supposed"*   Johnson, 51.
58 *"Milton had read"*   A. N. Wilson, 60.
59 *"[They] were condemned"*   Quoted in Johnson, 79.
60 *"set out to abolish"*   Holbrook Jackson, *Fear of Books*, 17.
60 *"erasure of indecent"*   Franklin, 232.

60 *"In which nothing"*   Ibid., 242.

61 *"tattooed and beplaistered"*   Quoted in Perrin, 87.

61 *"Three or four"*   Perrin, viii.

61 *"Traditional bowdlerism"*   Ibid., vii.

62 *"is vain and foolish"*   Ravitch, 11.

62 *"trivial"*   Ibid., 3.

62 *"Both right-wingers"*   Ibid., 79.

63 *"McCarthy's lists"*   See oral history of Catherine Heniford Lewis at www.libsci .sc.edu/histories/oralhistory/lewispage.htm.

63 *Unabomber*   For full text of manifesto see *New York Times* and *Washington Post*, Sept. 19, 1995. See also Robert D. McFadden, "From a Child of Promise to the Unabomb Suspect," and David Johnson and Janny Scott, "Brother Tells of a Painful Decision," in the *New York Times*, May 26, 1996; and Cynthia Hubert, "Scientists: Unabomber Lacks Formal Schooling," *Sacramento Bee*, August 4, 1995.

Chapter 4: Silent Witnesses

70 *solemn oath*   For the full text of the oath, see Basbanes, *Patience & Fortitude*, 425.

70 *"The ship brought up"*   Heffernan, 26.

70 *"This was the first"*   Quoted in Heffernan, 190–91. The full title of the Owen Chase book: *Narrative of the Most Extraordinary and Distressing Shipwreck of the Whale-Ship Essex of Nantucket; Which was Attacked and Finally Destroyed by a Large Spermaceti Whale in the Pacific Ocean; with an Account of the Unparalleled Sufferings of the Captain and Crew During a Space of Ninety-three Days at Sea in Open Boats in the Years 1819 and 1820*. See also *American Sea Writing* (New York: Library of America, 2000). Heffernan writes that the person Melville borrowed the book from was William Henry Chase, the son of Owen Chase; for detail on Melville's use of the *Essex Narrative*, including facsimiles of his marginal markings and underscorings, most of which relate to the whale's attack, see appendix A in Heffernan.

71 Sir Gawain and the Green Knight   For details on the preservation of the unique manuscript by Sir Robert Cotton (1571–1631), see Basbanes, *Gentle Madness*, 89–96.

72 *"The matchless style"*   Carter and Muir, 17.

72 *"Twins of Genius"*   Perry, 134–37; see also Justin Kaplan, *Mr. Clemens and Mark Twain* (New York: Simon & Schuster, 1966), 266–67, and Arlin Turner, *Mark Twain and George W. Cable* (Ann Arbor: University of Michigan Press, 1960), passim.

73 *"I came upon a sentence"*   Philip Roth, "The Story Behind *The Plot Against America*," *New York Times Book Review*, September 19, 2004.

73 *"The resulting dispersal"*   Kelley and Coley, ix.

74 *"I climbed the hill . . . myth-creating powers"*   Edel, 1–14.

76 *"Throughout his life"*   Tintner, xix.

76 *"ferociously literary"*   Ibid., xx.

77 *"The greatest artists"*   Edel, 11.

77 *"In every novel"*   Quoted in Tintner, xxiv.

78 *"not half of which"*   Luther Farnham, *A Glance at Private Libraries*, 1855 (facsimile edition, Weston, Mass.: M & S Books, 1991). See Basbanes, *A Gentle Madness*, 155–56, for a discussion of this important nineteenth-century survey.

78 *"I have always endeavoured"*   Edward Gibbon, *The History of the Decline and Fall of the Roman Empire*, ed. by David Womersley (New York: Penguin, 1994), vol. 4 of the history, in vol. 2 of this edition, 520.

78 *"high form of literary art"*   Grafton, 1.

78 *"The mind of Man"*   Keynes, 3.

79 *"the true mother . . . intellectual stature"*   Gibbon, 36–37.

79 *"idle and unprofitable"*   Ibid., 48.

80 *"an illiterate cripple"*   Ibid., 40.

80 *"Our family collection"*   Ibid., 42.

80 *"a dissertation of eight"*   Ibid., 76.

80 *"While coaches were rattling"*   Ibid., 94.

80 *"this slender beginning . . . prodesset"*   Ibid., 97.

81 *"energy of style"*   Ibid., 78.

81 *"Montesquieu was clearly"*   Patricia B. Craddock, *Edward Gibbon: Luminous Historian 1772–1794* (Baltimore: Johns Hopkins University Press, 1989), 8.

82 *"After glancing my eye"*   Gibbon, 98.

82 A New Method of a Common Place Book   Excerpts from *The Works of John Locke* (London: C. & J. Rivington, 1824), v. 9 (Posthumous Works).

82 *Commonplace books*   See William H. Sherman, introduction to *Renaissance Commonplace Books from the British Library*, www.ampltd.co.uk/collections_az/RenCpbks-BL/editorial-introduction.aspx. For a comprehensive study of the use of commonplace books in the Renaissance as an early form of information retrieval system, see Moss, passim.

84 *"tens of thousands"*   Richard Yeo, "A Philosopher and His Notebooks: John Locke (1632–1704) on Memory and Information," a professional lecture delivered at Griffith University, May 20, 2004, which includes superb information on the history and practice of commonplace books. The full text of Yeo's remarks is available at www.griffith.edu.au/ins/collections/proflects/yeo04.pdf.

85 *"which I do not strictly recommend"*   Gibbon, 79.

85 *"show clear signs . . . been fully realized"*   Harrison, 11–27.

88 *"I do not know"*   Quoted in Hawking, xviii.

Chapter 5: In the Margins

89 *"I have read almost"*   Lowes, ix.

90 *"what touched the springs"*   Ibid., 32.

90 *"It is, on the whole"*   Ibid., 5–6.

91 "How did Coleridge"   Ibid., 30.

91 *"Darwin, that is to say"*   Ibid., 34.

91 *"One after another"*   Holbrook Jackson, *Reading of Books*, 34–35.

93 *"The* in *and* un *struggle"*   H. J. Jackson, "Writing in Books and Other Marginal Activities," *University of Toronto Quarterly* 62, no. 2 (Winter 1992/3).

94 "Si Dieu n'existait pas"   See the official Web site of La Bibliothèque de Voltaire: http://voltaire.nlr.ru:8101/fr/page4.htm.

95 *"Great Princess"*   Furbank, 300–301; see also chap. 17, "Catherine the Great's Librarian," 290–309.

96 *"until their margins"*   Rosenthal, 10. For a detailed profile of Bernard M. Rosenthal, and the experiences of his family through three generations of bookselling, see Basbanes, *Patience & Fortitude*, 278–82.

96 *"restless, gloomy, superstitious"*   Ibid., 135–36.

97 *"His extravagant aim"*   Stern, 137.

97 "Romanae Historiae Principis"   See Anthony Grafton and Lisa Jardine, " 'Studied for Action': How Gabriel Harvey Read His Livy," *Past & Present* 129 (1990): 30–78.

98 *"interpreting, mediating"*   Sharpe, 66.

98 *"far from spoiling . . . in the period"*   H. J. Jackson, *Marginalia*, 104–10.

99 *"It is hard . . . largely unaware"*   Ibid., 124–37.

101 *"touched early"*   For more on James Logan and Isaiah Thomas, see Basbanes, *A Gentle Madness*, 129–35, 144–48. For more on the Mather Family Library, see the Web site of the American Antiquarian Society, www.americanantiquarian.org/matherlib.htm. For more on an American library that was in place before the one used by Cotton Mather, see Douglas Anderson.

104 *ExLibris*   See http://palimpsest.stanford.edu/byform/mailing-lists/exlibris/. For the University of Texas collection of authors' books, see www.hrc.utexas.edu/collections/books/holdings/libraries/.

107 *"The collection, which includes"*   Michelle Pauli, "Kingston University Buys Murdoch Library," *Guardian*, April 15, 2004.

110 *"The abbé's library"*   Gray, 27. For a discussion of Sade's library when he was an adult, see Gray, chap. 21, "Reading and Writing: The Budding Novelist," 262–86.

110 *"He knew all the nooks"*   Lever, 57.

110 *"Such books, such images"*   Gray, 26–27.

111 *"the most widely read"*   Wheen, 116; also Carter and Muir, 198.

111 *"Marx lives a very retired life"*   Quoted in Wheen, 118.

111 *"The stuff, on which I work"*   Padover, 71.

111 *"You'll certainly fancy"*   Ibid., 250.

111 *"book-worming"*   Wheen, 387–88.

112 *"Few people in Russia"*   Carter and Muir, 218.

112 *"The Art of Reading"*   Hitler, 46–50.

113 *Hitler's books*   See Timothy W. Ryback, "Hitler's Forgotten Library: The Man, His Books, and His Search for God," *Atlantic Monthly*, May 2003.

115 *"I was in the Reich Chancellery"*   Quoted in Basbanes, *A Gentle Madness*, 363–64.

118 *"promoter and patron . . . society and politics"*   Sharpe, 66–75.

118 *"shattered notions"*   Secord, 516.

119 *"readable as a romance"*   Ibid., 1.

119 *"No one would accuse"*   Ibid., 429–33.

119 *"denounced and praised"*   Ibid., 390.

120 *"the role of the printed word"*   Ibid., 3.

120 *"The contemporaneous canon . . . was Byron"*   St Clair, 216.

121 *"Of all the literary works . . . reading nation"*   Ibid., 357–65.

123 *"Why bother to identify"*   Darnton, *Forbidden Best-Sellers*, xxi–xxiii.

Chapter 6: Paving the Way

127 *"These are the times"*   Paine, 835.

128 *"At first sight"*   Adam Smith, *Wealth of Nations*, Book Four, "Of Systems of Political Economy," chap. VII, "Of Colonies," full-text online edition: www.adamsmith.org/smith/won-b4-c7-pt-3.htm.

128 *"which continues"*   Carter and Muir, 134.

129 *"All through . . . look for more"*   Churchill, 125–30.

130 *"He was no Moses . . . while writing it"*   Maier, 98–124.

132 *"Your father's zeal"*   McCullough, *John Adams*, 619.

132 *"never stopped reading . . . and set flowing"*   McCullough, *John Adams and the Good Life of the Mind*, 6.

133 *"We can't understand"*   Ibid., 4.

133 *Nathaniel Greene and Henry Knox*   For more on the backgrounds of these two American generals, see Billias, 109–36, 239–59. In *1776* (see bibliography), David McCullough identified *Memoirs Concerning the Art of War* (1757), by Marshal Maurice de Saxe, "one of the outstanding commanders of the era" (23), as one of the books Green used to train himself for the military.

136 *"Read somewhat . . . and porcelain"*   McCullough, *Good Life of the Mind*, 4–6.

138 *"the choicest editions"*   Basbanes, *A Gentle Madness*, 149–51. See also Gilreath and Wilson, 1–10.

138 *"One of the most systematic"*   Malone, 169–70.

139 *"Since his library"*   Quoted in Gilreath and Wilson, 4.

139 *"the aggregate"*   Lincoln, 161–62.

140 *"When he was young"*   Herndon and Weik, v. 2, 302.

140 *"Wherever he was"*   Ibid., vol. 1, 102.

140 *"To some indeterminable extent"*   Quoted in Douglas L. Wilson, "What Jefferson and Lincoln Read," in *Atlantic Monthly*, January 1991, 51.

142 *"Does history suggest"*   Harold Evans, "White House Book Club," *New York Times Book Review*, January 14, 2001. Evans's complete list of presidential bibliophiles: George Washington, John Adams, Thomas Jefferson, James Madison, James Monroe, John Quincy Adams, Millard Fillmore, James Buchanan, Abraham Lincoln, Rutherford Hayes, James Garfield, Theodore Roosevelt, William Howard Taft, Woodrow Wilson, Herbert Hoover, Franklin Roosevelt, Harry Truman, Dwight Eisenhower, John Kennedy, Richard Nixon, Jimmy Carter, and Bill Clinton. For more on presidents as readers, see Judith Miller, "President Turns a Page: So Might History," *New York Times*, May 9, 1998. Among the disclosures: During the Cuban Missile Crisis, John Kennedy read Barbara Tuchman's history of World War I, *The Guns of August*, for insight on how easily wars start; Richard Nixon, according to his daughter, Julie Nixon Eisenhower, carefully read books about towering figures from recent history, Joseph Stalin, Charles De Gaulle, and Huey P. Long among them, during his administration.

143 Bibliotheca De Re Metallica   See David Kuhner, "The Herbert Hoover Collection: A Gift and a Story," *Honnold Library Record*, vol. XII, no. 1 (Spring 1971). Online text: http://voxlibris.claremont.edu/sc/pubs/record/hlr-v12n1-low.pdf.

143 *The presidential memoirists*   James Buchanan, Ulysses S. Grant, Theodore Roosevelt, Calvin Coolidge, Herbert Hoover, Harry S Truman, Dwight D.

Eisenhower, Lyndon B. Johnson, Richard M. Nixon, Gerald Ford, Jimmy Carter, Ronald Reagan, William Jefferson Clinton. See "First in Line: Presidential Memoirs Accustomed to Slow Starts," in *Fine Books & Collections*, September/October 2004, 10.

144 *"Although frequently urged"*   Ulysses S. Grant, *Personal Memoirs of U. S. Grant* (New York: Charles L. Webster, 1885), v. 1, 7–8.

144 *ten thousand words*   Perry, 163.

144 *"I first wanted"*   Quoted in Perry, 225.

145 *"this record"*   Wilson, *Portable Edmund Wilson*, 489–90.

146 *"But perhaps more important"*   Evans, op. cit.

147 *"a collector* par excellence"   Carley, 14.

147 *"When a book"*   Ibid., 100.

147 *"Henry annotated"*   Ibid., 140.

147 *"She talks French"*   Quoted in Pryor, 17. See also: Alison Weir, *The Life of Elizabeth I* (New York: Alfred A. Knopf, 1998).

148 *"Boethius's influence"*   John Marenbon, *Boethius* (Oxford: Oxford University Press, 2003), 164. She also Margaret Gibson, ed., *Boethius: His Life, Thought and Influence* (Oxford: Basil Blackwell, 1981).

148 *"The text deals"*   John Morris Jackson and Noel Harold Kaylor Jr., "The Early Education of Queen Elizabeth I and Her Later Translation of Boethius's *De Consolatione Philosophiae*, in *Medieval English Studies* vol. 10, no. 2 (2002): 183–98; full text available online at www.sogang.ac.kr/~anthony/mesak/mes102/Kaylor.htm.

149 *"I may say"*   In Simon Keynes and Michael Lapidge, *Alfred the Great: Asser's Life of King Alfred and Other Contemporary Sources* (London: Penguin, 1983), 133.

Chapter 7: A Terrible Beauty

151 *"new readers make new texts"*   Cavallo and Chartier, 3.

155 *"The* Aeneid *is a cautionary tale"*   See Chris Hedges, "Bridge Between the Classics and the Masses," *New York Times*, April 13, 2004.

157 *"The Classics!"*   Quoted in Homer, *The Iliad*, tr. by Robert Fagles (New York: Viking, 1990), xiv.

160 *"his Achilles sometimes"*   Quoted in the online catalog of the University of Reading exhibition of Homer in English translation, www.library.rdg.ac.uk/colls/special/exhibitions/classics/homer.html.

160 *"poetical wonder"*   Johnson, 394.

161 *"I am a young Irishman"*   Ellmann, 71.

161 *"set himself to master"*   Ibid., 376.

161 *"the Dante of Dublin"*   Ibid., 75.

161 *"Just think"*   Ibid., 408.

161 *"imperfect acquaintance"*   Ibid., 408.

162 *"In a translation"*   Gass, 47.

162 *"translation is a form"*   Ibid., 51.

162 *"Most of the hands"*   Ibid., 63.

163 *"Those who have"*   Jorge Luis Borges, "Pierre Menard, Author of the *Quixote*," in *Collected Fictions*, tran. by Andrew Hurley (New York: Viking, 1998), 91.

164 Remembrance of Things Past   Another recent translator, Andreas Mayor, chose *The Past Recaptured* as the title in English; see Shattuck, chap. 8, for a full discussion of Proust in English translation. Proust, apparently, was unhappy with all of the English titles; see Shattuck, 191.

164 *"Anyone who can . . . read the novel"*   Shattuck, 23–24.

165 *"duty and task"*   Proust, xiii.

165 *"A tragedy by Racine"*   Ibid., 165.

166 *"I believe that my obligation"*   Grossman, in Cervantes, xix–xx.

167 *"cramped and weary voyagers"*   Leonard, 271.

167 *"too ill to read"*   Ibid., 285.

167 *"gather during their time off"*   Grossman, 267.

168 "Don Quixote *is one*"   Carter and Muir, 66–67.

168 *"an immortality"*   Ibid., 110.

172 *"all about translation . . . of this book"*   Hofstadter, xiii–xxiv.

173 *"all great texts"*   Walter Benjamin, "The Task of the Translator," in *Selected Writings*, vol. 1, ed. Marcus Bullock and Michael W. Jennings (Cambridge: Harvard University Press, 1996), 253–63.

Chapter 8: Gospel Truth

176 *Nag Hammadi Library*   See Basbanes, *Splendor of Letters*, 80–82.

178 *"urge all those with whom"*   Pagels, *Gnostic Gospels*, xviii.

178 *"secret and illegitimate"*   Pagels, *Beyond Belief*, 96.

179 *"acceptable"*   Ibid., 97.

180 *"As I stood . . . into creeds"*   Ibid., 3–5.

181 *"Americans revere the Bible"*   George Gallup and Jim Castilli, *The People's Religion: American Faith in the '90s* (New York: Macmillan, 1989), and George Gallup Jr. and D. Michael Lindsay, *Surveying the Religious Landscape: Trends in U.S. Beliefs* (Harrisburg, Penn.: Morehouse Publishers, 1999).

182 The Da Vinci Code   On the occasion of the second anniversary of the publication of Dan Brown's novel in March 2005, sales figures were reported to be 25 million copies worldwide, 10 million in North America alone, with editions released in forty-four languages. "That is 10 times the average sales of industry titans like John Grisham and Nora Roberts, making the book one of the fastest-selling adult novels of all time," the *New York Times* reported on March 21, 2005. The book made its debut at No. 1 on the *Times* best-seller list on April 6, 2003, and remained there for 103 weeks, 51 of them ranked No. 1, and never going below No. 5.

183 *"The New Testament"*   Ehrman, *Lost Scriptures*, 1.

184 *"The Bible is a book"*   Schniedewind, 1.

184 *"ultimately more important . . . call the Bible"*   Ibid., 5.

185 *"Both texts"*   Pelikan, 7.

186 *"accept the authority"*   Ibid., 15.

186 *"text-centered tradition"*   Halbertal, 1–44.

186 *"To a remarkable"*   Akenson, 7–8.

187 *"The Qur'an is"*   Haleem, ix.

189 *"It is like this"*   Neil MacFarquhar, "Muslim Scholars Increasingly Debate Unholy War," *New York Times*, December 10, 2004.

190 *"Reformed Egyptian"*   Grolier 100, 37.

190 *"One of the most salient"*   Gill, 209; see all of chap. 9 of Gill for publishing history.

191 *"Our next printer"*   Ibid., 218.

Chapter 9: Harvest of Riches

193 *"senior pack rat"*   Charles McGrath, "Fitzgerald as Screenwriter: No Hollywood Ending," *New York Times*, April 22, 2004.

194 *"He really loves books"*   Quoted in William W. Starr, "Matthew Bruccoli: At Home at USC," *State* (Columbia, SC), May 4, 2003.

203 *"Research begets research"*   Bruccoli, in Bucker, xii. See the catalog for detailed entries on all of the items in the Bruccoli Fitzgerald collection.

205 *"For Ned Griffith"*   Bucker, 54.

206 *"For Annah Williamson"*   Ibid., 62.

207 *"Dear Mr. Fitzgerald"*   Ibid., 218.

209 *"last of the great"*   Wilson, *Portable Edmund Wilson*, xi.

209 *"moral and intellectual"*   Aaron, in Wilson, *Letters on Literature*, xxix; see also John E. McIntyre, "The Likes of Edmund Wilson May Never Be Seen Again," *Baltimore Sun*, July 28, 2002.

213 *"If we can squander . . . wishes to stand"*   Wilson, *Fruits*, 6–10; see also Meyers, 464–66.
215 *"Without wishing to agitate"*   Letter to the Editor, *New York Times Book Review*, September 13, 1981.
218 *"and in shifting"*   Aaron, *American Notes*, xi.
218 *"observer and reporter"*   Ibid., ix.
219 *"I am grateful"*   Ibid., xxix–xxx.

Chapter 10: Born to Grapple

223 *"The flesh is sad, alas"*   See Basbanes, *Patience & Fortitude*, 370; the full line, in French, from the Mallarmé poem, "Brise Marine" (Sea Breeze), is "La chair est triste, hélas! et j'ai lu tous les livres."
225 *"He gets at the substance"*   Boswell, 802.
225 *"knew more books than"*   Ibid., 35.
225 *"with a view to urge"*   Ibid., 325–27.
226 Oxford English Dictionary   See Simon Winchester, *The Professor and the Madman* (New York: HarperCollins, 1998), and K. M. Elisabeth Murray, *Caught in the Web of Words: James A. H. Murray and the Oxford English Dictionary* (New Haven: Yale University Press, 1977).
226 *"the first dictionary"*   Quoted in Reddick, 2.
226 *"as one of the greatest"*   Bate, 240.
226 *"a copious"*   Quoted in Reddick, 35.
227 *"found him very busy"*   Boswell, 616.
227 *"a great deal in a desultory manner"*   Ibid., 27–28.
228 *"can claim the distinction"*   Greene, *Samuel Johnson's Library*, 5.
228 *"bold enterprise"*   Alter, 10–12.
229 first time in *"modern history"*   *Reading at Risk*, passim. For the full text online, see www.nea.gov/pub/ReadingAtRisk.pdf. On what qualifies as literary reading, the report offered this: "The distinction between reading literary works and reading any books is important to the analysis. . . . Books can be of any type and cover a vast array of subjects, literary and non-literary alike, and for the purposes of the survey, the respondents need to have read as a leisure time activity, not for work or school. Literature, of course, can be found in sources other than books. Poetry, drama, and fiction can be read in magazines and literary journals, even on subway and bus placards."
229 *"ancients and the moderns"*   The critic and literary journalist James Atlas used a

quotation from Swift's 1704 essay "The Battle of the Books" as the epigraph for his 1990 book on the curriculum debate in America, and paid the ultimate compliment to the author by using the same title for his examination.

231 *"siege on the canon . . . be used so easily"*   Barbara Herrnstein Smith, text of Presidential Address, "Limelight: Reflections on a Public Year," delivered at the annual convention of the MLA, in New Orleans in December 1988, copy of remarks furnished to the author. In an interview earlier that year, on January 6, 1988, with Joseph Berger of the *New York Times*, Herrnstein Smith expressed the division more succinctly: "What is being questioned is whether power, beauty, greatness as experienced by one group of people is locked into the work so that those who don't experience that are pathological, or alternatively, whether the two different experiences reflect differences about those groups, differences in the historical and social situations."

233 *"Basking in this unaccustomed level"*   John Strausbaugh, "Eggheads' Naughty Word Games," *New York Times*, December 27, 2004; see also Mark Bauerlein, "Liberal Groupthink Is Anti-Intellectual," *Chronicle of Higher Education*, November 12, 2004.

233 *"our reigning literary terrorist"*   Barbara Probst Solomon, "Moses and Feminism," *Washington Post*, September 16, 1990.

235 *"which might well be written up"*   Woolf, 1.

236 *"third sage of reading . . . Shakespeare"*   Bloom, *How to Read*, 21–24.

237 *"There is no one"*   John Taylor, "Bloom's Day: Hanging Out with the Reigning Genius of Lit Crit," *New York*, 1990.

238 *"Why should anyone"*   Dana Gioia, "Can Poetry Matter?," *Atlantic Monthly*, May 1991.

241 *"Ms. Vendler is so feared"*   Dinitia Smith, "A Woman of Power in the Ivory Tower," *New York Times*, November 22, 1997.

246 *"What I would hope"*   Henri Cole, "Helen Vendler: The Poem Unfolded: An Appreciation," *Humanities* 25, no. 3 (May/June 2004).

247 *"the page and the stage"*   For a detailed discussion of the issues involving the texts of Shakespeare's plays, see Marjorie Garber, *Shakespeare After All* (New York: Pantheon, 2004), 8–19.

254 *'Come, Madam, come'*   See Ricks, 157.

Chapter 11: The Healing Art

260 *Erik H. Erikson*   *Childhood and Society* (1950); *Young Man Luther: A Study in Psychoanalysis and History* (1958); *Gandhi's Truth: On the Origin of Militant*

Nonviolence (1969); *Vital Involvement in Old Age* (with J. M. Erikson and H. Kivnick, 1986); *The Life Cycle Completed* (with J. M. Erikson, 1997).

261 *"documentary child psychiatry"*   See Coles, *Spiritual Life of Children*, passim.

261 *Walker Percy*   For more on the life and work of Walker Percy, and his friendship with Robert Coles, see Samway; see also Coles's introduction to the Modern Library edition of Percy's novel *The Last Gentleman* (New York: Random House, 1997).

263 *"The place you find yourself"*   Handwritten letter from Walker Percy to a private individual, dated March 15, 1979, from the author's personal collection.

266 *"To write a book"*   Nicholl, 2.

267 *"most relentlessly curious"*   Quoted in Nicholl, 4.

267 *"inflate themselves"*   Ibid., 55. The full quotation: "Because I am not well-educated I know certain arrogant people think they can justifiably disparage me as an unlettered man."

268 *"Here, silent, speak"*   Nuland, *Doctors*, xvii.

269 *One Hundred Famous Books in Medicine*   The curator of the Grolier Club exhibition was Dr. Haskell F. Norman, one of the great collectors of books on science and medicine; see Basbanes, *A Gentle Madness*, 457–64. A number of Dr. Norman's books, including the presentation copy of the Vesalius, were among the books displayed. Dr. Norman's 2,500-volume library was sold at Christie's in New York for a total of $18.6 million. His Vesalius was hammered down at $1.6 million.

269 *"Aristotle quoted from"*   Mayo, in Norman, 5.

270 *"Because he wrote"*   Nuland, *Doctors*, 100.

270 *"There is hardly a phase"*   Norman, 169–70.

271 *"the most famous series"*   Norman, 70.

274 *"Poets, essayists, chroniclers"*   Nuland, *How We Die*, 8.

276 *"author's epistolary dedicatory"*   *The Complete Works of Doctor François Rabelais*, tr. from the French by Sir Thomas Urquhart and Peter Motteux (New York: Boni and Liveright, 1927), vol. 2, 219–20. See vol. 1 for an excellent biographical introduction by J. Lewis May.

277 *"a stylistically beautiful"*   Michael Bliss, *William Osler: A Life in Medicine* (New York: Oxford University Press, 1999), 45–46.

278 *"legal wife"*   Quoted in Henri Troyat, *Chekhov* (New York: E. P. Dutton, 1986), 78–79.

278 *"I write and doctor"*   Ibid., 69.

280 *"I learned to love Goethe"*   Schweitzer, *Goethe*, 23–24.

280 *"Proudly we remind"*   Ibid., 68.

281 *"what is now taking place . . . should hear"*   Ibid., 96–98.

Chapter 12: Reaching Out

284 *"I began my life"*   Sartre, 40. On Sartre's declining the Nobel Prize, see Jean-Paul Sartre, "Sartre on the Nobel Prize," tr. by Richard Howard, *New York Review of Books* 3, no. 9, December 17, 1964.

284 *"regarded world literature"*   Sartre, 65.

284 *"In my grandfather's"*   Ibid., 40.

284 *"I had found"*   Ibid., 59.

284 *"first friends"*   Ibid., 64.

285 *"a miniature adult"*   Ibid., 69.

285 *"breathe the rarefied air"*   Ibid., 60.

285 *"I didn't recognize . . . shake off"*   Ibid., 51.

286 *"My mother taught me"*   Quoted in Israel, 7.

287 *"Ah Shakespeare!"*   Ibid., 29.

289 *"Edison's marginalia . . . in their margins"*   Theresa M. Collins and Lisa Gitelman, "Reading as Invention: Thomas Edison and His Books," unpublished paper, 1998, copy furnished to the author, and used with permission.

290 *"We walked down"*   Keller, 88. For two contemporary accounts of reading-impaired adults and reading, see Finke, passim, and Kuusisto.

291 *"I read my first"*   Ibid., 90.

292 *"The frequent hearing . . . in ignorance"*   Douglass, 214–16. For other anecdotal accounts of African Americans, reading, and self-education during the years of slavery, see Heather Andrea Williams, passim.

293 *top one thousand books*   See www.oclc.org/research/top1000/complete.htm.

295 *"reading aloud"*   See Spock, 629–58.

300 *"When I think"*   Perri Klass, "Reach Out and Read: Literacy Promotion in Pediatrics," text of a speech, at http://fund4colorado.org/pdf/Perri%20Klass.pdf. See also Robert Needlman, Perri Klass, and Barry Zuckerman, "Reach Out and Get Your Patients to Read," *Contemporary Pediatrics* (January 2002): 51–69; Pamela C. High, Linda LaGasse, Samuel Becker, Ingrid Ahlgren, and Adrian Gardner, "Literacy Promotion in Primary Care Pediatrics: Can We Make a Difference?," *Pediatrics* 105, no. 4 (Supplement April 2000): 927–34. For Web site of Reach Out and Read: www.reachoutandread.org/.

304 *"As you can imagine . . . help the black man"*   Malcolm X, chap. 11, "Saved," 172–94.

306 *"Sonny's Blues"*   See James Baldwin, *Early Novels and Stories* (New York: Library of America, 1998), 831–64.

307 *"I had never"*   Ibid., 861–63.

310 *"break the dull . . . very thin indeed"*   Waxler and Trounstine, 1–10. For more on Changing Lives Through Literature, see http://cltl.umassd.edu/home-flash.cfm.

311 *"matched comparison group"*   G. Roger Jarjoura and Susan T. Krumholz, "Combining Bibliotherapy and Positive Role Modeling as an Alternative to Incarceration," *Journal of Offender Rehabilitation* 28 (1/2) (1998): 127–39.

Full Circle: A Final Stroke

314 *"an uneasy . . . valuable testament"*   Brown, 1–12.

BIBLIOGRAPHY

Aaron, Daniel. *American Notes: Selected Essays*. Boston: Northeastern University Press, 1994.

——. *The Unwritten War: American Writers and the Civil War*. New York: Alfred A. Knopf, 1973.

Adams, Henry. *Henry Adams: Novels, Mont Saint Michel, The Education*, ed. Ernest Samuels and Jayne N. Samuels. New York: Library of America, 1983.

Akenson, Donald Harman. *Surpassing Wonder: The Invention of the Bible and the Talmuds*. Chicago: University of Chicago Press, 2001.

Alter, Robert. *The Pleasures of Reading in an Ideological Age*. New York: Simon & Schuster, 1989.

Anderson, Douglas. *William Bradford's Books: Of Plimmoth Plantation and the Printed Word*. Baltimore: Johns Hopkins University Press, 2003.

Appelt, Kathi, and Jeanne Cannella Schmitzer. *Down Cut Shin Creek: The Pack Horse Librarians of Kentucky*. New York: HarperCollins, 2001.

Atkins, Peter. *Galileo's Finger: The Ten Great Ideas of Science*. Oxford: Oxford University Press, 2003.

Atlas, James. *Battle of the Books: The Curriculum Debate in America*. New York: W. W. Norton, 1992.

Ayer, A. J. *Voltaire*. New York: Random House, 1986.

Barnes, Bertram. *Goethe's Knowledge of French Literature*. Oxford: Oxford University Press, 1937.

Barnouw, David, and Gerrold van der Stroom, eds., tr. from the Dutch by Arnold J. Pomerans, B. M. Mooyaart-Doubleday, and Susan Massotty. *The Diary of Anne Frank: The Revised Critical Edition*. New York: Doubleday, 2003.

Basbanes, Nicholas A. *A Gentle Madness: Bibliophiles, Bibliomanes, and the Eternal Passion for Books*. New York: Henry Holt, 1995.

——. *Patience & Fortitude: A Roving Chronicle of Book People, Book Places, and Book Culture*. New York: HarperCollins, 2001.

——. *A Splendor of Letters: The Permanence of Books in an Impermanent World*. New York: HarperCollins, 2003.

Bate, W. Jackson. *Samuel Johnson*. New York: Harcourt Brace Jovanovich, 1975.

Becker, May Lamberton. *A Reader's Guide Book*. New York: Henry Holt, 1924.

Billias, George Athan, ed. *George Washington's Generals*. New York: William Morrow, 1964.

Bloom, Harold, ed. *The Best Poems of the English Language: From Chaucer Through Frost*. New York: HarperCollins, 2004.

———. *Genius: A Mosaic of One Hundred Exemplary Creative Minds*. New York: Warner Books, 2002.

———. *How to Read and Why*. New York: Scribner, 2000.

Bluestone, George. *Novels Into Film*. Baltimore: Johns Hopkins University Press, 1957 (paperback edition issued 2003).

Boswell, Jackson Campbell. *Milton's Library: A Catalogue of the Remains of John Milton's Library and an Annotated Reconstruction of Milton's Library and Ancillary Readings*. New York: Garland Publishing, 1975.

Boswell, James. *The Life of Samuel Johnson, L.L.D.* New York: The Modern Library, 1931.

Boyer, Paul S. *Purity in Print: Book Censorship in America*. New York: Charles Scribner's Sons, 1968.

Brown, Michelle P. *The Lindisfarne Gospels: Society, Spirituality and the Scribe*. London: The British Library, 2003.

Bucker, Park, ed. *The Matthew J. and Arlyn Bruccoli Collection of F. Scott Fitzgerald at the University of South Carolina*. Columbia: University of South Carolina Press, 2004.

Buell, Lawrence. *Emerson*. Cambridge, Mass.: Harvard University Press, 2003.

Calvino, Italo. *Why Read the Classics?* New York: Pantheon, 1999.

Canavaggio, Jean. *Cervantes*, tr. from the French by J. R. Jones. New York: W. W. Norton, 1986.

Carley, James P. *The Books of Henry VIII and His Wives*. London: The British Library, 2004.

Carnes, Mark C., ed. *Novel History: Historians and Novelists Confront America's Past (and Each Other)*. New York: Simon & Schuster, 2001.

Carter, John, and Percy H. Muir, eds., assisted by Nicolas Barker, H. A. Feisenberger, Howard Nixon, and S. H. Steinberg, with an introductory essay by Denys Hay. *Printing and the Mind of Man: The Impact of Print on the Evolution of Western Civilization During Five Centuries*. London and New York: Cassell and Co., and Holt, Rinehart and Winston, 1967.

Cavallo, Guglielmo, and Roger Chartier, eds. *A History of Reading in the West*. Amherst: University of Massachusetts Press, 1999.

Cervantes, Miguel de. *Don Quixote*, tr. from the Spanish by Edith Grossman, intro. by Harold Bloom. New York: Ecco, 2003.

Churchill, Winston. *My Early Life: A Roving Commission*. London: Thornton Butterworth, 1930.

Coetzee, J. M. *Giving Offense: Essays on Censorship*. Chicago: University of Chicago Press, 1996.

Coles, Robert. *The Call of Stories: Teaching the Moral Imagination*. Boston: Houghton Mifflin, 1989.

————. *The Moral Intelligence of Children*. New York: Random House, 1997.

————. *The Spiritual Life of Children*. Boston: Houghton Mifflin, 1990.

————. *Teaching Stories: An Anthology on the Power of Learning and Literature*. New York: Modern Library, 2004.

Cowley, Malcolm, and Bernard Smith, eds. *Books That Changed Our Minds: A Symposium*. New York: Kelmscott Editions, 1938.

Craig, Alec. *Suppressed Books: A History of the Conception of Literary Obscenity*. Cleveland: World Publishing Co., 1963.

Dalsimer, Katherine. *Virginia Woolf: Becoming a Writer*. New Haven: Yale University Press, 2001.

Darnton, Robert. *The Corpus of Clandestine Literature in France 1769–1789*. New York: W. W. Norton, 1995.

————. *The Forbidden Best-Sellers of Pre-Revolutionary France*. New York: W. W. Norton, 1995.

————. *The Great Cat Massacre and Other Episodes in French Cultural History*. New York: Basic Books, 1984.

————. *The Literary Underground of the Old Regime*. Cambridge, Mass.: Harvard University Press, 1982.

Darnton, Robert, and Daniel Roche, eds. *Revolution in Print: The Press in France, 1775–1800*. Berkeley: University of California Press, in collaboration with the New York Public Library, 1989.

Devine, C. Maury, Claudia M. Dissel, and Kim D. Parrish, eds. *The Harvard Guide to Influential Books*. New York: Harper & Row, 1986.

Dickinson, Asa Don. *The Best Books of Our Time*. New York: H. W. Wilson, 1931.

Donoghue, Denis. *The American Classics: A Personal Essay*. New Haven: Yale University Press, 2005.

————. *The Practice of Reading*. New Haven: Yale University Press, 1998.

Douglass, Frederick. *Frederick Douglass: Autobiographies*, ed. Henry Louis Gates Jr. New York: The Library of America, 1994.

Doyle, Arthur Conan. *Through the Magic Door*. New York: McClure Company, 1908.

Eastman, Fred. *Books That Have Changed the World*. Chicago: American Library Association, 1937.

Eco, Umberto. *On Literature*. New York: Harcourt, 2004.

Edel, Leon, and Adeline R. Tintner, eds. *The Library of Henry James*. Ann Arbor, Mich.: UMI Research Press, 1987.

Ehrman, Bart D. *Lost Christianities: The Battles for Scripture and the Faiths We Never Knew*. New York: Oxford University Press, 2003.

————. *Lost Scriptures: Books That Did Not Make It Into the New Testament*. New York: Oxford University Press, 2003.

Eisenstein, Elizabeth L. *The Printing Press as an Agent of Change: Communications and Cultural Transformations in Early-Modern Europe*, volumes I and II. Cambridge, England: Cambridge University Press, 1980.

Elie, Paul. *The Life You Save May Be Your Own: An American Pilgrimage*. New York: Farrar, Straus and Giroux, 2003.

Ellis, John M. *Literature Lost: Social Agendas and the Corruption of the Humanities*. New Haven: Yale University Press, 1997.

Ellmann, Richard. *James Joyce: New and Revised Edition*. New York: Oxford University Press, 1982.

Erasmus, Desiderius. *The Praise of Folly*, tr. from the Latin, with commentary, by Hoyt Hopewell Hudson. Princeton: Princeton University Press, 1941.

Febvre, Lucien, and Henri-Jean Martin. *The Coming of the Book: The Impact of Printing 1450–1800*, tr. from the French by David Gerard. London: Verso, 1990.

Finke, Beth. *Long Time No See*. Urbana: University of Illinois Press, 2003.

Fitzgerald, F. Scott. *Trimalchio: An Early Version of "The Great Gatsby,"* ed. James L. W. West III. Cambridge, England: Cambridge University Press, 2000.

Frank, Anne, ed. by David Barnouw and Gerrold van der Stroom, tr. from the Dutch by Arnold J. Pomerans, B. M. Mooyaart-Doubleday, and Susan Massotty. *The Diary of Anne Frank: The Revised Critical Edition*. New York: Doubleday, 2003.

Franklin, Colin. "The Bowdlers and Their Family Shakespeare," in the *Book Collector* 49:2 (summer 2000): 227–43.

Furbank, P. N. *Diderot: A Critical Biography*. New York: Alfred A. Knopf, 1992.

Gass, William H. *Reading Rilke: Reflections on the Problems of Translation*. New York: Alfred A. Knopf, 1999.

Gaukroger, Stephen. *Descartes: An Intellectual Biography*. Oxford: Oxford University Press, 1995.

Gibbon, Edward. *Memoirs of My Life*, ed. Georges Bonnard. New York: Funk & Wagnalls, 1966.

Gilreath, James, and Douglas L. Wilson. *Thomas Jefferson's Library: A Catalog with the Entries in His Own Order*. Washington, D.C.: Library of Congress, 1989.

Gill, Gillian. *Mary Baker Eddy*. Reading, Mass.: Perseus Books, 1998.

Gingerich, Owen. *The Book Nobody Read: Chasing the Revolutions of Nicolaus Copernicus.* New York: Walker, 2004.

Ginsburg, Carlo. *The Cheese and the Worms: The Cosmos of a Sixteenth-Century Miller,* tr. from the Italian by John and Anne Tedeschi. New York: Penguin, 1982.

Grafton, Anthony. *The Footnote: A Curious History.* Cambridge, Mass.: Harvard University Press, 1997.

Gray, Francine du Plessix. *At Home With the Marquis de Sade.* New York: Simon & Schuster, 1998.

Greene, Donald. *Samuel Johnson's Library: An Annotated Guide.* Victoria, B.C.: English Literary Studies / University of Victoria, 1975.

Griswold, Jerry. *Audacious Kids: Coming of Age in America's Classic Children's Books.* New York and Oxford: Oxford University Press, 1992.

Haffner, Sebastian. *Defying Hitler: A Memoir,* tr. from the German by Oliver Pretzel. New York: Farrar, Straus and Giroux, 2002.

Halbertal, Moshe. *People of the Book: Canon, Meaning, and Authority.* Cambridge, Mass.: Harvard University Press, 1997.

Haleem, M. A. S. Abdel, tr. from the Arabic, with an introduction. *The Qur'an: A New Translation.* New York: Oxford University Press, 2004.

Harrison, John. *The Library of Isaac Newton.* Cambridge, England: Cambridge University Press, 1978.

Harrison, John, and Peter Laslett, eds. *The Library of John Locke.* Oxford: Oxford Bibliographical Society / Oxford University Press, 1965.

Havens, George R. *The Age of Ideas: From Reaction to Revolution in Eighteenth-Century France.* New York: Henry Holt, 1955.

Hawking, Stephen, ed. *The Illustrated "On the Shoulders of Giants": The Great Works of Physics and Astronomy.* Philadelphia: Running Press, 2004.

Heffernan, Thomas Farel. *Stove by a Whale: Owen Chase and the Essex.* Middletown, Conn.: Wesleyan University Press, 1981.

Herndon, William H., and Jesse W. Weik. *Abraham Lincoln: The True Story of a Great Life.* 2 vols. New York: D. Appleton, 1917.

Hitler, Adolf. *Mein Kampf,* tr. from the German by Alvin Johnson. New York: Reynal & Hitchcock, 1939.

Hofstadter, Douglas R. *Le Ton Beau de Marot: In Praise of the Music of Language.* New York: Basic Books, 1997.

Howell, Kenneth J. *God's Two Books: Copernican Cosmology and Biblical Interpretation in Early Modern Science.* Notre Dame, Ind.: University of Notre Dame Press, 2002.

Hughes, Langston. *The Big Sea: An Autobiography.* New York: Hill and Wang, 1963.

Israel, Paul. *Edison: A Life of Invention.* New York: John Wiley & Sons, 1998.

Jackson, H. J. *Marginalia: Readers Writing in Books*. New Haven: Yale University Press, 2001.

———. *Romantic Readers: The Evidence of Marginalia*. New Haven: Yale University Press, 2005.

Jackson, Holbrook. *The Fear of Books*. New York: Charles Scribner's Sons, 1932.

———. *The Reading of Books*. New York: Charles Scribner's Sons, 1947.

Jardine, Lisa. *Erasmus, Man of Letters*. Princeton: Princeton University Press, 1993.

Jefferson, Thomas. *The Jefferson Bible: The Life and Morals of Jesus of Nazareth*, intro. by Forest Church, afterword by Jaroslav Pelikan. Boston: Beacon Press, 2001.

Johnson, Samuel. *Lives of the English Poets: A Selection*. London: Guernsey Press, 1975.

Kanigel, Robert. *Vintage Reading From Plato to Bradbury: A Personal Tour of Some of the World's Best Books*. Baltimore: Bancroft Press, 1997.

Keller, Helen. *The Story of My Life* (the restored edition, with supplementary accounts by Anne Sullivan, her teacher, and John Macy), ed. Roger Shattuck with Dorothy Herrmann. New York: W. W. Norton, Modern Library, 2003.

Kelley, Philip, and Betty A. Coley, eds. *The Browning Collections: A Reconstruction With Other Memorabilia*. Winfield, Kans.: Wedgestone Press, 1984.

Kernan, Alvin. *Printing Technology, Letters and Samuel Johnson*. Princeton: Princeton University Press, 1987.

Keynes, Geoffrey. *The Library of Edward Gibbon*. Dorchester, England: St. Paul's Bibliographies, 1980.

Kiefer, Monica. *American Children Through Their Books, 1700–1835*. Philadelphia: University of Pennsylvania Press, 1948.

Kriwaczek, Paul. *In Search of Zarathustra: The First Prophet and the Ideas That Changed the World*. New York: Alfred A. Knopf, 2003.

Kuusisto, Stephen. *Planet of the Blind: A Memoir*. New York: The Dial Press, 1998.

Lee, Hermione. *Virginia Woolf*. New York: Alfred A. Knopf, 1997.

Leonard, Irving A., with a new introduction by Rolena Adorno. *Books of the Brave: Being an Account of Books and of Men in the Spanish Conquest and Settlement of the Sixteenth-Century New World*. Berkeley: University of California Press, 1992 [originally published in 1949].

Lever, Maurice. *Sade: A Biography*, tr. from the French by Arthur Goldhammer. New York: Farrar, Straus and Giroux, 1993.

Lincoln, Abraham. *Abraham Lincoln: Speeches and Writings, 1859–1865*, ed. Don E. Fehrenbacher. New York: Library of America, 1989.

Link, Henry C., and Harry Arthur Hope. *People and Books: A Study of Reading and Book-Buying Habits*. New York: Book Industry Committee of the Book Manufacturers' Institute, 1946.

Loewen, James W. *Lies My Teacher Told Me: Everything Your American History Textbook Got Wrong*. New York: The New Press, 1995.

Longino, Helen E. *The Fate of Knowledge*. Princeton: Princeton University Press, 2001.

Lowes, John Livingston. *On Reading Books*. Cambridge, Mass.: The Riverside Press, 1929.

———. *The Road to Xanadu: A Study in the Ways of the Imagination*. New York: Vintage Books, 1959.

Mack, Maynard. *Alexander Pope: A Life*. New York: W. W. Norton, 1985.

Maier, Pauline. *American Scripture: Making the Declaration of Independence*. New York: Alfred A. Knopf, 1997.

Malcolm X, with Alex Haley, foreword by Attallah Shabazz. *The Autobiography of Malcolm X*. New York: Ballantine, 1999 (paperback edition of 1964 hardcover edition).

Malless, Stanley, and Jeffrey McQuain. *Coined by God: Words and Phrases That First Appear in the English Translation of the Bible*. New York: W. W. Norton, 2003.

Malone, Dumas. *The Sage of Monticello*. Boston: Little, Brown, 1981.

Martin-Rodríguez, Manuel M. *Life in Search of Readers: Reading (in) Chicano/a Literature*. Albuquerque: University of New Mexico Press, 2003.

McCrossan, John A. *Books and Reading in the Lives of Notable Americans: A Biographical Sourcebook*. Westport, Conn.: Greenwood Press, 2000.

McCullough, David. *John Adams*. New York: Simon & Schuster, 2001.

———. *John Adams and the Good Life of the Mind*. Boston: Boston Athenæum, 2004.

———. *1776*. New York: Simon & Schuster, 2005.

Meyers, Jeffrey. *Edmund Wilson: A Biography*. Boston: Houghton Mifflin, 1995.

Mitchell, Stephen, tr. *Gilgamesh: A New English Version*. New York: Free Press, 2004.

Montaigne, Michel de. *The Complete Essays*, tr. from the French by M. A. Screech. London: Penguin, 1991.

Moreau, Geneviève. *The Restless Journey of James Agee*, tr. from the French by Miriam Kleiger. New York: William Morrow, 1977.

Moss, Ann. *Printed Commonplace-Books and the Structuring of Renaissance Thought*. Oxford: Oxford University Press, 1996.

Muir, Percy H. "Ian Fleming: A Personal Memoir," in *Book Collector* 14, no. 1 (Spring 1965): 24–33.

Nafisi, Azar. *Reading Lolita in Tehran: A Memoir in Books*. New York: Random House, 2003.

Nell, Victor. *Lost in a Book: The Psychology of Reading for Pleasure*. New Haven: Yale University Press, 1988.

Nicholl, Charles. *Leonardo da Vinci: Flights of the Mind*. New York: Viking, 2004.

Norman, Haskell F. *One Hundred Books Famous in Medicine*, ed. Hope Mayo. New York: The Grolier Club, 1995.

Nuland, Sherwin B. *Doctors: The Biography of Medicine*. New York: Alfred A. Knopf, 1988.

————. *How We Die: Reflections on Life's Final Chapter*. New York: Alfred A. Knopf, 1994.

Ogburn, Charlton. *The Mysterious William Shakespeare: The Myth and the Reality*. New York: Dodd, Mead, 1984.

Ondaatje, Michael, Michael Redhill, Esta Spalding, and Linda Spalding, eds. *Lost Classics: Writers on Books Loved and Lost, Overlooked, Under-read, Unavailable, Stolen, Extinct, or Otherwise Out of Commission*. New York: Anchor Books, 2001.

One Hundred Influential American Books Printed Before 1900. An exhibition at the Grolier Club, New York, April 18 to June 16, 1946, catalog and text of addresses. New York: Grolier Club, 1947.

Padover, Saul K., ed. *The Letters of Karl Marx: Selected and Translated with Explanatory Notes and an Introduction*. Englewood Cliffs, N.J.: Prentice-Hall, 1979.

Pagels, Elaine. *Beyond Belief: The Secret Gospel of Thomas*. New York: Random House, 2003.

————. *The Gnostic Gospels*. New York: Random House, 1979.

Paine, Thomas. *Collected Writings*, ed. and with notes by Eric Foner. New York: Library of America, 1984.

Pastoureau, M., ed. *En Français dans le texte: Dix siècles de lumières par le livre*. Paris: Bibliothèque Nationale, 1990.

Pelikan, Jaroslav. *Interpreting the Bible and the Constitution*. New Haven: Yale University Press, 2004.

Perrin, Noel. *Dr. Bowdler's Legacy: A History of Expurgated Books in England and America*. Boston: David R. Godine, 1992 (paperback of 1969 edition includes a new chapter on contemporary bowdlerism).

Perry, Mark. *Grant and Twain: The Story of a Friendship That Changed America*. New York: Random House, 2004.

Pierpont, Claudia Roth. *Passionate Minds: Women Rewriting the World*. New York: Alfred A. Knopf, 2000.

Popol Vuh [The Mayan Book of the Dawn of Life and the Glories of Gods and Kings], tr. from the Quiché by Dennis Tedlock. New York: Simon & Schuster, 1985.

Printing and the Mind of Man: Catalogue of the Exhibitions at the British Museum and at Earls Court, London, 16–27 July 1963. London: F.W. Bridges & Sons and the Association of British Manufacturers of Printers' Machinery/Trustees of The British Museum, 1963.

Printing and the Mind of Man. Catalog of a tenth-anniversary exhibition of the 1963 London exhibition at the Lilly Library, foreword by David A. Randall. Bloomington, Ind.: Lilly Library, 1973.

Printing and the Mind of Man. Catalog of an auction sale of high-spots based on the 1963 London exhibition. London: Christie's, 1999.

Proust, Marcel. *On Reading Ruskin,* tr. from the French by Jean Autret, William Burford, and Phillip J. Wolfe. New Haven: Yale University Press, 1987.

Pryor, Felix. *Elizabeth I: Her Life in Letters.* Berkeley: University of California Press, 2003.

Quindlen, Anna. *How Reading Changed My Life.* New York: Ballantine, 1998.

Ravitch, Diane. *The Language Police: How Pressure Groups Restrict What Students Learn.* New York: Alfred A. Knopf, 2003.

Reading at Risk: A Survey of Literary Reading in America. Washington: National Endowment for the Arts, 2004.

Reddick, Allen. *The Making of Johnson's Dictionary 1746–1773.* Cambridge, England: Cambridge University Press, 1990.

Rexroth, Kenneth. *Classics Revisited,* afterword by Bradford Morrow. New York: New Directions, 1986.

———. *More Classics Revisited,* ed. Bradford Morrow. New York: New Directions, 1989.

Ricks, Christopher. *Dylan's Visions of Sin.* New York: Ecco Press, 2004.

Rosenthal, Bernard M. *The Rosenthal Collection of Printed Books With Manuscript Annotations: A Catalog of 242 Editions Mostly Before 1600, Annotated by Contemporary or Near-Contemporary Readers.* New Haven: Beinecke Rare Book and Manuscript Library/Yale University, 1997.

Rowse, A. L. *What Shakespeare Read and Thought.* New York: Coward, McCann & Geoghegan, 1981.

Rummel, Erika. *Erasmus as a Translator of the Classics.* Toronto: University of Toronto Press, 1985.

The Sale Catalogue of Samuel Johnson's Library: A Facsimile Edition. With an introduction and notes by J. D. Fleeman. Victoria, B.C.: English Literary Studies/University of Victoria, 1975.

Samway, Patrick, S. J. *Walker Percy: A Life.* New York: Farrar, Straus and Giroux, 1997.

Sanders, Barry. *A Is for Ox: Violence, Electronic Media, and the Silencing of the Written Word.* New York: Pantheon, 1994.

Sartre, Jean-Paul. *The Words,* tr. from the French by Bernard Frechtman. New York: George Braziller, 1964.

Schniedewind, William M. *How the Bible Became a Book.* Cambridge: Cambridge University Press, 2004.

Schoenbaum, S. *Shakespeare and Others.* Washington, D.C.: Folger Books, 1985.

Scholes, Robert. *The Crafty Reader.* New Haven: Yale University Press, 2001.

Schweitzer, Albert. *Goethe: Five Studies*, tr. from the German by Charles R. Joy. Boston: Beacon Press, 1961.

————. *Out of My Life and Thought: An Autobiography*, tr. from the German by C. T. Campion, with a postscript by Everett Skillings. New York: Henry Holt, 1949.

Secord, James. A. *Victorian Sensation: The Extraordinary Publication, Reception, and Secret Authorship of "Vestiges of the Natural History of Creation."* Chicago: University of Chicago Press, 2001.

Sharpe, Kevin. *Reading Revolutions: The Politics of Reading in Early Modern England.* New Haven: Yale University Press, 2000.

Shattuck, Roger. *Proust's Way: A Field Guide to "In Search of Lost Time."* New York: W. W. Norton, 2000.

Sherman, William H. *John Dee: The Politics of Reading and Writing in the English Renaissance.* Amherst: University of Massachusetts Press, 1995.

Silvey, Anita. *100 Best Books for Children.* Boston: Houghton Mifflin, 2004.

Sisman, Adam. *Boswell's Presumptuous Task: The Making of the Life of Dr. Johnson.* New York: Farrar, Straus and Giroux, 2000.

Sledd, James H., and Gwin J. Kolb. *Dr. Johnson's Dictionary: Essays in the Biography of a Book.* Chicago: University of Chicago Press, 1955.

Sorell, Tom, ed. *The Cambridge Companion to Hobbes.* Cambridge, England: Cambridge University Press, 1996.

Spevack, Marvin, ed. *Isaac D'Israeli on Books: Pre-Victorian Essays on the History of Literature.* London, and New Castle, Del.: British Library and Oak Knoll Press, 2004.

Spock, Benjamin. *Dr. Spock's Baby and Child Care*, 8th ed., updated and revised by Robert Needlman. New York: Pocket Books, 2004.

Spufford, Francis. *The Child That Books Built: A Life in Reading.* New York: Metropolitan Books, 2002.

St. Clair, William. *The Reading Nation in the Romantic Period.* Cambridge, England: Cambridge University Press, 2004.

Steiner, George, ed., with Aminadav Dykman. *Homer in English.* New York: Penguin, 1996.

Stern, Virginia F. *Gabriel Harvey: His Life, Marginalia, and Library.* Oxford: Oxford University Press, 1979.

Tintner, Adeline R. *The Book World of Henry James: Appropriating the Classics.* Ann Arbor, Mich.: UMI Research Press, 1987.

Tracy, James D. *Erasmus of the Low Countries.* Berkeley: University of California Press, 1998.

Tribble, Evelyn B. *Margins and Marginality: The Printed Page in Early Modern England*. Charlottesville: University Press of Virginia, 1993.

Vendler, Helen. *Coming of Age as a Poet: Milton, Keats, Eliot, Plath*. Cambridge, Mass.: Harvard University Press, 2003.

————. *Soul Says: On Recent Poetry*. Cambridge, Mass.: Harvard University Press, 1995.

Vendler, Helen, ed. *Voices and Visions: The Poet in America*. New York: Random House, 1987.

Waite, Terry. *Footfalls in Memory: Readings and Reflections From Solitude*. New York: Doubleday, 1997.

————. *Taken on Trust*. New York: Harcourt Brace, 1993.

Waxler, Robert P., and Jean R. Trounstine, eds. *Changing Lives Through Literature*. Notre Dame, Ind.: Notre Dame University Press, 1999.

Wheen, Francis. *Karl Marx: A Life*. New York: W. W. Norton, 1999.

Williams, Heather Andrea. *Self-Taught: African American Education in Slavery and Freedom*. Chapel Hill: University of North Carolina Press, 2005.

Wilson, A. N. *The Life of John Milton*. New York: Oxford University Press, 1983.

Wilson, Douglas L., and Rodney O. Davis, eds. *Herndon's Informants: Letters, Interviews and Statements about Abraham Lincoln*. Urbana: University of Illinois Press, 1998.

Wilson, Edmund. *The Fruits of the MLA*. New York: A New York Review Book, 1968.

————. *The Portable Edmund Wilson*, ed. Lewis M. Dabney. New York: Viking, 1983.

————. *Letters on Literature and Politics, 1912–1972*, ed. Elena Wilson, intro. by Daniel Aaron. Farrar, Straus and Giroux, 1977.

Woodward, W. E. *Tom Paine: America's Godfather, 1737–1809*. New York: E. P. Dutton, 1945.

Woolf, Virginia. *The Common Reader: First Series*, ed. Andrew McNeillie. San Diego: Harvest/Harcourt Brace, 1984.

INDEX

Index

Index